LA GRAN LÍNEA

LA GRAN

PAULA REBERT

LÍNEA

Mapping the

United States–Mexico

Boundary, 1849–1857

UNIVERSITY OF TEXAS PRESS, AUSTIN

Printed in the United States of America

First edition, 2001

Requests for permission to reproduce material from this work
should be sent to Permissions, University of Texas Press,
P.O. Box 7819, Austin, TX 78713-7819.

∞ The paper used in this book meets the minimum requirements
of ANSI/NISO Z39.48-1992 (R1997) (Permanence of Paper).

Library of Congress Cataloging-in-Publication Data

Rebert, Paula, 1948–

    La Gran Línea : mapping the United States–Mexico boundary, 1849–1857/by
Paula Rebert—1st ed.

      p.   cm.

Includes bibliographical references and index.

ISBN 0-292-77110-x (cloth : alk. paper) — ISBN 0-292-77111-8 (pbk : alk. paper)

1. United States—Boundaries—Mexico.   2. Mexico—Boundaries—United
States.   3. International Boundary Commission, United States and Mexico.
4. Surveying—Mexican-American Border Region—History—19th century.
5. Cartography—Mexico—History—19th century.   6. Cartography—United
States—History—19th century.   7. Mexican-American Border Region—Maps.
I. Title.

F786 .R43   2001
911′.721—dc21   00-041771

For Philip

Trabajarán con la buena armonía e inteligencia, que siempre ha reinado entre nosotros y . . . formarán un plano tan exacto como interesante de la gran línea astronómica que les está confiada.

They will work with the good harmony and understanding that has always prevailed between us and . . . make a map as accurate as [it is] interesting of the great astronomical line that is entrusted to them.

First Engineer Francisco Jiménez,
Mexican Boundary Commission,
to Lieutenant Nathaniel Michler,
U.S. Boundary Commission,
23 June 1855

CONTENTS

ILLUSTRATIONS

PREFACE

THE HISTORY OF THE UNITED STATES–MEXICO BOUND-
ary survey, combining important historical themes with dramatic
events and exciting adventure as it does, has interested many writers
and readers, but few have thought of the maps created from the survey
as central to its story. Yet when surveyors from the United States and
Mexico went into the distant borderlands, their mission was to map the
boundary as well as to locate and mark it. This study considers the
United States–Mexico boundary survey as a mapping enterprise. It
examines the efforts of surveyors and mapmakers from both the United
States and Mexico, compares their maps of the boundary and the country it crossed, and reflects on the significance of their cartographic en-
deavor for boundary history.

I have thought of my work as a contribution to the history of cartography—a vast and rich field of study that deserves to be more widely
known. I hope, however, that it will also find readers who are interested
from other points of view in the history of the boundary and the culture
of the borderlands. I've included brief explanations that I hope readers
will find helpful for technical terms from surveying and cartography. For
quotations from Spanish-language sources, I've given English translations; the translations are my own, unless otherwise noted. Notes cite
the original Spanish sources from which the translations were made. I
have transcribed quotations from primary sources so that they are true-
to-source in spelling. Nineteenth-century writing (in both English and
Spanish) sometimes varied from current standards in spelling and use
of diacritical marks, but the words are readily recognizable.

The boundary maps that I discuss are illustrated here in photographic
reproductions. The original boundary maps made by the representatives

of the United States and Mexico have been preserved and are now housed in the national archives of the two nations. The maps are manuscripts, drawn in pen and ink, and they remain in good condition. Many of the maps kept in the United States National Archives are in need of cleaning, however, as they are covered with a dark coat of varnish that partially obscures the image. The layer of varnish is apparent in some of the illustrations.

Research for this study was supported by a National Science Foundation Doctoral Dissertation Improvement Award (SES-9207169), a Library of Congress Junior Fellowship (Geography and Map Division), and a travel grant from the University of Wisconsin–Madison Graduate School. Many individuals, as well, supported my efforts in many ways, and it gives me great pleasure to acknowledge their help. I am deeply grateful to my Ph.D. advisor, David Woodward, who guided, criticized, and encouraged my research and writing through to the completion of my dissertation, and whose support for my assistantship on the *History of Cartography* Project and for my grant proposals were essential to making the work financially possible. I am also especially grateful to Ralph Ehrenberg, Chief of the Geography and Map Division, Library of Congress, with whom I first discussed the idea for this project and who offered much helpful advice, especially in locating primary source materials, and support for my work at the Library of Congress. I owe special thanks for the help offered by Ronald Grim, Specialist in Cartographic History, Geography and Map Division, Library of Congress, who was my guide to the possibilities, and through the complexities, of research at the Library and at the National Archives. I would also particularly like to thank Victor Hernández Ortiz, Chief of the Mapoteca Manuel Orozco y Berra, for his patient and generous assistance. Many individuals at other archives and libraries assisted me with their thorough knowledge of their collections, and to them, too, I owe my gratitude. Thank you also to many friends who offered their insights into research methods, references and sources, the boundary survey, and the history of cartography.

For their assistance in reading drafts and providing valuable commentary, I would like to thank Phillip Muehrcke, Thomas Vale, Robert Dott, and Robert Ostergren, at the University of Wisconsin–Madison, Robert Czerniak, of New Mexico State University–Las Cruces, and Daniel Arreola, of Arizona State University–Tempe. For reading and commenting on drafts at an early stage of the project, I am grateful to Dorothy Sack, of Ohio University, and Allan Bogue, of the University of Wisconsin–Madison. For advice and encouragement in rewriting my manuscript as a book, I am thankful to my sponsoring editor at the University of Texas Press, Shannon Davies; and I thank Bill Bishel, sponsoring editor, and all the staff members of the University of Texas Press for their continuing skillful assistance with the manuscript.

There is one person to whom I am most thankful, and to whom this book owes its existence above all others, and that is my husband, Philip Melnick. Not only were his encouragement and support critical, but his photographic skills and computer expertise have contributed greatly to the finished work. He made the photographs of the maps of the Mexican commission and the prints of all the maps that appear in this book, and I am deeply grateful to him.

INDEX MAPS

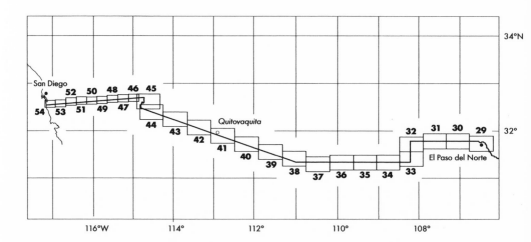

INDEX MAP 1. (*above*) Index of sectional map sheets of the boundary between the United States and Mexico, land boundary section. The map sheets made by both the U.S. Boundary Commission and the Comisión de Límites Mexicana covered approximately the same geographical areas and used the same numbering system. Source: [U.S. Boundary Commission], *Index Map No. 3 and Index Map No. 4.*

INDEX MAP 2. (*opposite*) Index of sectional map sheets of the boundary between the United States and Mexico, Rio Grande section. The U.S. Boundary Commission and the Comisión de Límites Mexicana used the same index for their final boundary maps. Source: [U.S. Boundary Commission], *Index Map No. 1 and Index Map No. 2.*

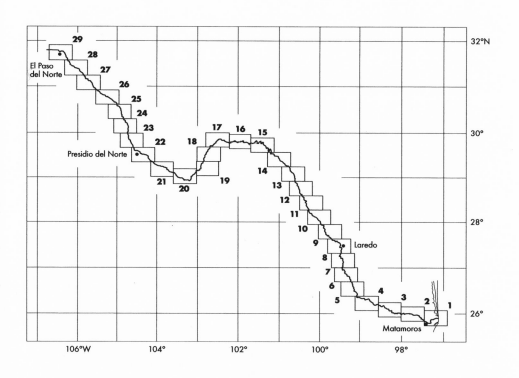

29
28
27
El Paso
del Norte
26
25
24
23
22
21
20
Presidio del Norte
18
17
16
15
14
13
12
11
10
9
19
Laredo
8
7
6
5
4
3
2
1
Matamoros
32°N
30°
28°
26°
106°W
104°
102°
100°
98°

LA GRAN LÍNEA

INTRODUCTION

Boundaries, when definite, are always marked upon the earth's
surface by natural features, such as mountains or streams, or
else by specific lines or curves; such boundaries when projected
upon a map are easily understood.

Astronomer Amiel W. Whipple to U.S. Commissioner John R. Bartlett,
12 December 1850

*T*HE MAKING OF THE BOUNDARY BETWEEN THE UNITED
States and Mexico was a matter of maps. Before the boundary existed on the land, treaty negotiators traced out the line on maps. They
planned for surveyors, guided by the treaty maps, to fix the boundary
on the ground and to demonstrate the results in authoritative maps. U.S.
and Mexican surveys of the remote frontier and the maps created from
them brought the boundary into being. The boundary maps made from
the first surveys later became important in the evolution of boundary
relations and defined the United States–Mexico boundary in a manner
unexpected at the time of their making.

The boundary had its painful beginning in the U.S.-Mexican War,
which was brought to an end with the Treaty of Peace, Friendship,
Limits, and Settlement, signed at Guadalupe Hidalgo, 2 February 1848.
At the treaty conferences, two of the four main stages in the process of
boundary making were fulfilled. The first stage, the allocation of territory, was a matter of political negotiation and resulted in Mexico's cession of the states of Alta California, Nuevo México, and the northern
portions of Tamaulipas, Coahuila, and Sonora—territory that would
become the U.S. states of California, Nevada, Utah, Texas, and parts of

Colorado, Arizona, and New Mexico. The cession opened up a vast new domain to the United States, while for Mexico, it was a grievous loss of half its territory. The second step, delimitation of the boundary—the choice of its location and its definition in written terms—was realized in the treaty itself. The new boundary superseded the dividing line between the territories of Mexico and the United States that had originally been defined in treaties between Spain and the United States.[1] The third stage of boundary making, demarcation, was assigned by the treaty writers to government commissions that would locate and mark the boundary on the ground. Because the treaty delimitation could not define the line as exactly as surveyors would place it, the commissions would make fine decisions regarding the location of the boundary.[2]

The writers of the Treaty of Guadalupe Hidalgo devised boundaries that followed both geometrical lines and rivers. Geometrical boundaries were frequently employed by diplomats who, lacking accurate geographic knowledge of the territory through which a boundary was to run, ruled a line upon a map. The ruled line was likely to conflict with the shape of the terrain, making access difficult for surveyors and demanding complex surveys to establish a flat map line on the curving earth. Rivers also were often chosen as boundaries because they were conspicuous features on maps of little-known territories. A number of different lines following the banks or channels could be interpreted as a river boundary, however, and each presented different problems in surveying. In addition, river instability was likely to produce problems in the fourth stage of boundary making, maintenance, and administration. The lines the treaty writers chose afforded solutions for their deficient knowledge of the new United States–Mexico borderlands, but they were replete with possibilities for uncertainty and controversy.[3]

The Treaty of Guadalupe Hidalgo described the boundary as it would run from east to west. The dividing line began offshore, as the delimitation explained: "The Boundary line between the two Republics shall commence in the Gulf of Mexico, three leagues from land, opposite the mouth of the Rio Grande, otherwise called Rio Bravo del Norte, or opposite the mouth of it's [sic] deepest branch, if it should have more than one branch emptying directly into the sea."[4] At the time of the treaty, as now, the offshore waters or marginal sea were considered to be part of the national territory of a coastal nation; but the extent of the marginal sea has often been a matter of negotiation and has varied considerably with different nations at different times. In the nineteenth century, the extent of the marginal sea was generally accepted as three nautical miles, equivalent to one marine league, distant from the low-water mark on the coast. Both the United States and Mexico supported the three-mile doctrine, but the Treaty of Guadalupe Hidalgo specified, nevertheless, a boundary of three leagues, or nine miles, into the Gulf of Mexico. The provision was derived from an earlier act of the Republic of Texas.[5]

By designating the river's deepest channel as the boundary, the treaty writers forestalled the possibility of contention in case the Rio Grande were discovered to have more than one outlet into the Gulf. Positioned, then, opposite the deepest branch of the Rio Grande, the boundary continued, "from thence, up the middle of that river, following the deepest channel, where it has more than one to the point where it strikes the Southern boundary of New Mexico."[6] The treaty line followed the Rio Grande, the "Great River," known in Mexico as the Río Bravo (Great or Wild River) or the Río del Norte (River of the North). It was implemented as the boundary as a matter of political necessity, since a U.S. claim to the Rio Grande as the boundary of Texas had been a precipitating cause of the U.S.-Mexican War. The Rio Grande had not yet been fully explored when the treaty negotiators found it prominently, although inaccurately, represented on the map they used in their discussions, the *Mapa de los Estados Unidos de Méjico* (Map of the United States of Mexico) by John Disturnell (fig. I-1).[7]

From the delimitation given in the Treaty of Guadalupe Hidalgo, two different lines in the Rio Grande could be understood as the boundary. The treaty used the words, "up the middle of that river," an expression that appeared to refer to the median line, a line everywhere equidistant from the nearest points on the opposite banks of the river; but the treaty also said, "following the deepest channel," designating a particular line in the river that depended upon depth soundings. In general, a median line marks the boundary in rivers that are not used for navigation, while navigable rivers are usually divided along the main channel, allowing access to the river by vessels of both nations—a concept known as "the principle of thalweg." Since the delimitation was ambiguous, its meaning had to be deduced from other statements in the treaty. Because another article guaranteed the right of navigation on the river, the contradictory language was usually construed in favor of the deepest channel, a construction that was complicated by the fact that much of the Rio Grande was not truly navigable.[8]

The end of the Rio Grande boundary, where the southern boundary of New Mexico struck the river, was also shown on Disturnell's map. The treaty line then ran along generally straight lines, connecting several "turning points," positions assumed to be correctly known and precisely located.[9] It followed the southern boundary of New Mexico to its western termination, then turned northward until it intersected the southernmost branch of the Gila River. In the words of the treaty, the line was to continue from the Rio Grande,

> thence, westwardly along the whole Southern Boundary of New Mexico (which runs north of the town called *Paso*) to it's [*sic*] western termination; thence, northward, along the western line of New Mexico, until it intersects the first branch of the river Gila; (or if it should not intersect any branch of that river, then, to the point on the said line nearest to such branch, and thence in a direct line to the same;) thence down the middle of the said branch and of the said river, until it empties into the Rio Colorado; thence, across the Rio Colorado, following the division line between Upper and Lower California, to the Pacific Ocean.

The "town called Paso" was located where Ciudad Juárez now stands and was also called El Paso or Paso del Norte after the nearby mountain pass of the same name. It was the important center of settlement in the area, as the Texas city of El Paso had not yet been established.

In order to clarify the delimitation, the treaty writers referred to Disturnell's map to illustrate their language and made the map a part of the treaty. The delimitation continued:

> The southern and western limits of New Mexico, mentioned in this Article, are those laid down in the Map, entitled *"Map of the United Mexican States, as organized and defined by various acts of the Congress of said Republic, and constructed according to the best authorities. Revised edition. Published at New York in 1847 by J. Disturnell:"* Of which Map a Copy is added to this Treaty, bearing the signatures and seals of the Undersigned Plenipotentiaries.[10]

FIG. I-1. John Disturnell, *Mapa de los Estados Unidos de Méjico, 1847*, attached to the U.S. copy of the Treaty of Guadalupe Hidalgo. (National Archives)

The treaty writers reconciled their language with the representation in Disturnell's map, but they did not confirm that the map image agreed with geographical reality. In fact, the map contained a number of serious errors, particularly in its depiction of the Rio Grande and the town of Paso, important features named in the written delimitation of the boundary. In spite of its recent publication date, Disturnell's map was based on old information. It was copied with few changes from *A Map of North America*, published by Henry S. Tanner of Philadelphia in 1822. The depiction of northern Mexico in Tanner's map had depended upon several sources, including Alexander von Humboldt, Pedro Walker, Zebulon Pike, and William Darby, all authorities dating from about the first decade of the nineteenth century. Although these authorities had not yet been superseded in 1846, when Disturnell took over the map, the age of the sources demonstrated the lack of up-to-date information about the geography of northern Mexico that existed at midcentury. Disturnell, who was not a cartographer himself but rather a business-man who published directories, guidebooks, and maps, brought out the *Mapa de los Estados Unidos de Méjico* in response to public interest gen-erated by the U.S.-Mexican War. In 1847, the year that treaty negotia-tions began, Disturnell published seven different printings of the map, each with additions and changes, which he termed "editions."[11]

A copy of the seventh edition of Disturnell's map was carried to Mex-ico City for use in the negotiations by Nicholas P. Trist, the U.S. treaty commissioner. Trist did not think highly of Disturnell's map; he consid-ered that it was "suddenly got up, as the mere speculation of an engraver or bookseller, to meet the demand in our country for Maps of Mex-ico."[12] Trist and the Mexican treaty commissioners searched for more reliable geographic information than that provided by Disturnell's map but were unable to find a satisfactory authority. When diplomacy was concluded, the map that Trist had carried with him was attached to the U.S. copy of the Treaty of Guadalupe Hidalgo. The map that was at-tached to Mexico's copy of the treaty was the twelfth edition, also pub-lished in 1847. It is not likely that the negotiators realized that they had placed two different editions of Disturnell's map with the treaty, but the differences between the two editions apparently caused no complica-tions in the boundary survey.[13]

The errors present in both official editions of Disturnell's map, however, precipitated controversy. In relation to the graticule of the map, the Rio Grande was placed farther to the east than its true position, and the town of Paso was located too far north on the Rio Grande. Paso was actually located about two degrees farther west and thirty minutes farther south than shown on Disturnell's map. In addition, the displacement of the Rio Grande on Disturnell's map made the southern boundary of New Mexico appear to be about three degrees long, whereas the southern boundary actually reached about one degree west of the Rio Grande. The southern boundary of New Mexico was shown as though it were an established entity, when in fact it had never been demarcated. The U.S. Boundary Commission and the Comisión de Límites Mexicana (Mexican Boundary Commission) appointed under the Treaty of Guadalupe Hidalgo discovered the problems in Disturnell's map when they arrived at Paso in December 1850, although the errors had been suspected well before then.[14]

The map's discrepancies raised doubts about the correct location of the boundary line west of the Rio Grande. Because Disturnell's map was an integral part of the Treaty of Guadalupe Hidalgo, U.S. Boundary Commissioner John Russell Bartlett and Mexican Boundary Commissioner Pedro García Conde had to decide whether the line should be determined by the latitude shown on the map or by its position relative to the town of Paso, as shown on the map. After extensive discussions, the commissioners directed an engineer from the Mexican commission, José Salazar, and an engineer from the U.S. commission, Amiel Whipple, to examine Disturnell's map, make measurements on the map, and prepare a written report. The engineers' findings served as the basis for an agreement between the commissioners that became known as the Bartlett–García Conde compromise. Salazar and Whipple reported as follows:

> With a certified copy of the Treaty Map before us, we proceeded to make a scale of minutes of latitude, by dividing into 120 equal parts, the length of that portion of a meridian laid down upon the Map between the parallels of 32° + 34° of North latitude.

> In a similar manner we found a scale of minutes of longitude for that degree of latitude, which passes through points of the Southern Boundary Line of New Mexico as indicated upon the same Map.

Then, measuring the distance from the point where the middle of the Rio Grande strikes the Southern Boundary of New Mexico, South to the parallel of latitude marked 32°, and applying it to our scale of minutes of latitude, we found the length equal to 22′ of arc. This reduced by Francoeur's tables is equal to 40659 metres = 25¼ english miles = 21.92 Geographical miles.

Finally, taking the distance from the point aforesaid to the extreme Western limit of the Southern Boundary of New Mexico, and applying this distance to our scale of minutes of arc in longitude, we found it to be 3°; which in this latitude, according to tables of Francoeur is equal to 282220.2 metres = 175.28 English miles = 154.14 Geographical miles.

Therefore, according to this determination, the point where the middle of the Rio Grande strikes the Southern Boundary of New Mexico, is 22′ of arc North of the parallel of latitude marked 32° upon the Map. From the same point thence the Southern Boundary of New Mexico extends 3° to its Western termination.[15]

The commissioners upheld the engineers' verdict that the boundary should run along the 32°22′ parallel, further north than its position on Disturnell's map relative to the town of Paso, for three degrees west from the Rio Grande, as shown on the map (see Location Map 3). The Bartlett–García Conde compromise gave the United States more territory to the west than the true southern boundary of New Mexico would have enclosed and gave Mexico more territory to the north than the true position of Paso would have allowed. The commissions proceeded to establish the initial point of the boundary on the 32°22′ parallel at the Rio Grande, near the town of Doña Ana; and the Mexican commission, satisfied with the Bartlett–García Conde agreement, continued to survey the entire southern boundary of New Mexico.[16] Discontent with the newly established initial point began to disrupt the U.S. commission, however, as some commission members argued that the initial point had been located much farther north than intended by the Treaty of Guadalupe Hidalgo. The controversy grew until many people were drawn into it, including residents of the border area and the governments of New Mexico and Chihuahua. Public opinion in the United States increasingly found the Bartlett–García Conde compro-

mise unacceptable and demanded renegotiation of the boundary delimitation. Meanwhile, U.S. survey operations stagnated, until at length
Congress suspended appropriations, and the boundary commission was
recalled.

Before the survey collapsed, the U.S. and Mexican commissions completed the Gila River survey and the California line. The boundary followed the middle of the Gila River to its confluence with the Colorado
River, crossed the Colorado, and struck a straight line to a point one
marine league due south of the southernmost point of the port of San
Diego. The dividing line between Alta California, allocated to the
United States, and Baja California, still a Mexican possession, had been
strongly debated in the negotiation of the Treaty of Guadalupe Hidalgo.
The Mexican diplomats had specific instructions not to relinquish the
port of San Diego, while for the U.S. commissioner, the acquisition of
San Diego was a fundamental goal. Mexico ultimately surrendered San
Diego because the town had been perceived as part of Alta California
since the time of its founding, but the boundary between the Californias
was particularly carefully defined in the treaty.[17]

Another map was consulted to support the delimitation of the California line. "In order to preclude all difficulty in tracing upon the ground
the limit separating Upper from Lower California," the treaty stated,

> it is agreed that the said limit shall consist of a straight line, drawn
> from the middle of the Rio Gila, where it unites with the Colorado,
> to a point on the Coast of the Pacific Ocean, distant one marine
> league due south of the southernmost point of the Port of San Diego,
> according to the plan of said port, made in the year 1782, by Don
> Juan Pantoja, second sailing-Master of the Spanish fleet, and pub-
> lished at Madrid in the year 1802, in the Atlas to the voyage of the
> schooners *Sutil* and *Mexicana:* of which plan a Copy is hereunto
> added, signed and sealed by the respective Plenipotentiaries.[18]

Duplicates of the plan of the port of San Diego were attached to the
U.S. and Mexican copies of the treaty (fig. I-2). The duplicates were
tracings made from the Spanish atlas named in the treaty, drawn at
Mexico City while the treaty was being negotiated; the Mexican tracing
was signed by Romualdo Rivera and the U.S. tracing was made or directed by Captain Robert E. Lee of the U.S. Army.[19] The boundary line
was added to the tracings of the Pantoja map. Labeled "Boundary Line

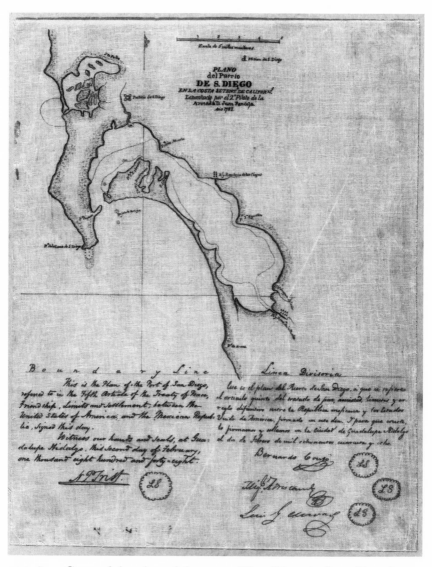

FIG. I-2. Copy of the plan of the port of San Diego by Juan Pantoja, attached to the U.S. copy of the Treaty of Guadalupe Hidalgo. (National Archives)

Linea Divisoria," it ran just below Punto de Arena, on the coast south of the bay. No designations of latitude or longitude were given anywhere on the tracing of Pantoja's plan, so that the boundary between the Californias was delimited in relationship to the topography, the features of the land surface.

The impasse that resulted from U.S. rejection of the Bartlett–García Conde compromise was resolved only through settlement of a new boundary treaty. While treaty negotiations were under way, U.S. and Mexican Boundary Commissions returned to the field and completed the survey of the Rio Grande. On 30 December 1853, the treaty commissioners in Mexico City signed a new treaty, and after extended debate in the U.S. Congress, ratifications were exchanged on 30 June 1854. Referred to by the participating diplomats as the treaty "of clarification of the Treaty of Guadalupe," the Treaty of 1853 nullified or revised several articles of the earlier treaty and provided a new boundary delimitation. It replaced the southern boundary of New Mexico as shown on Disturnell's map and the line in the Gila River with a boundary south of the Gila that followed specified geometrical lines connecting several new turning points, and a short jog along the Colorado River. As part of the treaty, the United States purchased from Mexico the territory between the Gila River and the new boundary. In the United States, the treaty became known as the Gadsden Treaty or the Gadsden Purchase after its U.S. negotiator; in Mexico it was called the Tratado de la Mesilla, named for the principal area in controversy, the Mesilla Valley, that was settled by the treaty. Both nations used the more neutral name, Treaty of 1853.[20]

The new treaty noted that the dividing line between the Californias would remain as already defined and established and repeated the delimitation of the Rio Grande boundary that had been given in the 1848 treaty. The Treaty of 1853 specified the limits in the Rio Grande as follows: "Beginning in the Gulf of Mexico, three leagues from land, opposite the mouth of the Rio Grande as provided in the fifth article of the Treaty of Guadalupe Hidalgo, thence as defined in the said article, up the middle of that river." The new portion of the boundary was to begin at

the point where the parallel of 31°47′ north latitude crosses the same [Rio Grande], thence due west one hundred miles, thence south to

the parallel of 31°20′ north latitude, thence along the said parallel of
31°20′ to the 111th meridian of longitude west of Greenwich, thence
in a straight line to a point on the Colorado river twenty English
miles below the junction of the Gila and Colorado rivers, thence up
the middle of the said river Colorado until it intersects the present
line between the United States and Mexico.[21]

Thus the new delimitation retained much of the boundary that had already been surveyed while it required new surveys in order to connect
the Rio Grande boundary and the California line.

Shortly after ratification of the Treaty of 1853, the U.S. and Mexican
Boundary Commissions renewed their surveying operations, completing the fieldwork in 1855. The surveys established a boundary 1,952 miles
(3,141 km) long, excluding maritime boundaries, from the Gulf of Mexico to the Pacific Ocean: 1,254 miles (2,019 km) on the Rio Grande;
533 miles (858 km) from the Rio Grande to the Colorado River; 24 miles
(38 km) on the Colorado River; and 141 miles (226 km) from the Colorado River to the Pacific Ocean.[22] The work of the boundary commissions was not over, however, for with the boundary surveyed and
marked in the field, the second of its two distinct but interdependent
projects remained to be completed: that of compiling and producing
authoritative maps of the line surveyed and marked. The final boundary
maps were completed two years later, in 1857, with the U.S. commission
and the Mexican commission each depositing a set of maps with their
respective governments, to be held as legal records of the boundary.

The maps contributed at once to the nineteenth century's expanding
geographical knowledge of the world. The region that had become the
borderlands through settlement of the U.S.-Mexican War was little
known, and the maps produced by the boundary commissions were the
first to portray the extensive area from an organized, scientific survey. In
the surveying and mapping operations of the joint commission, as well
as in the scientific investigations carried out in conjunction with the
survey, the work was conceived by its practitioners as a contribution to
world scientific knowledge. A U.S. scientist who traveled to Europe
while the survey was in progress, carrying with him copies of some of
the early boundary maps completed by the U.S. commission, wrote to
the commissioner to describe their European reception: "And how are
you coming on with your maps?" he asked; "The four first of which you
gave me copies to take along and distribute in Europe have created

general attention among men of science[,] geographers especially, both as works of art, as on account of their intrinsic value for the knowledge of that part of the globe[']s surface. I have left copies with the Geographical Societies of Berlin, Frankfort and other places and with Baron Von Humboldt, who expressed himself as being familiar with your name and as highly pleased with the whole work."[23] Historians later recognized the high achievement that the boundary surveys represented. William Goetzmann named the boundary survey as "one of the best of the surveys" of the U.S. Corps of Topographical Engineers, and Manuel Orozco y Berra marked the boundary survey as one of the best works carried out by the Mexican engineers.[24]

The results of the boundary surveys were incorporated into national maps of Mexico and the United States. In Mexico political turmoil had prevented orderly surveying and mapping of the new nation in the years following independence in 1821. The Sociedad Mexicana de Geografía y Estadística (Mexican Society of Geography and Statistics), at its founding in 1833, organized a project to produce a general map of the nation, but the map was not completed until 1850. Compiled from many sources, and including the northern territories that had been lost to the United States, Mexico's most authoritative national map was already outdated at the time of the boundary survey.[25] With the survey's conclusion, efforts to map the national domain were renewed. An atlas that presented a national map and maps of the Mexican states with geographical and statistical information, compiled by engineer, geographer, and writer Antonio García y Cubas and supported by the Ministerio de Fomento (Department of Development), was published in 1858, a year after the boundary maps were completed. The atlas's long list of map authorities—persons who had gathered the survey data on which the maps were based or who had contributed to their making—included members of both the Mexican and U.S. Boundary Commissions.[26]

In the United States, survey results contributed to two important maps of the western states and territories. The U.S. Boundary Commission prepared a general map of the Transmississippi West, one of the first to present an overall view of the West as a compilation of U.S. government surveys, that was published with the commission's final *Report* in 1857–58. The officer who had charge of the map's printing noted that "The map now is considered one of the best maps ever published and great demands are made daily for copies of it."[27] It did not long retain its standing as the master map of the Transmississippi West,

however, for even as it was being prepared, another map was being raced
to publication. Topographical Engineer Gouverneur Warren, working
in the Office of Pacific Railroad Surveys, produced a map of the West
nearly simultaneously with that of the boundary commission. Drawn at
a larger scale than the boundary commission's map, Warren's map was
compiled by comparing and analyzing the data from a large number of
surveys and included an image of the new U.S. borderlands based on
boundary survey information. Some historians have judged Warren's
map of the West to be a landmark map, the culmination of six decades
of exploration and mapping.[28]

Some forty years after the original survey, the geometric boundaries
were resurveyed by U.S. and Mexican engineers. The original demarcation had been made with only a few, widely spaced monuments, many
of which were destroyed in time, so that the boundary was poorly
marked. Because of disputes over the exact location of the boundary that
arose as adjacent lands became more settled, the United States and
Mexico agreed to restore the boundary monuments and erect new ones
to mark the line where it ran overland. An International Boundary
Commission performed the resurvey in the years 1891 to 1896 and prepared a new set of maps of the land boundary. The plan of operations
drawn up between U.S. and Mexican engineers was based on relocating
the original monuments; the terms of their agreement stated that "all
monuments whose position, after verification, are found to be as located
by the International Boundary Commission of 1849–56 shall be accepted as positive boundary marks."[29] The maps of the original survey
were crucial in recovering the monuments on the land and in verifying
that the markers found were in fact those erected in 1849–56.

The maps of the original survey also aided in maintaining the boundary in the Colorado River and the Rio Grande. An International Boundary Commission to resolve problems relating to the river boundaries was
first created in a treaty between the United States and Mexico in 1889.[30]
The commission was to investigate changes that had occurred in the
course of the Rio Grande and, in each case, decide upon sovereignty of
the adjoining lands. Locating the old bed of the river and ascertaining
the extent and location of change was often assisted by reference to the
maps of the original survey. The maps were also called upon as evidence
in international hearings to resolve boundary questions. The role of the
maps in providing evidence became most important when judicial con-

cern fell upon the boundary maps' authority and the permanence of the Rio Grande boundary.

Another concern, the management of water resources, became increasingly important as population in the borderlands grew, and several new treaties clarified water management and boundary issues. The Treaty of 1944 made extensive provisions for the utilization of the waters of the Rio Grande, Colorado, and Tijuana Rivers and renamed the boundary commission as the International Boundary and Water Commission (Comisión Internacional de Límites y Aguas), charging it with carrying out the terms of the treaty.[31] In 1970 the Treaty to Resolve Pending Boundary Differences and Maintain the Rio Grande and the Colorado River as the International Boundary continued the commission's jurisdiction over boundary matters.[32] Mapping requirements spelled out in the Treaty of 1970 maintain surveying and mapping among the commission's important activities. The International Boundary and Water Commission coordinates mapping projects with U.S. and Mexican national mapping agencies, embracing cooperation on many cartographic issues, such as the exchange of data, map materials, and information on mapping programs, shared geodetic control along the border, publication of cartographic information furnished by the other country, and acquisition and distribution of aerial photography.[33]

The example for cooperation in boundary work by specialists from both the United States and Mexico was set in the original surveying and mapping project of 1849–57. The participation by representatives of both nations in the surveys and the reflection of their proceedings in the final maps are important themes for boundary history. The decisions and agreements of the original U.S. and Mexican Boundary Commissions became the foundation for future boundary relations, initiating open and professional negotiations for boundary administration. The maps they produced, on the other hand, became significant because each commission maintained independence in its surveying and mapping operations. The existence of two sets of official boundary maps, one made by the United States and one by Mexico, would later have consequences for the development of boundary relations between the United States and Mexico; but these consequences were not revealed until half a century after the original survey was completed. The making of maps by the U.S. and Mexican commissions set the course of boundary history.

CHAPTER ONE

ON THE LINE

Field Surveys

I take the liberty to believe that . . . the most modern methods
of observation and calculation have been employed, that up to
now had not been used in the country, and that for that reason
the results obtained correspond to their object.

First Engineer Francisco Jiménez,
"Diario-memoria de los trabajos científicos"

T HE WORK OF THE U.S. AND MEXICAN BOUNDARY COM-
missions began with the field surveys. By means of the surveys, the
commissions established on the ground the boundary line that had first
existed only in words and treaty maps. The authoritative bases for the
formation of the U.S. Boundary Commission and the Comisión de
Límites Mexicana were given in the Treaty of 1848 and later the Treaty
of 1853, which delegated responsibility for boundary demarcation to
them. Sponsored by the U.S. and Mexican governments, the commissions pursued their duties in the field for over six years, from July 1849
to October 1855. During that time, many individuals joined and left the
surveys and participated in the making of the boundary.

The Treaty of Guadalupe Hidalgo required that the United States
and Mexico should each appoint a commissioner and a surveyor. Their
duties, "to run and mark the said Boundary," were defined more fully
as, "to designate the Boundary line with due precision, upon authoritative maps, and to establish upon the ground landmarks which shall show
the limits of both Republics, as described in the present Article." The
commissioner and surveyor were endowed with considerable power, as

the treaty further specified that "the result, agreed upon by them, shall be deemed a part of this treaty, and shall have the same force as if it were inserted therein." This statement gave the four appointees authority to interpret the boundary delimitation contained in the treaty and made their determination final. The two governments were to provide the commissioners and surveyors with escorts and whatever might be necessary for their work.[1]

Within the U.S. commission, the appointments made under the Treaty of Guadalupe Hidalgo resulted in distracting struggles for authority, so the negotiators of the Treaty of 1853 sought to avoid further disruptions by combining the duties of the commissioner and surveyor. The new treaty mandated that "each of the two Governments shall nominate one Commissioner," whose duty it would be to "survey and mark out upon the land the dividing line stipulated by this article." The commissioners would have exclusive authority: "that line shall be alone established upon which the Commissioners may fix, their consent in this particular being considered decisive and an integral part of this Treaty, without necessity of ulterior ratification or approval, and without room for interpretation of any kind by either of the Parties contracting." To further prevent contention, the treaty noted that the commissioners would have assistants, but they were to have no jurisdiction: the concurrence of "Scientific or other assistants, such as Astronomers and Surveyors" would "not be considered necessary for the settlement and ratification of a true line of division between the two Republics."[2]

The Mexican government appointed four boundary commissions between the years 1849 and 1857, three of them to carry out fieldwork and one to prepare maps. The first and second Mexican Boundary Commissions were appointed under the Treaty of Guadalupe Hidalgo in 1848 and 1850 and worked from bases in San Diego and Paso, respectively. The third commission was appointed in 1854 to operate from Paso under the Treaty of 1853. The Mexican commissions were composed of well-educated engineers, often military personnel, and many continued to work from one commission to the next. Although a great deal has been written about the power struggles and personal interactions in the U.S. commission, little is known about the internal relations of the Mexican commission. In general, the appointments to the Comisión de Límites Mexicana were characterized by stability and continuity.[3]

By the time of the boundary survey, the occupation of the topo-

graphical engineer or surveyor was well-established in Mexico. Colonial
New Spain had witnessed the surveying and mapping activities of the
Spanish Royal Corps of Engineers, many of whose members resided for
long periods in New Spain. All of the professional members of the
Mexican Boundary Commission had been educated at either the Colegio de Minería, founded in Mexico City in 1783 and, at mid-nineteenth
century, having a broad curriculum in science and mathematics; or at
the Colegio Militar, founded in 1822, shortly after Mexican independence, and to which a Corps of Engineers was added in 1833. Early in
the survey, the U.S. chief astronomer sized up the Mexican commission
and remarked that it was "composed of well educated and scientific
men."[4] The members of the U.S. and Mexican commissions recipro-
cated respect and cordiality; the personal friendships that developed between the officers of the two commissions often contrasted with the
prejudiced attitudes of the members of the U.S. commission toward
Mexicans in general.[5]

The first Mexican Boundary Commission was organized in Mexico
City late in 1848. A distinguished army engineer and former director of
the Colegio Militar, General Don Pedro García Conde, was selected as
commissioner. He was experienced in surveying and mapping and was
familiar with the border region, having conducted a notable survey of
Chihuahua that resulted in a manuscript map of the state and a published account.[6] García Conde's role in the boundary survey was primarily administrative and diplomatic. The position of *agrimensor* or *geó-
metra* (surveyor) was held by a civilian engineer, José Salazar Ylarregui.
Salazar had received his education at the Colegio de Minería, where he
studied with a renowned professor of mineralogy, Andrés Manuel del
Río, and later held teaching and administrative positions.[7] Salazar was
to play a heroic role in the Mexican commission, similar to that of William H. Emory in the U.S. commission, staying with the work throughout its entire course and ending up as commissioner.

In addition to the commissioner and surveyor required by treaty, four
engineers and an interpreter were appointed. Salazar's principal assistant
in the California survey was First Engineer Francisco Martínez de
Chavero, from the Colegio Militar, who was also named secretary of
the Mexican commission.[8] Francisco Jiménez, captain of engineers and
professor of mechanics at the Colegio Militar, was appointed as another first engineer. There were two second engineers: Agustín García

Conde, a military engineer and son of the commissioner, and Ricardo Ramírez, a civilian appointed as surveyor and naturalist. Felipe de Iturbide accompanied the engineers as translator and interpreter.[9]

In the early spring of 1850, with most of the survey in California completed, the joint boundary commission agreed to adjourn and meet again in Paso in November. Ramírez, assisted by a young engineer named Samora, remained in California to work with Captain E. L. F. Hardcastle of the U.S. commission in erecting the monuments on the boundary. The rest of the commission returned to Mexico City, where the second Comisión de Límites was organized, with García Conde remaining at its head and Salazar still the official surveyor. Jiménez stood as first engineer, to carry out much of the astronomical work; he also became the leader of the survey of the Río Gila, locating a boundary that was later superseded by the Treaty of 1853. Agustín García Conde was now also a first engineer. New mapping personnel included Juan B. Espejo, second engineer; and Manuel Alemán, Agustín Díaz, and Luis Díaz, who each had the title of *agregado* (assistant).[10]

Espejo was a military engineer from the Colegio Militar; as a member of the second commission, he worked on the survey of the Bartlett–García Conde line that was later overthrown.[11] Luis Díaz and Agustín Díaz, two brothers who were both lieutenants of engineers at the Colegio Militar, were Espejo's assistants on the expedition. For Agustín Díaz, the boundary survey was the first important assignment in a career that eventually placed him as Mexico's foremost cartographer, founding and directing the government mapping agency, the Comisión Geográfico-Exploradora. The Díaz brothers specialized in triangulation and topography, while Manuel Alemán, the third new assistant on the Comisión de Límites, was an astronomer. Like the Díaz brothers, Alemán had been a student at the Colegio Militar.[12]

In December 1851, while the Mexican engineers were engaged in the survey west from Paso del Norte, García Conde contracted a fatal illness and was taken to his native town of Arizpe, Sonora, where he died. Agustín learned of his father's death upon returning from the survey of the Río Gila and departed directly for Mexico, never rejoining the commissions formed later. Salazar was appointed interim commissioner early in 1852. The second commission turned to work on the Río Bravo, then straggled back to Mexico City to await a resolution of the controversy over the Bartlett–García Conde compromise. Agustín Díaz was the last Mexican engineer left working on the river in spring 1854, alone after the rest of the members of the Comisión de Límites had returned to Mexico City and well after the U.S. commission had departed.[13]

The third commission, appointed under the Treaty of 1853, was composed equally of experienced boundary surveyors and new mapping personnel. Salazar, who had participated in the negotiation of the treaty, was named commissioner, the position now including the official function of the former surveyor. The commission was divided into three sections, each charged with the survey of a part of the boundary. The *sección de Sonora*, responsible for the survey of the Río Colorado and the line eastward from the Colorado, was led by First Engineer Francisco Jiménez, assisted by the astronomer, Manuel Alemán, now promoted to captain; and the experienced topographers Agustín Díaz, newly promoted captain and second engineer; and Luis Díaz. The *sección del Río Bravo*, made up of Manuel Fernández Leal, Francisco Herrera, and Miguel Iglesias, was to complete the survey of the river between Paso and Laredo. The *sección del norte*, composed of Salazar and new engineers Ignacio Molina and Antonio Contreras, was bound for Paso to meet with the U.S. commission.[14]

All three engineers of the *sección del Río Bravo* were new to the boundary. Manuel Fernández Leal, skilled in topographical surveying and drawing, had graduated from the Colegio de Minería, and later became a minister in the Mexican government. When the United States–Mexico boundary was resurveyed in 1891–96, the name of Manuel Fernández Leal, who had jurisdiction over the Mexican commission as minister of development, was commemorated in a document deposited in the monument on the Pacific Ocean. Francisco Herrera was another engineer who received his training at the Colegio de Minería, as probably did Miguel Iglesias.[15]

The *sección del norte* had the task of establishing the new initial point on the Rio Grande. When Salazar and his party reached Paso ahead of the U.S. engineers, their arrival was described by a messenger for the U.S. commission:

> On Sunday evening the 5th Ultimo, Señor Salazar[,] the Mex[n]
> Boundary Commiss[r][,] accompanied by two officers of his party,
> Señor Molinar [*sic*], and Senor Contretras [*sic*], arrived at El Paso,
> having left the City of Mexico Septr 14th. . . . I believe the two Gen-

tlemen with Sen. S. are officers in the Mex[n] Engineer Corps. Sen
Moliner [sic][,] the elder of the two[,] I should imagine to be 25 yrs.
of age, and Sen Contreras about 17. This is I think their first experience in the boundary.[16]

Captain Molina was a military engineer educated at both the Colegio
Militar and the Colegio de Minería. Contreras was a young assistant
who had not yet completed his training at the Colegio de Minería. As
commissioner, Salazar faced great trials when political events in Mexico
City led to his arrest and imprisonment for several months in 1855.[17]
Restored to his position, Salazar and the engineers of the *sección del norte*
and the *sección del Río Bravo* were the last members of either commission
to leave the field, remaining to work on the line west from Paso after
the survey was officially closed.

Compared to the Comisión de Límites Mexicana, the United States
Boundary Commission was more complex and more varied in its activities. The official staff of the U.S. commission was much larger and, over
time, was not so clearly renewed as several distinct entities as was the
Mexican commission. Political partisanship, personal bickering, conflicts between military and civilian personnel, and the agendas of various
interest groups continually disrupted the U.S. commission. In addition,
a number of scientists and artists, intrigued by the prospect of exploring
the untracked territory newly acquired by the United States, traveled to
the borderlands with the U.S. commission to pursue personal projects
or institutional programs of research.

During the course of the field surveys, four different U.S. commissioners were appointed, and the commission was generally called after
the commissioner who headed it. The Weller commission of 1849,
which convened in San Diego, was the first U.S. Boundary Commission. It was followed by the Bartlett commission of 1850 in Paso del
Norte; the Campbell commission for the survey of the Rio Grande in
1853; and the Emory commission, appointed in 1854 to meet once again
in Paso. There were many changes in personnel with the appointment
of each commissioner, and commission members were apt to be of
widely varying abilities.

John B. Weller, a political appointee, headed a large commission.
The military provided not only a protective escort but also officers from
the elite Corps of Topographical Engineers, a division of the pre–Civil

War U.S. Army dedicated to scientific exploration and mapping and civil engineering projects. Like most of the Topographical Engineers, the officers of the Weller commission, Major William H. Emory, Captain E. L. F. Hardcastle, and Lieutenant Amiel W. Whipple, were graduates of the Military Academy at West Point, the leading institution for the training of engineers in the United States at that time.[18] Both Major Emory, the chief astronomer, and Andrew B. Gray, the official surveyor and a civilian, were charged with the technical work that would locate the boundary on the ground. Some of the mapping personnel were subordinate to Emory, while others were assistants to Gray.

William Hemsley Emory held prominent positions in the U.S. Boundary Commission throughout its duration and has been credited with the achievement of the boundary survey more than any other one person. Earlier experience had prepared Emory well for his service on the boundary. When the Corps of Topographical Engineers was formed in 1838, he was appointed first lieutenant, and he was assigned to assist in making a map from surveys by Joseph Nicollet, a French scientist who introduced new scientific methods of cartography to the United States. Emory also compiled a regional map of Texas, served as a principal assistant on the northeast boundary survey between the United States and the British Provinces, and acted as chief engineer officer on the U.S. Army's march to California during the U.S.-Mexican War, producing an important map of the army's route across the border region. Thus to his work on the United States–Mexico boundary, Emory brought his training in scientific and mathematical cartography, experience in boundary surveying, and authoritative knowledge of the borderlands.[19]

Emory's principal assistants in California were Edmund La Fayette Hardcastle and Amiel Weeks Whipple, who both held positions as assistant astronomers. Hardcastle had done reconnaissance mapping in Mexico during the war, and Whipple had previous experience as an assistant astronomer on the northeast boundary survey. Other members of Emory's party included civilians James Nooney, principal computer (responsible for calculating geographical positions from the astronomers' and surveyors' observations); Charles Christopher Parry, assistant computer, geologist, and botanist; and George Clinton Gardner and Edward Ingraham, junior computers.[20]

Legal responsibility for the survey belonged to the U.S. surveyor, Andrew Belcher Gray. Gray lacked the scientific and mathematical expertise of the Topographical Engineers but was an experienced surveyor who had represented the Republic of Texas on the U.S.-Texas Boundary Commission in 1839–40.[21] Surveyor Gray's party was made up of Charles J. Whiting, principal assistant; Henry Clayton, draftsman and first assistant; John H. Forster, first subassistant; and several additional assistants.

When the boundary survey moved to Paso del Norte in November 1850, the U.S. commission was almost entirely reconstituted. The new commissioner was John Russell Bartlett, another political appointee without qualifications in surveying or cartography. He did have literary and artistic talents, however, and produced records of the boundary survey of lasting artistic merit; but his quarrelsome temperament and his misdirection of the commission eventually led to its breakdown.[22] Although Bartlett was commissioner for two years and numerous surveys were conducted during his tenure, none of them contributed to the final boundary maps. The surveys he supervised connected the California boundary with the initial point on the Rio Grande, along the line proposed by the Bartlett–García Conde compromise, and all of the surveys were abrogated by the Treaty of 1853. Most of the Rio Grande boundary was also surveyed during Bartlett's administration, but the work was entirely under Emory's control.

Emory eventually became both U.S. surveyor and the chief astronomer of the Bartlett commission, although at the outset, Gray, detained in Washington by illness, was still surveyor. When the original appointee as chief astronomer was removed before he had accomplished anything on the boundary, Bartlett appointed Lieutenant Whipple as chief astronomer and acting surveyor—an appointment that was later contended to be illegal. Nevertheless, as an acting officer, Whipple established the initial point on the Rio Grande at the 32°22' parallel, supporting the soon-to-be disputed Bartlett–García Conde compromise. Whipple also took charge of the survey of the Gila River, producing, according to an inventory by Bartlett, fifty-one maps of the river boundary.[23]

Whipple's duties were soon taken over by a new chief astronomer, Brevet Lieutenant Colonel James Duncan Graham, and Surveyor Gray. Graham was eminently qualified for his position, having formerly been principal astronomer of the northeast boundary survey, but he became embroiled in the commission's feuds and also accomplished little. Gray, late to arrive in Paso, fell into conflict with the U.S. commissioner when he rejoined the survey. Refusing to accept the Bartlett–García Conde compromise, Gray insisted that the initial point must be established farther south. Because of his refusal to sign the agreement, Gray was removed from his position by the secretary of the interior.[24] The replacement of both Graham and Gray by Emory removed two argumentative individuals and simplified the U.S. commission. Emory's combined duties of chief astronomer and surveyor made his position similar to that held in the Mexican commission by Salazar.

By the time Emory received his dual appointment, the need to simplify the U.S. commission was great. Not only was internal dissension a problem but the commission had simply grown too large to function efficiently. The number of assistants that Bartlett brought to the frontier—even those strictly of the "surveying, astronomical, and topographical division"—were too many to list here.[25] Furthermore, few of them were qualified to do the work they were appointed to perform. The Mexican commissioner was of the opinion that "Mr. Bartlett, who presides over it [the U.S. commission], is a fine fellow, but without an idea of the work that we have to do; he brought 120 engineers, of whom not one knows his duty in determining the line, and, excepting two or three fairly good ones among them, the rest don't know a word nor do they obey the Commissioner."[26] Graham thought that there were "not more than three or four, out of some dozen or so, that are at all instructed in surveying, and the rest are of no use in the world. They are amiable, and worthy young men," he said, "but I cannot make use of them in surveying, nor could I possibly be responsible for their work."[27]

Several competent assistants accompanied Graham and Emory to the field, however, and they remained on the frontier to become largely responsible for the survey of the Rio Grande. Some of Bartlett's employees also continued in service and made contributions. Accompanying Graham were a civilian surveyor, Charles Radziminski; a computer, John H. Clark; and the assistant astronomer and Topographical Engineer, William F. Smith. Charles Radziminski, a Polish refugee, had worked on the Northeast Boundary Commission directed by Graham. On the Rio Grande, Radziminski carried out a variety of administrative duties and held the title of principal assistant surveyor.[28] John Henry Clark's appointment was arranged with Graham by Spencer F. Baird of the Smithsonian Institution; Clark was to serve on the boundary survey as a collector of zoological specimens. Clark did send shipments of specimens, but he made that effort in addition to steady work as a computer; under Emory's direction, he gained training as an astronomer.[29] Lieutenant William Farrar Smith had been working on wagon road surveys in West Texas just prior to his assignment to the boundary commission. Smith fell into bitter disagreements with Emory and, at his own request, was soon relieved from duty on the boundary commission.[30]

Emory's assistants were a lieutenant of Topographical Engineers, Nathaniel Michler; Arthur Schott, a civilian surveyor; and Gardner and Ingraham, assistants who had been with Emory in California. Nathaniel Michler was a graduate of West Point who first served as a Topographical Engineer making road and river surveys in Texas, including a reconnaissance of the Rio Grande between Ringgold Barracks and the Big Bend.[31] The name of Arthur Carl Victor Schott appeared on the final boundary maps more often than that of any other person except Emory. In addition to his work as a surveyor, Schott made drawings of the borderlands and collected plant, animal, fossil, and mineral specimens. An immigrant from Germany, Schott had received his education at the gymnasium and technical school at Stuttgart, his native city, and additional training at the Institute of Agriculture at Hohenheim.[32]

Two employees who performed difficult duties as leaders of surveying parties were hired originally by Bartlett for other work on the commission. Marine Tyler Wickham Chandler, a congressman's son, was employed by Bartlett as a meteorological and magnetic observer; he later prepared the sections on meteorology and barometric heights for the final *Report*. He held a master's degree from the University of Pennsylvania and had worked as an engineer and surveyor for the city of Philadelphia.[33] Maurice von Hippel was hired as a draftsman. Not long after the commission's arrival in Paso, Hippel and two other draftsmen resigned in protest of their low status and inadequate salaries. Hippel soon came back, after the additional resignation of the principal topographic draftsman, Augustus de Vaudricourt, and was the only draftsman on the Bartlett commission.[34] He remained to hold several important positions as an assistant surveyor.

Other employees hired by Bartlett whose names appeared on the final boundary maps included Frank Wheaton and Hugh Campbell. Wheaton was a student in the Scientific Department of Brown University and a city engineer in Providence, Rhode Island, at the time of his appointment to the boundary commission.[35] Being very young, Wheaton was placed at the level of a sixth assistant; later he gained experience as a topographer. Hugh Campbell followed a similar career in the U.S. commission, beginning as a junior assistant and gaining experience.

There were a few other appointees of Bartlett's whose names were not included on the boundary maps but who made significant contributions to the surveys and continued their work on later commissions. E. A. Phillips came to Bartlett's commission as a subassistant surveyor; John O'Donoghue was hired as a computer; and James H. Prioleau served as a first assistant surveyor.[36] James H. Houston, Malcolm Seaton, and Thomas Walter Jones likewise began as assistants with Bartlett and continued with the next commissioner. There were several others employed by Bartlett who must have been qualified surveyors but who made no contribution to the final boundary maps because their work was superseded by the Treaty of 1853. Possibly the only extant field book made by a member of the U.S. Boundary Commission was kept by John Bull, first assistant surveyor in charge of surveys on the Gila River, during the commission's march across Texas to Paso in 1850.[37]

In contrast to the Bartlett commission, the Campbell commission was short-lived and efficient. It was headed by Robert Blair Campbell, another political appointee without scientific or technical qualifications, with Emory in place as surveyor and chief astronomer. Emory controlled much of the decision making, although Campbell remained active in overseeing the fieldwork. The commission completed the survey of the Rio Grande, dividing the work among four small parties headed by Michler, Schott, Radziminski, and Emory. Most of the surveying and mapping personnel of the Campbell commission continued from the earlier commissions, with a notable newcomer in the person of John E. Weyss. Weyss was an immigrant from Austria, where he had been trained as a scientist and engineer; he worked on the boundary survey as a surveyor, topographer, and illustrator.[38]

With ratification of the Treaty of 1853, a new boundary commission was appointed in 1854 with Emory as commissioner. Veterans of the Rio Grande survey were organized into two parties. The larger group, headed by Emory, returned to Paso to press the survey westward; the other team, under the direction of Nathaniel Michler, was bound for "the Pacific side" to work eastward.[39]

Emory's group included assistants Campbell, Chandler, Clark, Hippel, Houston, and Weyss. He was aided in administrative and logistical duties by Charles Radziminski and Charles Turnbull. Radziminski held the position of secretary to the commission, and there is no evidence that he assisted as a surveyor under the Treaty of 1853, despite his earlier successful surveys of the Rio Grande. Charles Nesbit Turnbull was the only assistant who was new to the boundary; a Topographical Engineer recently graduated from the U.S. Military Academy, he worked as a computer in addition to serving on Emory's field staff.[40] With Michler on the Pacific side were the assistant surveyor, Arthur Schott; sub-assistant, E. A. Phillips; and assistant astronomer, John O'Donoghue. Michler's party and the Mexican commission's *sección de Sonora* together officially completed the location of the line delimited in the Treaty of 1853 and closed the boundary survey in October 1855.

In the task of surveying and marking the line, the U.S. and Mexican commissions used similar methods. In general, both commissions divided the work between astronomers, who determined the latitude and longitude from astronomical observations at points along the line, and topographers, who investigated the forms of landscape features and ascertained their locations relative to the astronomers' positions. The surveying procedures of the two commissions differed primarily in emphasis. The U.S. commission stressed astronomical determinations for rapid location of the line, while the Mexican commission emphasized triangulation and topographical mapping and limited astronomical observations.

The U.S. approach to the survey was based on a plan devised by Emory. En route to California, Emory drew up a comprehensive plan for the boundary survey that included astronomy, topography and demarcation of the line, and auxiliary scientific activities. The location of the line would depend upon astronomy. He reasoned that "the most rigid mode of operating would be to cover the whole ground by triangulation; but the expense and the time required by this method, exclude it from consideration. The next method in order of accuracy, and that which presents itself as the only practicable one, is to base the entire work on astronomical determinations of latitude, longitude and azimuth."[41]

Because the boundary from the Pacific Ocean to the mouth of the Río Bravo would extend for nearly two thousand miles, it would be necessary to connect the astronomical stations in a geodetic survey. Calculations employing astronomical data to determine positions, directions, and distances would have to be formulated to take into account the curvature of the earth; thus a more complex mathematics would be required than that used for plane surveys of small areas, based on the assumption that the earth's surface is flat. "It will be seen by those conversant with geodetic matters," Emory cautioned, "that the determination I had undertaken was of no ordinary kind, and required for its success the most accurate and elaborate observations, and a skilful application of those observations by analytic formulae, involving the figure of the earth and other elements, a perfect knowledge of which has not yet been attained, although researches upon the subject have occupied the minds of the great astronomers."[42] The knowledge of scientific theory and mathematics required for the astronomers' work conferred on them a prestigious position among the scientific corps.

Emory's plans for topographical surveying were limited. He proposed that "all determinations of the line of actual boundary, and the topography for one mile on each side, must be based on actual measurement," and that each surveying party would be required to make sketches of the country and barometric levelings of the section surveyed "and note the general character of the country, in its applicability to agriculture, roads and navigation." Each survey party would also be required to keep meteorological records. Emory thus directed much of the topographers' effort toward auxiliary scientific activities.[43]

In contrast to the U.S. commission, the Mexican engineers relied upon triangulation as the survey method they most often preferred. Triangulation is based upon trigonometric principles: from a measured baseline and two measured angles, the remaining measurements of a triangle may be calculated, and from the known positions of the original stations, a network of triangles may be extended and the geographical positions of all the vertices known. Triangulation, although slow and therefore costly, was the most accurate survey method available. The chief advantages of Emory's plan for depending on astronomical determinations rather than triangulation surveys were the shorter length of time and, ideally, fewer workers required, therefore saving in cost. The Mexican commission, however, chose to establish fewer astronomical stations and attempted to carry out triangulation surveys in sections of the boundary where the U.S. commission was satisfied with a rapid traverse.

Both the U.S. and Mexican commissions established primary and secondary astronomical stations and used the same methods for finding latitude and longitude. Primary stations were those whose geographical positions were determined directly by elaborate astronomical observations with large instruments, distinguished from second-class stations where the positions were determined by means of smaller instruments and the transmission of chronometers from primary stations, or by simultaneous observations of gunpowder flashes. The U.S. commission fixed eighteen primary stations across the length of the border, including Camp Riley on the Pacific Coast; the junction of the Gila and Colorado Rivers; eight stations between the Colorado and the Rio Grande; Frontera; the initial point on the Rio Grande; San Elizario; and five other stations on the Rio Grande.[44] The Mexican astronomers fixed seven, possibly eight, primary stations along the length of the boundary. Primary observatories were established at San Diego and at the confluence of the Gila and Colorado Rivers by the first commission; Salazar and Jiménez both directed extensive observations at Paso; and Jiménez and Alemán established primary stations at the mouth of the Río Bravo, Matamoros, Nuevo Laredo, and Quitovaquita (Quitobaquito). It is also possible that Salazar carried out prolonged observations at Presidio del Norte.

Several methods of finding longitude were used, all basically dependent upon comparisons of time between places of unknown longitude and a known longitude position. At the primary stations, longitude was usually determined by means of lunar culminations, and occultation of stars might also be used. The lunar culmination method was based on observation of the moon's location on the celestial sphere at the time of culmination—the time of passage of the moon's center through the meridian. The location was found in comparison with several nearby stars. The longitude was then determined from the moon's hourly rate of motion and its distance from a position of known longitude, as given in an ephemeris, or star catalog. Calculations made at the time of observation, based on predicted star positions from the ephemeris, could be made more accurate later when the actual positions of the stars on the date of observation were known. The corresponding observations for a known longitude that were used in calculations by both the U.S. and Mexican commissions were those made at Greenwich, with observations at U.S. observatories used in a few cases. The occultation of stars—their disappearance behind the moon or other passing celestial body—could be timed at a station of unknown longitude and compared to observations at a station of known longitude; but because of the difficulty of obtaining corresponding observations, occultations were seldom used.[45]

The longitude of secondary stations was found by chronometer or by signals of gunpowder flashes. The chronometric method compared the time at a known longitude, as shown on the chronometer, to the local time at a new station, and converted the time difference to angular distance. The accuracy of the method was limited by the difficulty of maintaining correct time while the chronometers were transported under rugged travel conditions. Flashes of gunpowder would be used as signals that could be observed simultaneously between stations, the local time of the signals being recorded at each station, and the differences between the times giving the longitudes.

Finding the latitude was less difficult. Astronomical determination of latitude depended upon the measurement of the greatest daily altitude, called the meridian altitude, of a celestial object for which the declination—the location north or south of the celestial equator—at the time of the meridian transit was known. The boundary astronomers referred to the Greenwich catalog to find declinations. The latitude could then be computed from the observed meridian altitude. Emory stated specifically that he used a technique known as the Talcott method for finding latitude. It was a very accurate technique that depended on measurement of the zenith distances of stars. The zenith distance, the angle between the observer's zenith and a celestial object at the time of its meridian passage, is the complement of the meridian altitude. The Talcott method applied formulas that combined observations of the zenith distances of two stars of known declination, one star north and the other south of the observer's zenith.[46]

Once the necessary geographical positions had been determined, the boundary line could be traced across the terrain, a process that the U.S. surveyors referred to as "running the line"—a general term for several operations that they did not define. An engineer in the resurvey of 1891–96 explained that "the work on different parts of the boundary differed very much in theory, but the actual fieldwork was practically the same in all cases, and consisted in establishing as nearly as possible a long, straight line over a given stretch of country by successive prolongations of a given initial direction."[47] The theoretical differences depended upon whether the section of the boundary being run followed an azimuth line or a line of latitude.

Azimuth lines that the surveyors had to establish included the California boundary and the United States–Sonora line. These two lines, each conceived as the shortest distance connecting two points, were great circles when projected on the sphere of the earth. In the field, the astronomers calculated the horizontal angle between the projected boundary line and the meridian to obtain the azimuth. In making their geodetic calculations, both Jiménez and Emory followed Friedrich Wilhelm Bessel, the acclaimed Prussian mathematician and astronomer, as their authority for the shape and dimensions of the earth, and they used the formulas of the French mathematicians Louis Puissant and Louis-Benjamin Francoeur.[48] By observations on the pole star, the astronomers would be able to relate the calculated angle to the line's initial point and establish the direction of the line; the angle could then be measured on the ground with surveying instruments.

A general difficulty for both astronomers and surveyors was inconsistency in the systems of units they used in calculations and measurements. In preparing geodetic calculations for the United States–Sonora azimuth line, Jiménez noted that he applied Bessel's dimensions as given in meters, while Emory converted the dimensions to yards. The two commissions had no agreement about the relationship between the length of the meter and the yard. In order to carry out the azimuth-line survey, Jiménez and U.S. Engineer Michler referred to a publication of the Corps of Topographical Engineers, Lee's *Tables and Formulae,* for an equivalence between the yard and meter.[49] Both boundary commissions often worked in metric units, although they occasionally fell back on common standards of measurement inherited from British or Spanish usage; and since the boundary treaties relied upon common units of linear measurement in their delimitations, the commissions were required to use those units to fulfill treaty specifications.

In the resurvey of 1891–96, the calculated azimuth lines were traced by determining a series of straight lines that would approximate the theoretical straight line along the great circle. The engineers used several methods of taking foresights and backsights between two intervisible positions, and sights from intermediate points between the two positions. Each method of sighting would result in a different straight line—each, however, differing little from the others and from the theoretical line. The commission of 1891–96 found that, for the distances on the United States–Mexico boundary, lines traced by any of the several methods of sighting would be "sufficiently accurate," and "all of them were used at one time or another, as found most convenient."[50] The procedures used for tracing the azimuth lines in the resurvey were probably similar to the methods that the original boundary surveyors used.

Lines of latitude were demarcated by a different method than that used in running the azimuth lines. The 31°47′ and 31°20′ parallels west of El Paso were laid out by a technique called the tangent method, a method that was also used in the nineteenth-century U.S. public land surveys. The true meridian was determined at a latitude station on the parallel to be traced, and a tangent at 90° to the meridian was laid off. From the straight line of the prolonged tangent, which gradually departed from the curving parallel as it followed the sphere of the earth, offsets of previously calculated lengths could be measured to locate the position of the parallel.[51] The tangent lines used by the U.S. commission were up to thirty miles in length, and each tangent, surveyed with its offsets, was compared and adjusted to the next tangent determined at a new latitude station. The calculated angles and lengths of the offsets were provided to the surveyors in tables for use in the field to establish points on the parallels. The surveyors' measurements on the tangent and the offsets were generally made by chaining, sometimes by triangulation.[52]

Both azimuth lines and parallels were often aligned by a method of signals. The Mexican commission established the Bartlett–García Conde line on the 32°22′ parallel by using gunpowder signals, and the U.S. commission used signal fires to align the parallels delimited in the Treaty of 1853. The method was exemplified in a set of instructions to Assistant Surveyor Hippel in which Emory planned to find the tangent for the 31°20′ parallel at Espia by signal fires at night. Hippel was to build a signal fire on a hill in view from Emory's observatory. At his station, Emory would set off flashes of powder that, by a prearranged code, would direct Hippel to move his signal fire until it was in the line of the tangent. The next night, Emory would have a large fire built precisely where his instrument had stood, in order for Hippel to take a backsight and verify the line of the tangent, which he would then produce.[53]

In addition to running the line, the topographical surveys employed a variety of techniques, including traverse, triangulation, and barometric leveling. A traverse connected a series of points between which distances and directions were measured along a route, thus establishing the relative locations of the points. The points could be referred to an astronomical station in order to fix their positions; a survey made from a known position of latitude and longitude to find an unknown point is called a "tie." Distances were often found by chaining—measuring ground distances with a standard surveyor's chain. Both distances and directions could be found by triangulation. The use of a barometer to determine elevation from measurements of atmospheric pressure, a technique introduced to western exploration in the United States only a decade or so before the boundary survey, was thought appropriate because it was fast and required little equipment or personnel. The instruments were so fragile, however, that in practice they were usually broken in transport.

The general methods of topographical survey were outlined in U.S. plans for the survey of the Gila River. The primary objects of that survey were to locate the middle of the river, defined as the boundary in the Treaty of Guadalupe Hidalgo, and to make a topographical sketch of the adjacent country.[54] The survey was to start from a position on the river that had been fixed astronomically and marked. Chief Astronomer and Acting Surveyor Whipple instructed the leader of the topographical party as follows:

> The surveying and reconnoitering instruments will consist of Goniometer, chain, Tape, Magnetic compasses +c. . . . From this place [the position determined astronomically] your survey will commence following the direction of the stream. . . .

> The basis of your operations will be the line of the survey of the river. This line will connect the astronomical stations which should be numerous as may be, without greatly impeding the rapidity of the survey. Angles + courses will be measured by the various methods which the nature of the country will render most convenient and correct. The distance over precipice or other obstacle not easily chained may be determined by a hasty triangulation. By similar means you will obtain points upon the other bank of the river so as to be able to determine the middle of the river Gila. . . .

You will also please from time to time take angles or bearings to distant mountain peaks and other prominent features of the country to
aid in plotting the notes + sketches of the Topography in which all
distances will be estimated by the eye. . . .

Your field books should be kept in the most lucid and systematic
manner, with copious explanatory notes.[55]

The quantity and quality of the data produced from the U.S. and
Mexican surveys depended greatly upon the scientific instruments available to the engineers. The two commissions used not only the same
techniques but also the same types of instruments. Although the records
of the U.S. commission contain a great deal of information about its
scientific instruments, little has been written about them.[56] Those studies that consider the Mexican commission usually state that their instruments were poor and infer that the role of the Mexican commission was
therefore extremely limited. Early in the survey, U.S. Chief Astronomer
Emory presumed that he could look for "little or no aid from the Mexican Commission" because "their instruments were radically defective"
and would render the Mexican engineers ineffectual in performing the
geodetic works that Emory had instituted. Emory's statement became
the basis for U.S. historians' evaluation of the Mexican commission, the
quality of its survey, and its contribution in establishing the United
States–Mexico boundary.[57]

The Mexican commission suffered disheartening difficulties in obtaining instruments for the survey. In November 1848 the Mexican government allocated money for the purchase of instruments, which were
immediately ordered from Europe. They were to come from the workshops of Gambey and of Lerebours in France and from Troughton and
Simms of London—all prestigious precision-instrument makers. The
purchases were gathered together in Paris, where they were examined by
the director of the Royal Observatory, who judged them magnificent;
but the instruments were never delivered to the Mexican commission.
The instruments that eventually arrived in Mexico were of inferior quality and were not manufactured by the designated workshops. It was believed that poor instruments were substituted for the fine ones when the
instruments were packed. Consequently, in order to meet the deadline
set by the Treaty of Guadalupe Hidalgo, the Mexican commission was
obliged to solicit instruments from the Colegio de Minería and the Co-

legio Militar and to organize them quickly before departing for the north.[58]

The U.S. commission had its own problems in obtaining instruments. Like the Mexican engineers who had had to make arrangements with their military school, U.S. commission members were compelled to negotiate with the U.S. Military Academy to borrow instruments for the California survey. At Paso work was delayed when newly appointed Commissioner Bartlett arrived to find that most of the commission's instruments had been left in San Diego, for use in completing the work in California. Largely through the efforts of Chief Astronomer Graham, the U.S. commission eventually assembled on the Rio Grande a new collection of scientific instruments, of higher quality than those in California.[59]

The instruments used by the boundary commissions may be classified into six general groups. These include astronomical instruments, used for determining geographical positions from astronomical observations; chronometers, for precise timekeeping; surveying instruments, used for locating positions from angles and distances measured on the ground; instruments for measuring elevation; instruments for measuring natural phenomena—particularly those phenomena that would affect the accuracy of the position-finding instruments; and instruments for cartography. In each category, each commission had a number of different types of instruments, represented by a number of individual instruments that had been made by different makers, including examples of the work of nearly all the leading instrument makers of the time, both European and American.

The astronomical instruments were preeminent among the instruments, permitting a wider range of observations and greater precision than any others. The highest class of astronomical instruments were those used to determine the positions of primary stations. They were patterned after the stationary instruments used in observatories and were made as large as could be practically transported. Included in this class were astronomical transits, zenith telescopes, and other large telescopes mounted for angular measurements of celestial objects.

The astronomical transit was used to track the apparent motion of a celestial body across the observer's meridian, in conjunction with a precision time-keeping instrument. With tables and calculations, the observations could be applied to obtain the latitude, the correct time, and the longitude. Graham described one of the astronomical transits he brought to El Paso as follows:

> This is the largest and one of the most valuable astronomical instru-
> ments belonging to the survey. . . . It was made in the year 1844,
> under my special directions, by Troughton & Simms, of London, for
> use on the northeastern boundary. . . . It is the instrument with
> which the first determination of latitude was ever made in America,
> I believe, by observing the transits of stars over the prime vertical.[60]

The U.S. commission had at least three astronomical transits made by Troughton and Simms, the leading workshop in England.

Salazar reported an *anteojo de tránsitos*, an astronomical transit, as one of the Mexican commission's principal instruments. It came from the workshop of Troughton, but Salazar found a serious defect in it: the eyepiece reticle had been engraved by students under the supervision of a professor at the Colegio de Minería, and they had not succeeded in scribing the crosshairs exactly equidistant. Nevertheless, Salazar used the instrument successfully for many operations, including in his report on the commission's work in California some fifty pages of tables of astronomical observations.[61]

It was specifically in reference to astronomical operations that Emory criticized the Mexican commission's instruments, and Emory's dispar-agement was fortified by Salazar, who in his report on the California survey deplored the condition of his instruments. The instruments they had in California, however, were not all that the Mexican engineers used throughout the survey; they later acquired some new and better instruments.[62] Unfortunately, Salazar appears not to have written an in-ventory and description of the instruments used in the later surveys, but the reports of Jiménez and Díaz, and scattered documents such as Es-pejo's report on the survey of the Bartlett–García Conde line, contain references to instruments the engineers used as members of the second and third commissions.

Jiménez was especially pleased with a new zenith telescope. A por-table telescope used for measuring zenith distances, it was the preferred instrument for finding latitude. Jiménez explained that he determined the latitude at Paso with a "*telescopio zenital* of large dimensions, con-structed by Troughton & Simms of London, an instrument provided with a micrometer, a very sensitive level, good lenses, very well graduated, and entirely new." He judged that "when good [star] catalogs are had, it is a valuable instrument, especially on expeditions, like that of the boundary, where economy of time is essential."[63] In comparison, the U.S. commission had at least two zenith telescopes: one was made by Troughton and Simms and loaned to the commission by the Coast Survey, and the other was by William Wurdemann, a pioneer manufacturer of astronomical and geodetic instruments in the United States.[64] Other new instruments obtained by Jiménez that the Mexican commission had not had in California were at least one, and possibly two, transit instruments, also by Troughton and Simms; at least one additional chronometer; and several new micrometers, barometers, and compasses.

Both commissions were limited to methods and instruments suitable to the frontier conditions of the border region. In assembling equipment for the survey, Emory recommended that "the higher class of astronomical instruments—such as the Troughton and Semmes [sic] telescope, the transit, and the altitude and azimuth instrument—though admirably adapted for service on the northeastern boundary, intersected as that boundary was at many points by the great thoroughfares of travel, are, in consequence of their size, unsuited for general use on the Mexican boundary, and can only be used at or near points accessible by sea—San Diego and the mouth of the Del Norte."[65] For finding latitude and longitude at secondary stations, smaller, more portable instruments were required.

Less important positions were located with chronometers and reflecting instruments such as reflecting circles, repeating circles, and sextants. The various reflecting instruments were characterized by the basic technique for their use: two celestial objects whose angular distance was to be measured were brought into apparent coincidence by simultaneously viewing them, one directly and the other in a mirror; the mirror was mounted on an index arm that would indicate the angle between the objects. The accuracy of the reflecting instruments was evaluated by Emory as follows:

Where I had direct comparisons with results obtained by the large instrument, I ascertained that the latitude of a place determined by the Gambey sextant in the proper hands, in a single night, might be relied upon to within 3″ or 5″; and if the observation was repeated for two nights, the result might be relied upon to be within 2″ of the true position.[66]

Both the U.S. and Mexican engineers used reflecting instruments and chronometers in reconnaissance surveys and in daily work in fixing the line, although the U.S. commission had a far greater number of instruments to work with.[67]

An assortment of surveying instruments was available to both commissions. U.S. equipment lists included such items as surveyor's transits, railroad transits, theodolites, and goniometers—names for variations of the principal surveyor's instrument used for measuring horizontal and vertical angles; compasses of several sorts; measuring implements, including surveyor's chains, tapes, marking pins, and plumb bobs; standard measures; viameters; and many accessories. The Mexican commission's extensive reports on triangulation operations indicate that the commission was well equipped to carry out triangulation surveys. Salazar even included in his California inventory of instruments some surveying equipment, such as a theodolite and measuring tape, with which he found no fault. Agustín Díaz mentioned using two theodolites: one a large, heavy theodolite made by Ertel of Germany that belonged to the Mexican commission, the other a portable theodolite borrowed from the U.S. commission; of the two, the Ertel theodolite gave finer readings, and Díaz preferred it.[68]

Topographical elevations were not critical to the boundary survey and were not pursued consistently. The surveyors' equipment included barometers for altimetry and engineer's levels, tripods, and level rods for differential leveling.[69] The U.S. commission was well stocked with different types of barometers, including cistern, siphon, aneroid, and thermo-barometers, in an attempt to test them to find the most suitable type for fieldwork. The Mexican commission also carried a few barometers. Differential leveling was used to measure the differences in elevation between two points. Determination of elevation differences or slope angle was necessary for accurate baseline measurement over sloping or uneven terrain and may have been the procedure to which the leveling equipment was most often applied.

The U.S. commission carried equipment for ancillary investigations in order to fulfill its broad instructions to explore and gather information about the geography and natural history of the border country. Some data, such as observations for temperature and magnetism, were collected in order to account for their effect upon the readings of the surveying instruments. The Mexican commission did not have the personnel or instruments to attempt general scientific explorations.[70] Both commissions, however, carried supplies such as paper, pens, ink, watercolors, scales, curves, and protractors for drawing maps in the field, and the U.S. commission brought a camera lucida for copying and reducing.[71]

It appears that the Mexican commission possessed adequate instruments for topographical surveying and mapping, and any question about the quality of the Mexican instruments devolves on the instruments used for astronomy. Although the quality of the Mexican astronomical instruments used early in the survey may have been doubtful, some of the instruments obtained later in the survey were probably state of the art. First Engineer Jiménez was distressed more by a lack of quantity of instruments than by lack of quality, saying philosophically that some of them were good, some were defective, but in general the number of them was very small.[72] It is clear that the Mexican commission never had the quantity and variety of instruments that was available to the U.S. commission. From the Mexican engineers' own statements, the evidence is that the shortage of high-quality instruments impaired the quantity and quality of data the Mexican commission was able to collect. But the situation was by no means so bad as to cripple the Mexican commission, as U.S. authors have often implied.

Historians have often presented the boundary survey as the activity of politicians and commissioners. "It is the diplomats and politicians, if any, who are remembered in connection with the boundary survey," wrote Goetzmann; "the men who led the field parties through the heat and the hostile country . . . are now almost completely forgotten."[73] Reports, data, field maps, and the finished boundary maps provide ample evidence, however, of the field parties' contributions to the U.S. and Mexican surveys. The Mexican engineers are shown to have been professionally educated and experienced individuals who shared a similar scientific training and usually a military training as well and who worked with great energy and single-minded application, executing complex and extensive surveys. The more numerous employees of the U.S. commission came from a wide variety of backgrounds; some were highly trained and others gained their scientific proficiency as employees of the survey. Both commissions used the most advanced methods they could bring to the frontier and sought the best instruments they could find. The success of the boundary survey depended upon all of the surveyors, astronomers, topographers, and draftsmen who carried on the work of the U.S. and Mexican commissions. Their united efforts accomplished the fieldwork and continued in the office work in the making of the maps.

CHAPTER TWO

THE BOUNDARY OFFICE

Mapmaking

For marking the Boundary in a liberal acceptation is transferring
to paper and steel the Topography and views which perpetuate
the line and enable parties concerned to identify it. . . . In this
way the Mexican Commissioner and myself agreed to mark the
line by making maps, views &c.

U.S. Commissioner William H. Emory to Comptroller of the
Treasury Elisha Whittlesey, 15 January 1857

WORK ON THE UNITED STATES – MEXICO BOUNDARY MAPS
began while the survey was in progress. Although the Mexican
engineers, between field assignments, prepared early reports and calculations in Mexico City, both the U.S. and Mexican commissions completed the final maps at the boundary office in Washington, D.C. First
established in late 1850 and finally closed at the end of 1857, the boundary
office was the scene of seven years of mapmaking—a lengthier project
than the field work.

The Treaty of Guadalupe Hidalgo required the production of boundary maps. In providing for the creation of boundary monuments, jour-
nals, and maps, the treaty specifically mentioned maps twice. It declared
that the boundary must be designated "upon authoritative maps" and
stipulated that the U.S. and Mexican commissions were "to keep jour-
nals and make out plans of their operations." The Treaty of 1853 repeated the requirements of the earlier treaty that the commissions
should keep a journal and make "proper plans of their operations."[1]

In keeping with the treaties, the U.S. and Mexican governments gave instructions for making boundary maps to the commissions they first appointed. The U.S. commissioner was directed to "cause a true and accurate map to be made of the country through which [the boundary] passes, in its entire extent" and to prepare the map in duplicate. The sets of duplicate maps were to be certified by the U.S. and Mexican commissioners and surveyors.[2] The Mexican commission was instructed to make both a general map of the boundary and a series of more detailed sectional maps; united, the sectional maps were to portray the entire course of the line and add to knowledge of Mexico's national geography.[3]

Although new governments came into power and the personnel of the commissions changed over the years of the survey, the basic instructions to the first commissions were fulfilled in the production of the final boundary maps. The goals of the mapping process, however, were never clearly defined or agreed upon. The boundary treaties did not designate how the maps were to be made, what information they should contain, how they were to be used, or what their legal status should be. While the general instructions of the U.S. and Mexican governments supported the importance of the mapmaking effort, neither government offered an affirmation of the authority that the maps were to command.

The officers of the U.S. and Mexican commissions questioned whether maps should be made for certification during the field work. They held reservations because field maps in general were based on positional observations that might later be refined through additional mathematical calculations and were roughly drawn; but political motivations and the desire to speed the survey tempered their views. On occasion the Mexican commission urged the signing of official field maps. From the outset, however, as U.S. chief astronomer, Emory opposed the idea of attempting to make complete calculations and official maps in the field. In California he observed:

> This important matter of the record, which when printed and the copies are multiplied, forms the imperishable evidence of the Boundary, cannot be done in this country; neither can the necessary papers and books of reference be found here. It is a business never attempted in the field, nor away from the societies of the learned: it must be done at the proper place and by the persons who made the observations on

which the results depend, or the results must be lost to the country, to the individual and to the cause of science.[4]

Unresolved, the commissions' policy on certifying maps in the field wavered. Field maps of some sections of the boundary made by one or both commissions were agreed upon and signed by various U.S. and Mexican officers, but ultimately only the maps made in the Washington office became official maps.

The most famous production of the Washington office was the *Report on the United States and Mexican Boundary Survey*, prepared under Emory's direction and published between 1857 and 1859, containing an account of the U.S. survey, many illustrations, and essays on the geography and natural history of the borderlands. Although it was originally planned that the final *Report* would be accompanied by a set of general, or index, maps of the boundary and a few large-scale, sectional maps as well, the *Report* was printed without boundary maps. The final boundary maps were prepared in manuscript only. In time the scientists and artists of the boundary survey and their works in the *Report* became better known than the boundary maps and the computers and drafters who worked to create them. The final reports of the Mexican commission also were never published and remained, like the Mexican maps, little known.[5]

The Office of the U.S. and Mexican Boundary Survey began as the mapmaking office of the U.S. commission. The survey in California had been under way for nearly a year when the secretary of the interior, in response to Emory's petition, directed the chief astronomer to establish a boundary commission office. Emory was to remain in the field at San Diego until he had gathered "all the elements necessary for the calculations"; then, the secretary told him, "you will . . . repair to this place [Washington] for the purpose of making your calculations and maps, and you are authorized to bring with you such of your civil assistants as will be required on that duty."[6] Once established, the boundary office was sustained by the addition of many new employees to the U.S. commission. Emory had pointed out that continuity of the field personnel in office work was essential, but he also insisted that "in the duties of the office, a new class of employees becomes necessary."[7]

By spring 1851, Emory had made progress in the recomputation of astronomical and geodetic observations and had begun the projection and reduction of the maps. He was aided by Assistant Computer Joseph Stillman Hubbard, professor of mathematics and astronomer at the Naval Observatory in Washington, and by P. Harry, draftsman, who may have been Philip Harry, a portrait and landscape painter from Boston who lived in Washington at the time the boundary maps were being finished.[8] Before Emory was recalled to the field with the Bartlett commission, another artist, Joseph Welch, joined the staff. Welch had worked with Emory in drawing the route map of the U.S. Army's march to California in 1846. Emory considered Harry and Welch to be "two artists of the best ability in the country" and instructed his successor in supervising the office to allow no other persons but Harry and Welch to touch the finished maps.[9]

Although the office was at all times under the charge of the Corps of Topographical Engineers, the people who drew the boundary maps were hired from outside the army engineers. They came from various backgrounds—some were artists, some engineers, some engravers—but all were experienced topographers. A few talented individuals were skilled at both field surveying and topographical drafting, but most were either surveyors or drafters, exclusively. A distinction was also made between topographers and lettering specialists, although the division of labor may have been more strictly adhered to in engraving than in drawing maps. The artists' working situations were rather improvised, as in the case of Harry and Welch, described by Emory: "As they both have other engagements, I have employed them on the following terms, namely, Five hours work constitute a day, and for each day so made up, they earn each $3; the work of the two has heretofore been about equivalent to that of one artiste steadily employed."[10] As the office work progressed, many more drafters were added to the staff, some as regular employees, and many on an ad hoc basis. As Emory explained, "It sometimes becomes necessary to employ others [draftsmen], discharge those already engaged and again to re-employ them."[11]

Joseph Welch may have established a precedent, working on the staff of the boundary commission for several years, while his "other engagement" was at the Coast Survey, the U.S. government's preeminent scientific institution at mid-nineteenth century. The boundary commission and Coast Survey continued to share employees throughout the life of the boundary office. Welch had joined the drawing division of the Coast Survey in 1847, taking on such work as tracing, inking, reduction, and drawing of topography. By 1854 he was one of the leading drafts-men, "executing the reductions of topography of the finest class."[12] Meanwhile, he continued to work on the boundary maps. Welch's per diem salary was changed to a contract whereby he was paid by the square inch of drawing; he received a dollar and twenty-five cents per square inch of hill work and forty cents per square inch for grass and sand. Joseph Welch died, probably in early 1857, before the boundary maps were completed, having drawn six of the final sheets.[13]

Topographical Engineer E. L. F. Hardcastle assumed supervision of the office when Emory returned to the field. Because the office was forced to move into rented rooms in a building that was not fireproof, Hardcastle's foremost task was that of duplicating all the records of the survey for separate storage as a precaution against fire. He also furthered the cartographic work, which was already quite advanced. According to Emory's description, "the projection of the general map [of the boundary from the Pacific to the Gila River] and of the detailed maps is all completed and the actual line laid down. On several the Topography is nearly completed, but on the larger portion the topography is not yet sketched in." Emory instructed Hardcastle to have the topography drawn, "making the finished sheets," and to have the reconnaissances he had conducted in California plotted, reduced, and transferred to the general map.[14] Harry and Welch stayed on with Hardcastle, and there is evidence that Charles Preuss, the cartographer known for his maps of John Charles Frémont's expeditions, worked for a time in Hardcastle's office.[15]

In spring 1852, Hardcastle was detailed to another service and ordered to close the boundary office. Before leaving, he boxed and cataloged all the field notes and maps.[16] The catalog of maps included many field sketches and reconnaissance maps and two sets of final maps of the boundary line, called the "rough set" and the "finished set." Each set consisted of four sheets numbered 1 through 4 from the initial point on the Pacific eastward and an additional, unnumbered "junction sheet" that showed the junction of the Gila and Colorado Rivers. The stage of work on the rough set of maps ranged from "very incomplete" to "fin-ished," and on the finished set, from "merely projected" to "nearly com-pleted." Whether the maps cataloged by Hardcastle were integrated into the final map series is not clear, as Hardcastle's inventory numbers do not match those of the extant boundary maps. The final map showing the initial point on the Pacific, as well as the next four sheets eastward, however, were drawn by Harry and Welch.

The boundary commission office remained closed, the work in storage, for nearly a year. Meanwhile, Commissioner Bartlett planned with the Mexican commissioner to jointly prosecute the office work in Mexico City. It was agreed that the joint commission would meet there on the first of March or April 1854, presumably for the purpose of opening the office.[17] Emory, however, was opposed to working in Mexico City and argued against it when Campbell was appointed commissioner. "Mexico is remote from the Boundary, and possesses no facilities whatever," he contended. "If that agreement is binding it will cost a large sum of money, much greater than I have estimated."[18] Campbell succeeded in having the agreement rescinded, and later Emory, as commissioner, negotiated the meeting of the joint commission in Washington, even though the difficulty and expense of travel would then bear upon the Mexican commission. Before departing for the Rio Grande, Commissioner Campbell opened a new boundary office in the U.S. capital.

Emory's nominee for supervisor, Lieutenant of Topographical Engineers George Thom, was placed in charge. Thom was experienced in boundary surveying and mapping, having directed the office of the Northeast Boundary Commission under Graham after his graduation from the U.S. Military Academy. Thom resumed work on the California sheets and began the maps of the Rio Grande. Progress was slowed by the necessity of waiting to obtain astronomical data from U.S. and European observatories for use in calculating positions of latitude and longitude. Thom corresponded with observatories, coordinated some computations with the Coast Survey, performed calculations himself, submitted office budgets and disbursed funds, hired office staff, and managed contracts for engraving those maps and illustrations that were to be printed. In addition, about half of the finished boundary maps were verified and signed by Thom, showing that he had proofed the final maps by comparison with the original surveys.[19]

Thom supervised the United States–Mexico boundary office for three years while the fieldwork was ongoing. The offices were established in a large house, located opposite the Post Office and rented from a Mr. Barney, where Thom and his family also lived. Seven rooms in the house were set aside for the use of the expanded office staff. John O'Donoghue and Frank Wheaton stayed in Washington as computers rather than returning to the Rio Grande. M. T. W. Chandler and Christopher N. Thom also remained as office assistants. Harry and Welch continued as drafters on a per diem basis while Francis Herbst joined the drafting staff on a full-time basis. Prior to his employment at the boundary office, Herbst had worked on contract in the drawing division of the Coast Survey. He continued with the boundary commission for three years, drawing eight of the final boundary maps.[20]

Emory and Lieutenant Nathaniel Michler took up office work when they returned from the Rio Grande toward the end of 1853. Under Emory's direction, Michler opened a separate office in a room in the U.S. Patent Office building, where he computed and plotted the portion of the Rio Grande his party had surveyed. Emory became involved in another project, that of compiling a map of the western territories of the United States, with the assistance of two Topographical Engineers from the Pacific Railroad Office. That project became the foundation both of the famous map of the West compiled by Gouverneur K. Warren and of Emory's own western map to be executed in the boundary office.[21]

When the U.S. Boundary Commission was reorganized under the Treaty of 1853, Thom was again appointed to direct the office. As the survey was getting under way at Paso, he reported on the status of the cartographic work:

> The maps of the Rio Bravo continue to be executed in the same style of art. . . . [T]here still remains to be drawn about twenty sheets of that portion of the boundary (including the Islands and Soundings in their vicinity); also two large general index maps of the whole boundary from the Gulf of Mexico to the Pacific; also other maps connected with the geology and meteorology of the country; together with several maps of the country near the Gila.
>
> The numerous astronomical observations have all been computed, and are now being put in form and prepared for the final report.[22]

Six drafters were reported to be engaged in the office, with Francis Herbst as principal draftsman—the only one of the six positions providing a full-time salary.[23]

The slowness of the computations had previously made it unnecessary to increase the drafting force, but now that the office had been revitalized and the computations completed, Thom may have begun to hire additional artists by the hour, as he had earlier been authorized to do. Other members of the drawing staff probably included William Luce, Charles Mahon, Theodore H. Oehlschlager, and Charles László, all of whom drafted maps that Thom reported in progress. Herbst drew four of the maps of the Rio Grande boundary; Luce, five; Mahon, eight; and Oehlschlager, six. Oehlschlager also drew four maps of the California boundary, of "the country near the Gila." László drafted all five sheets showing islands in the Rio Grande. One Rio Grande map was drawn by J. R. P. Mechlin, one by M. C. Grilzner, and one by Edward Freyhold. There were also two maps of the Rio Grande and three maps of California drafted by Joseph Welch that may have been completed earlier, and one Rio Grande map that John Weyss drew when he returned to Washington from field duty.

In employing new drafting personnel, the boundary office extended its connections with the Coast Survey office. Luce, Mahon, and Oehlschlager, as well as Mechlin, Grilzner, and Freyhold, were employees of the Coast Survey. Luce, for example, had worked in the drawing division of the Coast Survey preparing projections, reductions, drawings, and tracings, and having charge of the electrotype apparatus. The boundary office employed him first by the square inch of drawing, then on a monthly salary. When the boundary maps were eventually completed, the Coast Survey was rather eager to regain the employees it had lost to the boundary commission.[24] Some of the artists, however, including Mahon, Oehlschlager, Mechlin, and Freyhold, found further employment in Washington at the Office of Pacific Railroad Surveys. Freyhold's Coast Survey work and his Rio Grande boundary map became early accomplishments in a lifetime devoted to drawing maps of the West for government-sponsored expeditions and surveys. His most noteworthy cartographic achievement was perhaps his drawing of Warren's western map, on which he was engaged at the same time that Emory's map of the West was being drawn in the boundary office.[25]

The artist who drew Emory's western map, Thomas Jekyll, was first engaged by the boundary office in fall 1854 for the specialized task of lettering the Rio Grande maps.[26] He signed his name to only one boundary map, "Index Map No. 3," which was probably the last index map to be completed and was drawn as a shared effort by Jekyll and Herbst. Jekyll was to remain with the commission for three years, until well after all of the other members of the drawing staff had left, in order to oversee the engraving of the maps selected for printing. After even Emory had left Washington, Jekyll stayed on to work with Albert H. Campbell of the Pacific Wagon Road Office and with Mrs. Emory to proof and correct the map of the West, keeping Emory updated on developments in the work. When the map was printed for the final *Report,* it carried the credit, "Projected and drawn . . . by Thomas Jekyll, C.E."

Major changes came to the boundary office late in 1855, as the fieldwork began to wind up. Emory wrote ahead to Thom, warning him that the astronomical and surveying parties would soon be arriving in Washington. The entire building that contained the commission offices would be needed as working space, and Emory directed Thom to vacate the rooms that he and his family had been occupying. Charles Radziminski took charge of disbanding the field personnel while Emory returned to Washington and assumed control of the office. In spring 1856, Thom was transferred to Minnesota Territory, and Michler took Thom's place as next-in-charge of the boundary office under Emory.[27]

A number of the field assistants became members of the office staff when they arrived in Washington. Hugh Campbell, M. T. W. Chandler, John Clark, and Christopher Thom were employed in making computations, and E. A. Phillips and John Weyss in topographical drawing. Maurice von Hippel prepared rough maps from his field notes before leaving in spring 1856, reporting to Emory that "all the field notes of the U.S. + Mex^n boundary line taken by me under your command are plotted and so far finished that they are ready for the draughtsman."[28] Arthur Schott's long and multifaceted service was rewarded with a promotion to principal assistant in Hippel's place, and he continued to work in the office at topographical drawing and collating and drawing natural history collections. His and Weyss's views of the boundary between the Rio Grande and the Colorado River were engraved and published in the final *Report.*[29]

The boundary office began to look forward to the arrival of the Mexican commission. Commissioners Salazar and Emory had agreed in Paso that they and their assistants would convene in the city of Washington for mapmaking. Salazar had desired to set a meeting date on the first of January 1857 to allow time for the Mexican engineers to complete their surveys, but Emory succeeded in gaining Salazar's consent to meet on the first of April 1856.[30] To provide space for the Mexican commission, Emory arranged to move the office into larger quarters. He signed an agreement with W. W. Corcoran and G. W. Riggs to rent the banking house at Fifteenth Street and Pennsylvania Avenue; the rent was to be one hundred dollars per month if the building were occupied by the U.S. commission alone, and one hundred and fifty dollars per month if occupied also by the Mexican commission, one-half the rent due from each commission. Boundary office records, showing that the U.S. commission regularly made rent payments of seventy-five dollars per month from the time that the Mexican commission arrived until the work was completed, indicate that the banking house served as the map office for both commissions.[31]

The members of the third Comisión de Límites Mexicana returned to Mexico City after closing the field work, the last of them, Manuel Alemán and Luis Díaz, arriving in February 1856 with all the papers and instruments of the *sección de Sonora*. A fourth commission, appointed to complete the calculations and cartography, traveled to Washington, where their arrival was much anticipated, reaching there toward the end of June. The banking house office, occupied by the U.S. commission since the first of June, then became known as the office of the joint commission.[32]

All but two of the members of the fourth commission had participated in the field surveys. Arriving in Washington with Commissioner Salazar were First Engineer Francisco Jiménez; Second Engineers Agustín Díaz, Luis Díaz, and Manuel Alemán; and Assistants Ignacio Molina, Julio Pinal, and Antonio Espinosa y Cervantes. The two new assistants, Pinal and Espinosa y Cervantes, were both designated as *dibujantes* (drafters or illustrators). Pinal was a captain, but his background is unknown. Espinosa y Cervantes was an engineer, apparently a civilian. During his tenure on the fourth commission, Agustín Díaz was promoted to first engineer.[33]

It was a small contingent to fulfill Mexico's large share of the office work. Their work as a group consisted of "calculating the observations, recalculating others, projecting and drawing the general and sectional maps until they were fully completed."[34] The calculation of geographical positions from the accumulated astronomical data was done by only two individuals, Jiménez and Alemán. The title of a report prepared by Agustín Díaz suggests that he may have directed the cartography: "Report explaining the manner in which the maps of a part of the boundary between Mexico and the United States were made, done according to the instructions of the Commissioner and Surveyor of the Mexican Commission, Don José Salazar Ilarregui, under the direction of the second engineer of the same, Don Agustín Díaz. Year of 1857."[35]

The maps drawn for the U.S. commission regularly carried the artist's name, but not so the maps of the Mexican commission. Only one map, sectional map "No. 14," bears a tiny signature by an artist, and it is that of Antonio Espinosa y Cervantes. It is likely that, in addition to those who came from Mexico City, drafters were also hired in Washington. A loan that the Mexican commission obtained while in Washington from the U.S. government was required especially to pay the foreign artists who had helped execute the maps.[36] Considering that many of the artists who worked for the U.S. commission were employed on a part-time or contract basis, it is possible that some of the individuals who drew maps for the United States also drafted maps for the Mexican commission.

The fourth commission worked on the boundary maps in Washington steadily for over a year. Since the Mexican engineers had not undertaken the execution of finished maps before their arrival in Washington, they must have worked strenuously to complete the calculations, projections, plotting, drawing, and copying of so many maps within the short time of their stay. Jiménez described his work with Alemán in making calculations as occupying them "without rest." He explained his desire that the two of them recalculate everything twice, in order to compare different individuals' results and be more satisfied that no error had been committed in the calculations; "but the observations are so many, and the time so limited," he said, "that it is impossible for two individuals to be sufficient for a task so arduous." He had to be satisfied with employing "all the means of rectification possible in our circumstances."[37]

On the U.S. side of the office of the joint commission, 1856 was the peak year of map production. More people worked in the office that year than at any other time, with many new individuals hired to do the drawing. New names that were listed as draftsmen in the office accounts in spring 1856 included A. de Zeyk, Henry C. Evans, Felix Nemegyei, John de la Camp, Paul Max von Engel, William Hesselbach, and John D. Hoffman. They stayed for varying lengths of time. A. de Zeyk, who signed boundary map "No. 36," may have been the same person as Albert Dezyick, an engraver, born in Hungary about 1825 and living in Washington during the 1860 census. Evans came to the boundary commission from the Coast Survey, where he had been an apprentice in the engraving division; he worked on only one final map, sharing the drawing on that sheet with Charles László. Nemegyei worked until he was honorably discharged in December 1856, completing two boundary maps.[38] The name of John de la Camp as draftsman was added in pencil to "Index Map No. 3." Several names that occurred regularly in the office accounts for monthly salaries did not appear on any of the boundary maps; von Engel, Hesselbach, and Hoffman fall into this category. They may have worked on compilations and rough sheets but did not draw final maps.

As Jekyll became increasingly committed to drafting the map of the West, another specialist was hired to do lettering; the name of lettering expert Frederick Courtenay appeared in the office accounts in spring 1856. A year later Courtenay worked with the engraver to letter the western map for the final *Report;* the printed map credited him, "Lettering by F. Courtenay." If he lettered any of the manuscript boundary maps, however, it was not acknowledged on the sheets. Courtenay went on to work for the Office of Explorations and Surveys, lettering the map of the Río Colorado drawn by the noted western cartographer, Frederick W. von Egloffstein.[39]

The U.S. and Mexican commissioners occasionally held official meetings. Shortly after his arrival, Salazar met with Emory to discuss both the surveys completed by the Mexican field parties after the U.S. commission had disbanded and the basic provisions for mapmaking. The discussion and planning went on for two days, on 24 and 25 June 1856. They agreed that the maps should be made in two scales: a series of detailed maps at a scale of 1:60,000, and a set of general maps on a scale of 1:600,000. Since the U.S. commission had already constructed detailed maps of the boundary between the Pacific Coast and the Colorado River on a scale of 1:30,000, an exception was made to allow for the larger scale in that section of the boundary. They also agreed that all the maps should be made in duplicate—one set to be deposited with the U.S. government and one set with the Mexican government. The finished maps would be signed by the commissioners, and the two commissions would exchange the topographical and astronomical data they had collected in the field.[40]

The commissioners' agreements were aimed at producing consistency between the U.S. and Mexican maps. Not long after their conference,

Salazar addressed a letter to Emory requesting a copy of the Greenwich tables for use in recomputing longitude determinations and inquiring about the projection to be used for the maps. "I make you these questions," he said, in the translation of his letter, "because I wish that my computations and the tracing of the projection agree with what you have done."[41]

Although the commissions worked side by side in the same building for over a year, they apparently kept few records of their interactions. A loan made to the Mexican commission for its support while in Washington, and the repayment of the loan by Salazar, were more fully documented than the intellectual exchanges among the members of the two commissions. Emory took the initiative in attempting to secure a loan for the Mexican engineers when, after they had resided in Washington for nearly a year, he became aware of their lack of means to continue. Emory's correspondence on the Mexican engineers' behalf offers evidence of the cooperation that existed between the two commissions. Proposing a loan to the secretary of the interior, Emory wrote that

> the disturbed state of the Interior of Mexico has prevented these gentlemen from receiving remittances and has left them here in a condition truly deplorable.

> The cordial and friendly relations which have existed between the two Commissions, places me necessarily in a position to know these difficulties, and to sympathise with the sufferers. . . .

> It will greatly facilitate the completion of the remaining business of the Joint Commission, and will be a graceful act of kindness to the distressed Officers of a neighboring and friendly power.

> This application is of course made without the knowledge or assent of Mr Salazar.[42]

The loan to the Mexican commission was advanced through Michler in the boundary office and was repaid by Salazar just before he departed from Washington. Also toward the end of his stay, Salazar assisted Emory in the preparation of the western map for the U.S. final *Report*, proofreading the place names, particularly those in Mexico, and suggesting many changes.[43]

As their last and most important official duty, the commissioners approved the finished boundary maps and views. On 3 July 1857, while the office work continued, they accepted and signed some of the maps. Later they met unofficially to examine and compare the maps remaining to be signed and found them to agree "in all essential matters appertaining to the Boundary." At an official meeting of the joint commission on 21 September 1857, Emory and Salazar signed the remaining maps to complete the entire series for both nations. They placed their signatures beneath a handwritten note on each map stating that it had been "examined, compared, and agreed to" (fig. 2-1). On 30 September 1857, the commissioners approved a number of views of the boundary and signed them, and thereupon, the boundary commission was finally adjourned.[44]

Emory delivered the manuscript maps to the department of the interior shortly after they were signed. For preservation he also sent six volumes of observations and computations for latitude and longitude. The U.S. commission's field notes, however, were sent with a recommendation that they be destroyed. Emory advised that "as the treaty makes the determination of the commissioners as expressed on the maps the final Boundary, these notes can be of no future use but may make confusion, and I recommend them to be burnt."[45] Emory's recommendation was apparently followed. The Comisión Mexicana returned to Mexico City, where Jiménez, on behalf of Salazar, delivered the commission's official documents to the minister of relations in February 1858. The documents included fifty-eight boundary maps, the minutes of the joint commission, and a collection of views of notable points along the line.[46]

The office of the joint commission on Pennsylvania Avenue was closed when the commission adjourned. Emory was relieved from duty as boundary commissioner and assigned to Fort Riley, Kansas Territory, although he retained general supervision of the final *Report*. He requested that the engraved plates for sectional maps *No. 1* and *No. 29* and index maps *No. 1* and *No. 2* be turned over directly to the superintendent of public printing and that the same be done with index maps *No. 3* and *No. 4* as soon as they were completely engraved. He made the recommendation, he said, "in consequence of learning the numerous applications made for these maps."[47] Emory's request was denied, although Pacific Wagon Road Office chief Campbell, who was left in charge of the plates, did eventually deliver them to the public printer, without a decision from Congress to print them. A number of proof impressions were made from the plates.[48]

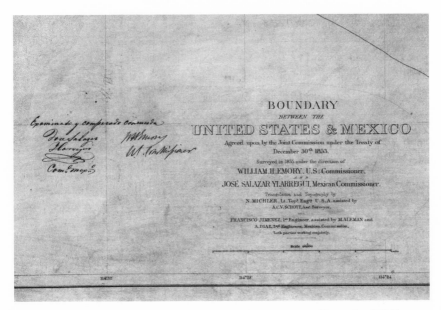

FIG. 2-1. Title panel and commissioners' signatures: Detail of U.S. map "No. 45." (National Archives)

The U.S. and Mexican commissions each produced a complete and unique set of final maps. The official boundary maps made by the U.S. commission consisted of fifty-four sectional sheets, plus five maps of islands in the Rio Grande, and four index sheets, all manuscripts. All of the U.S. maps were plotted and drawn by U.S. computers, topographers, and artists. The Mexican commission's final maps also consisted of fifty-four sectional sheets and four index maps in manuscript, but there were no island maps. Some of the Mexican maps were copied from U.S. sheets. In certain sections of the line, the Mexican commission lacked data for map compilation, having been unable to survey the entire boundary; and the pressure of the Mexican commission's limited time in Washington may have dictated some of the map copying. Most of the Mexican maps, however, were compiled by Mexican computers and topographers, and all were drawn by drafters employed by the Mexican commission.

Despite the lack of records of communication between the U.S. and Mexican mapmakers, the similarity of the maps made by the two commissions demonstrates that conferences did take place. Both commissions organized their maps in the same way: the sectional sheets were numbered consecutively from east to west, beginning with "No. 1" on the Gulf Coast and ending with "No. 54" on the Pacific; each commission's four index maps were likewise numbered from east to west. Map sheets identified by the same number in each commission's series covered comparable areas of land, although there were occasional, small variations in the territory depicted on the U.S. and Mexican maps. Each commission produced its maps as a unified series, and both within the series and between the series of the two commissions, the maps conformed to general specifications.

The sectional maps and the index maps were much alike. All maps were made upon similar, heavy rag paper. The size of the paper sheet for the U.S. maps was about 65 centimeters (25$^1/_2$ inches) by 98 cm (38$^1/_2$ in.), with slightly larger sheets of about 77 cm (30 in.) by 109 cm (43 in.) used for the Mexican maps. On both the U.S. and Mexican sectional sheets showing the boundary between the Gulf of Mexico and the Colorado River, the dimensions of the map image were approximately 59 cm (23 in.) by 92 cm (36 in.). The map field on the sectional sheets for the California boundary covered a somewhat smaller area, and on the four general maps, the image area was slightly larger. The maps were made at the three scales that the commissioners had agreed upon: 1:30,000 for the California maps, 1:60,000 for the sectional maps between the Gulf of Mexico and the Colorado River, and 1:600,000 for the general maps.

All maps were drawn in pen and black ink over a penciled compilation—the plot of the survey data—and were lettered similarly using roman and italic serif letters and large shaded block letters. The title of each map was given in a panel of text that contained the year of the survey, names of the authorities responsible for the field work, and map scale, including a graphic scale on the U.S. maps (see fig. 2-1). At the lower right corner of the sheet, the U.S. maps were signed by the artists who drew them. The lines of the graticule, the network of parallels and meridians, were drawn across the map image, spaced at intervals of four minutes on the 1:60,000 sheets, at two-minute intervals on the California maps, and every thirty minutes on the 1:600,000 index sheets. Both commissions utilized Greenwich as the prime meridian, since it was designated in the Treaty of 1853, although it would be nearly thirty years before Greenwich was generally approved as the international prime meridian.

The graticules of the U.S. and Mexican maps are alike, apparently drawn on the same projection, but the map scales are large enough that it is now difficult to determine the projection with certainty. Salazar's letter to Emory, in which he mentioned that he wished the Mexican maps to agree with those of the United States, offers clues about the projection they used. Salazar's letter asked, in translation, "Did you employ the french projection for the General Map? If so which Latitude did you adopt to the middle parallel, and which Longitude for the central Meridian, and, if you made the cone tangent or sextant [*sic*] [secant]?"[49] Salazar's allusion to "the French projection" may have signified the Bonne projection, a pseudoconic projection used in France since 1802 for the national topographic map series. The projection had received some recent application in the United States in Coast Survey charts and would have been a likely choice for the boundary maps. Considering the close relations between the U.S. boundary office and the Coast Survey, however, it is also likely that the U.S. Boundary Commission would have chosen the polyconic projection developed in the 1820s by Survey Superintendent Ferdinand Hassler and used regularly for Coast Survey charts. The polyconic and Bonne projections are similar in appearance, although the Bonne is an equal-area projection with concentric parallels and those features are lacking in the polyconic.[50] In any case, the evidence of Salazar's letter indicates that the U.S. commission chose the projection when it began constructing the final boundary maps some years ahead of the Mexican commission, and the Mexican engineers later adopted the selected projection.

The content of the U.S. and Mexican maps was also similar. Each map showed a portion of the boundary either as a river channel or as a line across the land, and the country near the line. The maps included only information gathered by the commissions' field parties, leaving blank the areas beyond their surveys. Surrounding the boundary were the physical features of a mostly wild landscape of mountains, deserts, canyons, and plateaus, and the region's few rivers, springs, and coastal lagoons. Patterns of symbols for vegetation or sand and gravel suggested the land cover on some maps. Cultural features included towns, forts, ranches, a few Indian villages, cultivated fields, roads and paths, and river fords and ferries. The cultural features and a few of the physical features were labeled with place names. Astronomical observatories and boundary monuments established by the commissions were also shown. Some of the maps included notes giving the geographical positions determined for certain stations.

The final maps made by the two commissions are presently housed in national repositories in Washington, D.C., and Mexico City.[51] At the U.S. National Archives and Records Administration, the separate sheets are stored in a large number of folders. Mounted on linen and heavily varnished, most of the map images are somewhat obscured by streaks of yellow-orange coating. Mexico's maps, stored in the Mapoteca Manuel Orozco y Berra, have been bound into four large portfolios. They are mounted on linen, but unvarnished, so that the black ink of the drawing contrasts with the white paper more nearly as it did when the maps were first drawn. Tracings of four of the U.S. island maps are stored as separate sheets, but the date of the tracings is not given.

The final maps were a great accomplishment, completed despite the physical, political, and financial obstacles that continually threatened to thwart the surveys and the office work. They satisfied treaty requirements and the U.S. and Mexican governments' general instructions to their boundary commissions. But beyond meeting requirements, the commissions worked together without directives to resolve questions about how the maps should be made and the survey data presented. The maps were elegantly designed and drawn and formally consistent. Furthermore, in placing their signatures on the maps, the commissioners were able to agree that the U.S. and Mexican maps were alike and correct in their boundary representations and that the maps officially marked the line. Only many years later would difficulties unfold from the commissioners' judgment of their maps. But before these difficulties were to be faced, the commissions first had to discover the geography of the boundary country, relate the treaty delimitations to the land, and map the line as they found it should lie on the ground.

CHAPTER THREE

CONSULTATION BETWEEN THE COMMISSIONS

Surveys on the Pacific and Gulf Coasts and the Colorado River

They had thus far carried on their operations separately, agreeing
and reporting upon the results, and, from the nature of things, it
was proved to be the better way.

*U.S. Surveyor Andrew B. Gray to Secretary of the Interior
Thomas Ewing, 20 February 1850*

*W*HEN THE OFFICERS OF THE MEXICAN BOUNDARY COM-
mission disembarked at the port of San Diego on 3 July 1849, they
were met by the officers of the U.S. commission, who escorted them
on horseback to the presidio and three days of dining, dancing, and a
Fourth of July celebration. At the end of the festivities, Commissioners
Weller and García Conde and Surveyors Gray and Salazar assembled
a meeting of the joint commission to begin the boundary work. The
surveyors were appointed to form a plan for the survey of the California line.

With the help of the interpreter to the Mexican commission, Felipe
de Iturbide, Gray and Salazar planned the steps to be taken in the California survey and established a general mode of working. The surveyors
agreed that either commission could begin the survey work whenever
ready and that each party would pursue its own methods to arrive at the
required result. When both commissions were satisfied with the survey
results, they would approve the placement of monuments at points on

the line. The surveyors anticipated that, "from time to time, as the work progresses, and information is obtained of the country through which any portion of the line will pass, the said parties can agree as to the plan of taking the topography or marking the line."[1]

The surveyors' plan for the two commissions to work independently, consulting in the field in order to adjust their survey methods and results, was applied at the beginning of the work in California but was sustained in only a few sections of the boundary. Most of the maps that were surveyed according to the surveyors' plan, including U.S. and Mexican maps "No. 1," "No. 44," "No. 45," "No. 53," and "No. 54," portrayed sections of the boundary that contained turning points defining the course of the line. Maps "No. 54" showed the initial point on the Pacific; maps "No. 44" and "No. 45" showed the Colorado River boundary, including the point where the Gila River flowed into the Colorado, as well as the initial point of the United States–Sonora azimuth line; and maps "No. 1" portrayed the initial point at the mouth of the Río Bravo.

The California survey was to begin with both astronomical observations and topographical surveys. The surveyors agreed that three points should be located on the ground: the southernmost point of the port of San Diego and the two extreme points of the straight line connecting the coast and the confluence of the Gila and Colorado Rivers (Location Map 1). From the southernmost point of the port of San Diego, one marine league would be measured south to the initial point on the Pacific. The latitude and longitude of the two extreme points would be determined in order to calculate the azimuth of the straight line, so that its course could be marked on the ground.

U.S. Chief Astronomer Emory and his assistants set up an observatory at a place he called Camp Riley, just east of the southern end of San Diego Bay, and began observations for latitude and longitude. Surveyor Gray, meanwhile, installed Camp Rough and Ready south of Emory's observatory. Salazar, as both surveyor and chief astronomer of the Mexican commission, established an observatory south of Gray's camp, designating it *el primer campo* (the first camp). The small corps of mapping personnel in the Mexican commission hoped to expedite their survey through individual exertion, in order to match the efforts of the large U.S. commission.[2]

Salazar first took up his duties as surveyor, using triangulation to

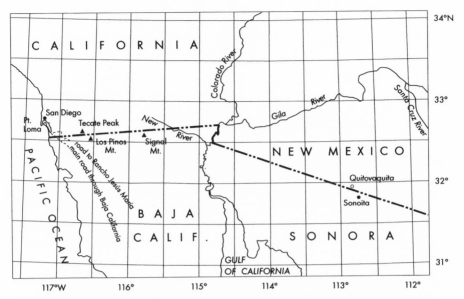

LOCATION MAP 1. Boundary between the United States and Mexico, showing the California azimuth line, the Colorado River, and part of the United States–Sonora azimuth line. Source: [U.S. Boundary Commission], *Index Map No. 4.*

locate the southernmost point of the port of San Diego. He directed the measurement of a baseline from Emory's observatory southward through the Mexican camp and then extended a network of triangles around the southern end of San Diego Bay. Salazar explained that the triangulation was necessary because of the difficulty of locating the shoreline: "If the bay in the southern part had been well determined and limited as in some places by rocks cut to sharp points, the determination of the most southern point could have been made in half an hour and with a hand compass; but it was not so, and the terrain, being flat, presented no obstacle to the water."[3] After drawing up a plan of the triangulation, Salazar selected one of the vertices that bordered on the bay as the southernmost point of the port of San Diego, reasoning that it was the most southern position on the average water line, halfway between the high and low levels of the bay.

Gray derived the southernmost point of the port of San Diego in a different way, relying on Pantoja's map (see fig. I-2). He had difficulty at first because he found that the configuration of the shoreline had changed almost entirely from Pantoja's delineation. In the course of his survey, however, Gray was able to identify a bluff that he considered to be identical with a point shown on the map. Using the treaty map, he measured by the map scale the distance from the bluff point to a line marked for the southern point of the harbor. Gray did not explain how he determined where to mark the southern point of the harbor on the Pantoja map, but he could have done so by measuring one marine league in the scale of the map northward from the boundary line drawn on the map, reversing the instructions in the treaty. Having figured the distance from the bluff to the southernmost point of the harbor from the map scale, Gray then laid off the same distance on the ground, beginning from the bluff in order to locate the desired point. According to Gray, it was the highest point at which indications of saltwater could be seen to reach. Gray also drew up a plan of his survey.[4]

The surveyors met to compare their maps and their determinations of the southernmost point of the harbor. Both agreed that their maps were in complete accord, but Salazar and Gray had chosen different southernmost points. Gray's southernmost point was situated about 3,500 feet to the south of the semicircle of vertices that Salazar had established outlining the average water level of the bay. Gray attributed the difference in the location of the points to changes in the features of the bay from the representation in Pantoja's map. A decision from the commissioners regarding the two opinions was needed but could not be obtained, for although García Conde was present and in approval of Salazar's determination, Weller was absent in San Francisco on a fund-raising trip. The surveyors found it necessary to resolve the problem for themselves.

The problem the surveyors debated was whether the southernmost point of the port of San Diego, a location named in the Treaty of Guadalupe Hidalgo, should be identified as a modern feature of the land or should be considered as a place drawn in the map to which the treaty specifically referred. If it was a feature of the land, a more precise definition of the southernmost point was needed; was it the high-water mark, for example, or the low-water mark, or some point in between? If the southernmost point of the port of San Diego was a point drawn in the treaty map, where its location was shown only in relation to other features, the map depiction had to be related to the present features of the bay, which had changed over time.

Salazar agreed with Gray that they were bound by the treaty to conform their selection of a southernmost point with the representation in Pantoja's map. The surveyors noted a point on the western shore of the bay depicted in the Pantoja map that was apparent in the landscape and could be identified in both of their plans. Salazar designated it *punto P* and, upon making measurements from point *P*, became convinced that Gray had located the correct southernmost point; he explained as follows:

> Point *P* located, it proved to be 2370 meters from *F* [Gray's southernmost point]; and point *P* being in Pantoja's plan 2360 meters from where we were directed to measure the league, it is clear that—disregarding the small difference between the two distances, arising from the difficulty of estimating from Pantoja's map because of its very small scale—point *F* is the most southern, conformable to the Treaty of Guadalupe Hidalgo.[5]

Salazar's determination of the average waterline was therefore rejected, and Gray's point was taken as the southernmost point of the port of San Diego.

The surveyors' next step was to measure off the marine league from the southernmost point of the harbor to the initial point. The simplicity of the delimitation was deceptive, for the marine league was not defined by any universally accepted standard. The treaty writers may have used the marine league because the Pantoja map contained a graphic scale in *millas marítimas* (nautical miles), a Spanish linear measure that reckoned three miles to the *legua marítima* (marine league). The Spanish marine league was a measure that had evolved over the centuries and, by the time Pantoja's map was drawn, was defined as one-twentieth of a degree of the great circle of the earth; the length of the marine league, therefore, depended upon knowledge of the circumference of the earth, a number subject to continual refinement.[6]

The surveyors had to agree upon the length of the marine league to be used in their measurement. Official instructions that had been given to García Conde regarding the length of the marine league guided Salazar in suggesting a figure that the surveyors adopted. Salazar and Gray both recorded that the length of the marine league they used was 5,564.6 meters; Gray stated that their authority was Louis Benjamin Francoeur, professor at the Ecole Polytechnique and the University of Paris and author of several works in mathematics, whose books were among those taken into the field for reference during the survey.[7] Salazar and Gray each measured out the marine league separately, using his commission's own steel measuring bar or tape. Both surveyors found that two offsets were required to avoid swampy and uneven ground. The independent measurements were completed with a difference of 1.4 meters, according to Salazar; Gray did not mention it.

After the measurement of the marine league, Salazar executed a triangulation from the observatory in the Mexican camp and found what he believed to be the most suitable situation for the initial point. The position was somewhat north of the termination of the marine league. Upon examination by the commissioners, however, the site was rejected, Weller claiming that it would be needed for the construction of a lighthouse. The commissioners selected a point located 168 meters away, at the midpoint between Salazar's position and the termination of the marine league. On the following day, a temporary monument was placed and formally dedicated. U.S. reports did not mention that an alternative initial-point location had been considered, but Salazar reported the proposal in detail because he felt gratified that the outcome partially compensated Mexico for the ground he had lost in the determination of the southernmost point of the port of San Diego.[8]

While Salazar was involved with topographical surveys, other members of the Mexican commission carried out the astronomical work. A transit telescope, vertical circle, and two chronometers—with all of which Salazar expressed dissatisfaction—were set up as the principal instruments in the observatory at the Mexican camp. Observations were made between 28 August and 13 October 1849, probably by Jiménez, Chavero, and Agustín García Conde. The engineers also made computations in camp, the Mexican commission having brought as references the British *Nautical Almanac* and Callet's *Tables*. The geographical position determined by the engineers for their camp was transferred to the initial point by means of the triangulation directed by Salazar, geodetic calculations providing the latitude and longitude of the initial point from the base length and observed angles of the triangulation.

Emory also began astronomical observations in late September. His principal instruments were a zenith telescope, transit instrument, and chronometers, the observations for latitude and longitude made by Emory personally. Only one triangle was needed to transfer the position determined for Camp Riley to the initial point. The base was measured twice: once with the U.S. commission's rods of seasoned redwood and once with steel wires belonging to the Mexican commission; and the average of the two measures was taken. The calculations for the latitude and longitude of the initial point made by each commission were then compared, and the differences were small enough that Salazar felt they could be eliminated by discarding one or two of the Mexican engineers' most extreme observations. "Considering the great number of observations made by Mr. W. H. Emory with magnificent instruments," Salazar said, he was inclined to accept the U.S. determinations. The numbers agreed upon in the field were corrected later in the boundary office with the corresponding observations from Greenwich.[9]

From the initial point on the Pacific, the boundary was to follow a straight line to a point at the middle of the Río Gila where it emptied into the Río Colorado. While Gray was engaged in locating the initial point on the Pacific and Emory in finding its position, another party from the U.S. commission, led by Lieutenant Whipple, was sent to the Colorado River to make observations for latitude and longitude. Surveyor Gray was to arrive shortly to perform the topographical survey. Gray, however, delegated the job to an assistant, John H. Forster, who prepared a sketch of the area that Gray submitted to Commissioner Weller. Weller strongly disapproved of the surveyor's delegation of work that should have been conducted under his personal authority and felt constrained to rely upon Whipple for an accurate survey of the confluence. The commissioner, therefore, empowered Whipple to "agree with Mr. Salazar on the point where the Gila empties into the Colorado, and make an accurate survey of the same, and also of the boundary line from that point to where it crosses the Colorado."[10]

Whipple established an observatory at the confluence in early October 1849, two months before Salazar was able to finish his work on the Pacific Coast, and completed his observations for latitude and longitude by the end of November. Salazar lamented his lack of a sufficient number of instruments to put survey teams to work at both ends of the line. Assistant Forster's sketch of the confluence was, meanwhile, utilized by Gray and Weller to designate the point where the Río Gila united with the Colorado. The position they chose was that to which Whipple was to obtain Salazar's assent.

For his consultation with the Mexican surveyor, Whipple prepared a plan of the confluence and transferred the point selected by Gray and Weller to his map. When the Mexican commission arrived at the confluence, García Conde, Salazar, and Whipple explored the area, and García Conde approved the point that had been marked on the map. A formal agreement, accompanied by Whipple's plan, was drawn up in English and Spanish by the interpreter Iturbide and signed by Salazar and Whipple.[11]

Emory remained at Camp Riley, where he prepared to work out the azimuth of the line between the Pacific and the Colorado River. He directed Captain Hardcastle to accompany Surveyor Gray on a reconnaissance of the Peninsular Ranges in order to investigate rumor of a mountain peak from which it was possible to see both the Pacific Ocean and the Colorado River. Emory hoped to ascertain the usefulness of the peak as a signal station. He planned to use signals for making simultaneous observations of time at the two extremes of the line to obtain their relative longitudes—determinations he needed for his azimuth calculations. A guide conducted Gray and Hardcastle to a peak called Sierra de los Pinos, where they were able to see the ocean about thirty-five miles distant but could not see the Colorado River.

The knowledge gained by the reconnaissance led Emory to revise his plan so that observations of signals would be made from a series of stations between the coast and the Colorado River. As soon as Whipple was installed at the Colorado, Hardcastle and his assistants were directed to occupy three peaks between the river and the coast. An elaborate program of signals by rockets and gunpowder flashes was worked out for each station.[12] Emory explained how the operation would furnish the relative longitude of the two ends of the line:

> Counting the stations, including the observatories, from west toward the east, and numbering them 1 to 5, it was believed that flashes could be seen from 1 to 2, from 4 to 5, and from 3 to both 2 and 4. Having the local time of flash at 2 observed from 1, the difference between the flash at 2 and the flash at 4, observed from 3, and the local time of the flash at 4, observed from 5, the difference in local time between 1 and 5 is given, and consequently, the difference of longitude.[13]

In practice, the design failed. The signals were produced for five nights, and the chain of observations was carried as far as four stations, but the observers at the confluence were unable to perceive the signals because of fogs that obstructed the view. Emory reluctantly abandoned the project, even though, he said, it "would have given me the difference in longitude, with nearly the same accuracy as a geodetic operation, and certainly as good as the telegraphic wire."[14] To make his calculations for the azimuth, Emory, therefore, had to rely upon the separate determinations of longitude made at each end of the line. Mexican engineers also used the determinations to compute the azimuth, and after examination of the two commissions' calculations, the azimuth was agreed upon.[15]

Whipple had begun to mark the azimuth line westward a few days before the Mexican commission arrived at the Colorado. He erected a stone pier on the first hill west of the confluence, designating it as the station from which astronomical observations would be made to prolong the azimuth line. From the stone monument, Whipple fixed two more stations: one on the next hill west from the confluence and one on the right (north) bank of the Gila near its junction with the Colorado. Upon his examination of the confluence, Salazar approved of the location of Whipple's stone monument. In their formal agreement, Whipple and Salazar noted the impossibility of measuring the azimuth line from the center of the river and elected the stone pier as a point for practical operations and as a monument on the boundary line.[16]

The survey at the junction of the Gila and Colorado Rivers yielded an unforeseen result. The U.S. commission discovered that the southward flowing Colorado River turned abruptly to the northwest after its union with the Gila and maintained a northwest direction for several miles before looping southward again (see figs. 3-3 and 3-4). The azimuth line going west from the confluence would therefore run south of the Colorado River, more or less parallel to it, for several miles before crossing the river, placing both banks of the Colorado in that extent of the river within U.S. territory. Both commissions explored the area and surveyed and mapped it in detail.[17]

The Mexican commissioner objected to placing the boundary south of the Colorado River, protesting that a literal interpretation of the boundary delimitation violated the spirit of the Treaty of Guadalupe Hidalgo. The treaty makers had clearly presumed that the Colorado River flowed directly south—to be bordered by the United States above and by Mexico below the junction with the Gila. García Conde proposed to the U.S. commissioner that the matter be referred to their respective governments for judgment, but Weller refused to do so. He maintained that the joint commission was invested with full power to reach a final verdict and must be guided by "the plain, unequivocal language of the treaty itself."[18] The Mexican commissioner capitulated, although he remained dissatisfied, reserving his opinion that the decision conflicted with the sense of the treaty. The issue disappeared when the boundary was redefined by the Treaty of 1853. Under the new treaty, the junction of the Gila and Colorado Rivers was contained within U.S. territory.

Whipple and his party returned to San Diego shortly after signing the agreement with Salazar, while the Mexican commission continued to work from its base at the confluence, *el segundo campo* (the second camp). After about a month's labor, spent in determining the latitude and longitude of the Mexican observatory, transferring the determination to the confluence, and rectifying the azimuth of the line by observations on the polestar, Commissioner García Conde departed with Engineers Jiménez, Chavero, and Agustín García Conde, to follow the azimuth line back to San Diego. Along the way, eight positions were astronomically located. Salazar and Ramírez remained at the confluence for several more weeks to complete the observations before returning to San Diego.[19]

The commissioners meanwhile met in San Diego to discuss the placement of monuments between the coast and the Colorado River. They decided that, at present, they would establish only one more monument. The placing of the remaining monuments would be delegated to one engineer from each commission, who would be left behind while the rest of the joint commission moved to the town of Paso on the Rio Grande. The one monument that would be erected immediately would be fixed by Astronomers Emory and Salazar, at the point where the boundary crossed the main road leading from San Diego to Baja California. Surveyor Gray protested against the U.S. commissioner's delegation of the task of locating the monument to Emory, but to no effect, for Weller was soon afterward dismissed and Emory placed in temporary charge of the U.S. commission.[20]

Emory and Salazar took charge of prolonging the azimuth line eastward from San Diego. During his residence at San Diego, Emory had fixed several positions on the line, which he designated as stations 2 through 5, counting eastward from station 1 at the initial point. The position on the road to Baja California, where the monument was to be placed, was determined by Emory as station 4. García Conde instructed Salazar to reach an agreement with Emory regarding station 4 and, in addition, to rectify the positions of Emory's other stations and to situate two more points on the azimuth line. García Conde and most of the Mexican commission then departed for Mexico City as the U.S. commission also began to break up.

The monument on the road to Baja California would be the first marker eastward from the initial point on the Pacific and, therefore, would project the azimuth of the line to the Colorado River. Salazar tested the position of Emory's station 4 with observations on Polaris and then signed a formal agreement with Emory endorsing the placement of the monument, adding a note that additional verification was to be done by Salazar: "As a further precaution, Jose Salazar Ylarregui undertakes to connect the same by triangulation with the initial point."[21] A temporary monument was erected at the road.

Salazar was assisted by Chavero in his further duties. They performed a triangulation of Emory's five stations, which they denominated by roman numerals, and added a station VI to the west, measuring the distance from the initial point to station II as a base. García Conde had ordered Salazar to locate his positions by sextant observations, but Salazar relied on the sextant alone for only station VII, which he added as his last station to the west, beyond the triangulation. Salazar explained that the triangulation allowed him to ascertain the distances between stations on the line, which would make recovery of the points more certain than sextant observations alone. The astronomical position, "even if very delicate observations are made," he pointed out, "is never the true one, speaking with complete rigor; and if by a certain astronomical position one must hunt for one point on a line of constant and invariable direction, it will never turn out to be on the line, but outside it."[22] As a result of the triangulation survey, Salazar found Emory's stations to be *bien elegidos* (well chosen) and supported their positions.

The station that gave Salazar and Chavero some difficulty was their own station VII. It was located on Cerro de Zecate (Tecate Peak), a summit that was much trouble to ascend. Salazar selected it because the peak gave a clear view toward the Colorado River and would be useful in extending the line. Emory later verified Salazar's position, as he described: "Señor Salazar undertook to establish on the Tecaté a signal in the prolongation of this line, and has succeeded in doing so; and the same has been verified under my orders."[23]

With station VII, the astronomers' work on the California boundary was finished. Sites had been chosen for four permanent monuments to

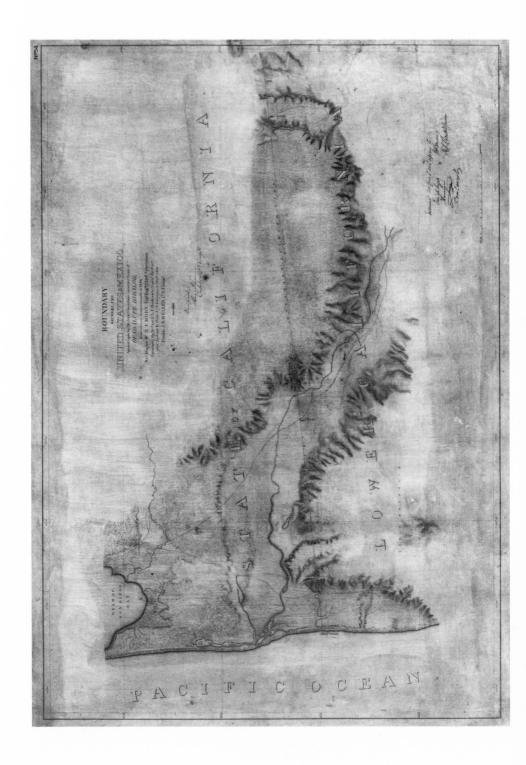

mark the line: the initial point on the Pacific; the intersection of the boundary with the road to Baja California; the left bank of the Colorado River, where it was crossed by the line; and the mouth of the Gila River. The four points together marked the ends of the line and established the azimuth between them. At a later time, three more sites for monuments at intermediate points on the boundary would be determined by the appointed engineers.

Maps "No. 54," the westernmost sheets of the U.S. and Mexican map series, exhibited the results of the commissions' work on the Pacific Coast (figs. 3-1 and 3-2). The information given in the title blocks confirmed that maps "No. 54" were based on independent surveys by the U.S. and Mexican commissions. U.S. map "No. 54" was "determined astronomically" by W. H. Emory, with topography by E. L. F. Hardcastle and Andrew B. Gray, while Mexican map "No. 54," according to the legend, was surveyed by José Salazar Ylarregui and Francisco M. de Chavero, with monumentation by Ricardo Ramírez and E. L. F. Hardcastle.

The images presented by the maps were generally similar, with small differences in content that may have been due to differences in the original data collected by the two commissions. In both maps, the image filled only part of the area bounded by the neatlines; approximately the same areas were left blank on each map; but the U.S. coastal survey extended slightly further south into Mexican territory. Each commission portrayed only its own observatory: Camp Riley on the U.S. map and Campo Mexicano on the Mexican map. The drawing styles were distinct enough to show two different hands. Both maps depicted relief by means of hachures (short lines drawn in the direction of slope), and land cover was shown by delicate patterns and stippling indicating chaparral and sand. The same topographical features were readily identifiable on both sheets, although the angles and turns of the slopes and canyons often did not match exactly. Creeks and lagoons varied in their outlines between the two maps, and the shores of San Diego Bay had a scalloped appearance on the U.S. map that they did not have on the Mexican map.

In the essential matter of the boundary line and its relationship to the

FIG. 3-1. U.S. map "No. 54." The image is partially obscured by a heavy coat of varnish on the manuscript map. (National Archives)

LINEA DIVISORIA

ENTRE

MEXICO Y LOS ESTADOS UNIDOS

conforme al tratado de Guadalupe Hidalgo

firmado en 1848 por

JOSE SALAZAR YLARREGUI

y

FRANCISCO M. DE CHAVERO

MAPA

Levantado por los ingenieros

SUMARIO EN SU LANGA EN 1851

bajo la dirección de los Commissionados respectivos

GENERAL PEDRO G. CONDE Y MAYOR W. H. EMORY

Ricardo Ramirez, y Capitan E.P.L. HARDCASTLE

C A L I F O R N I A

E S T A D O D E C A L I F O R N I A

B A J A C A L I F O R N I A

LIMITE

O C E A N O P A C I F I C O

Longitud Oeste de Greenwich

graticule, the maps agreed. The relationship of landforms to the boundary line was also highly consistent between the two maps. Both commissions presented the final results of the surveys and showed none of the measurements and triangulations that were carried out to establish the initial point and the stations on the azimuth line. On each map, three monuments were shown along the line and labeled: the first monument at the initial point on the Pacific; the second monument on the main road from San Diego to Baja California; and the third monument at the eastern edge of the map, established by Engineers Ramírez and Hardcastle a year after the original work by the joint commission. The U.S. map also labeled six of the stations that were located by Emory and Salazar on the azimuth line.

The California azimuth line was surveyed and marked according to the Treaty of Guadalupe Hidalgo, but the Treaty of 1853 altered the boundary at the Colorado River. The new treaty required that the junction of the Gila and Colorado Rivers should be the turning point where the boundary would turn south to follow the Colorado River, taking the middle of the river as the boundary for a distance of twenty English miles, before the line turned eastward across the Sonoran Desert. The position twenty miles below the confluence, where the land boundary departed from the river, became known to the boundary commission as the initial point on the Colorado River.

The new U.S. and Mexican Boundary Commissions under the Treaty of 1853 set out to perform independent surveys as the earlier commissions had done in California. In 1854 each commission sent a party to survey the Colorado River, the U.S. party traveling to California from Washington, D.C., while the Mexican contingent marched from Mexico City. For the United States, the "party for the Pacific side" was placed under the direction of Lieutenant Michler of the Corps of Topographical Engineers. His principal assistants were Schott, Phillips, and O'Donoghue, and in addition he was aided by five other assistants and instrument bearers, as well as laborers, teamsters, herdsmen, and an escort. The Mexican party, the *sección de Sonora* (Sonoran division), was headed by Jiménez, whose assistants were Engineers Alemán, Agustín Díaz, and Luis Díaz. The division was plagued by meager financial

FIG. 3-2. Mexican map "No. 54." (Mapoteca Manuel Orozco y Berra)

resources and lack of support from government authorities. Since the soldiers of the escort to the Mexican commission were expected to double as laborers and assistants to the engineers, Jiménez attempted to secure particular escort officers who had already had experience working with the boundary survey, but to his great chagrin, Jiménez found difficulty in obtaining any escort at all. Negotiations for an escort caused lengthy delays, until the *sección de Sonora* arrived at the Colorado River some four months later than the U.S. party, accompanied by only thirteen soldiers but with experienced officers in command.[24]

Jiménez had instructions from the Mexican commissioner to work in the customary manner—independently, but in agreement with the U.S. commission. Michler, however, had been instructed by the U.S. commissioner to proceed with operations without consideration of the Mexican party. In fact, Michler and Jiménez found it advantageous to consult on many technical matters involved in the fieldwork, although the Mexican section arrived at the river too late to effectively argue with any of the operations already carried out by the U.S. party.

Commissioner Emory had given Michler lengthy orders for the work on the Pacific side. Among them were instructions to measure the twenty miles beginning from the monument that marked the departure of the California azimuth line, near the junction of the Gila and Colorado Rivers. Since the geographical position of the monument had been elaborately calculated in office work following the field survey, Michler was to transfer its latitude and longitude by triangulation to the new initial point on the Colorado. In addition, he was to make astronomical observations for latitude at the initial point.[25]

In December 1854, Michler and his party arrived at newly established Fort Yuma, near the confluence of the Gila and Colorado Rivers, where they began triangulation toward the initial point on the Colorado. Cutting their way through the dense timber of the river bottom, the triangulation team reached the end of twenty miles by early March. The observatory that Michler constructed nearby was ready just as spring floods began. "I had commenced observing for Latitude," Michler related, "when after two nights the Observatory was flooded with water, and it was only by great labor that the Instruments were saved by wading and swimming nearly two miles." When the waters at length receded, Michler returned to his station and continued observations for latitude; as longitude, he took the position measured and calculated from the triangulation.[26]

The U.S. commission was still dislocated by the flood when the *sección de Sonora* reached the Colorado River. Jiménez had known that the U.S. party was working on the river and expected their operations to be well advanced. But Commissioner Salazar had authorized Jiménez to formally agree with the U.S. engineer about the initial point on the Colorado, so Jiménez was surprised to learn from Michler that his instructions did not require him to work in agreement with anyone—only to work with the greatest speed possible. Jiménez, therefore, quickly planned how the Mexican commission could carry out in a few days the operations that the U.S. commission had already practiced for four months.

The instructions for determining the initial point that Jiménez had received were somewhat different from Michler's. Salazar had specified the latitude of the confluence and directed Jiménez to measure the twenty miles beginning from that point; Jiménez was then to observe for two months for the longitude of the initial point. The method of measuring the twenty miles, not stated in the treaty, was to be agreed upon between Jiménez and the head of the U.S. section. Jiménez was to strive for an agreement that the twenty miles would be measured on the course of the river. As a second choice, he should agree to make the measurement on the hypotenuse of a triangle, and only if he failed to obtain one of those two methods, he should agree to measure the distance on the meridian.[27]

Jiménez requested a conference with Michler and was pleased to find that Michler responded "with the same obligingness and gentlemanly behavior that afterwards distinguished him in all his actions."[28] In their meeting, Jiménez said, he learned that Michler had been instructed to calculate the twenty miles by the second method, that is, as a hypotenuse, and that by using that method he had determined the initial point on the Colorado. Jiménez agreed to accept the initial point located by Michler, contingent upon the Mexican division's determination of latitude and longitude at the point. Once the coordinates of the confluence and the initial point were known, Jiménez noted, it would be easy to verify that the initial point was twenty miles below the confluence because the calculation of the distance could be reduced to the application of a formula.[29]

Although Jiménez understood that Michler had been directed to measure the twenty miles on the hypotenuse, Michler's instructions did not actually state so. When Emory later learned of the nature of the work that Michler had accomplished on the Colorado River, he apprehended that his orders to "take a point 20 miles below or south, of the junction of the Gila and Colorado" had not been strictly obeyed; rather, Michler had ascertained the point "by taking a radius of 20 miles, and with the junction of the Gila and Colorado as a centre, describing a circle, the point of intersection with the Colorado being adopted as the Initial Point on the River." Nevertheless, considering that Michler had, "of his own accord invited and received the concurrence of the Mexican Engineer," Emory gave his approval to the initial point Michler had established, for he believed it met the requirements of the treaty, which described the point "as simply *below* the junction." [30]

Jiménez and Alemán quickly established an observatory on the bank of the river near the initial point. They accomplished sixty observations for latitude during the first week of April and made computations from their observations for the position of Michler's observatory. Upon comparison with Michler's results, they found only a small difference in their determinations and agreed to take the average as the position that they would transfer to the initial point in the river. To find the longitude of the initial point, however, Jiménez could not spend the two months that Salazar had recommended, so he proposed to Michler that the longitude be checked by signal fires between the initial point and the confluence.

Michler agreed to observe signal fires for longitude on three nights and offered to reconnoiter the terrain to find locations for the signals. He was unable to find a suitable site, but Agustín Díaz discovered a spot where fires could be seen simultaneously from the old monument at the confluence and the observatory at the initial point. Díaz took charge of making the signals while Jiménez and Alemán observed at the confluence and Michler observed at the initial point. On two of the three nights appointed for the signals, heavy fog on the river prevented observations, resulting in only nine pairs of times for Jiménez to use to calculate the longitude difference. The outcome, over fifteen seconds of arc at variance with the longitude derived from Michler's triangulation, did not satisfy Jiménez. Not wishing to delay the eastward tracing of the line any longer and considering his results from the signal fires doubtful, Jiménez agreed to adopt Michler's longitude as true, meanwhile leaving Díaz at work upon a triangulation of the river that would yield a comparison to Michler's work. [31]

To test the position of the initial point, Jiménez calculated its distance from the confluence. For the latitude and longitude at the confluence, Jiménez used values slightly different from those supplied by Emory to Michler, but he used the position of the initial point that he and Michler had agreed upon. In his instructions to Jiménez, Salazar had given the distance of twenty English miles as 32,202 meters, an equivalent derived from Francoeur, which Jiménez applied. As a result of his computations, Jiménez found that the initial point had been established 32,208.2 meters below the confluence, or 6.2 meters too far south. He concluded that the distance was so small, being even less than the distance obtained from the difference in latitudes determined by the two commissions at the initial point, that the initial point should be accepted as an accurate determination. On 26 April 1855, Jiménez and Michler signed a formal agreement adopting the initial point on the Colorado and specifying its geographical position.[32]

Two months later, Jiménez was able to compare the triangulation surveys conducted by the Mexican and U.S. parties. Both the Díaz and Michler triangulations began from the monument near the confluence and transferred its latitude and longitude to the initial point on the Colorado. Jiménez reported that there was so little difference in the geographical coordinates for the initial point yielded by the two triangulations that he was entirely satisfied with the established initial point on the Colorado.[33]

In addition to the astronomical and geodetic work, Michler had instructions from Emory to make a topographical sketch of the Colorado River and the surrounding country—"as far as [he could] do so without much impeding . . . operations." Michler assigned the topographical survey to Schott, his assistant surveyor, who began on the Gila River a few miles above its mouth and continued downriver on the Colorado until Phillips was appointed to take over the work. Schott then drew field maps of his survey while Phillips was on the river. According to Michler, both Schott and Phillips conducted their surveys separately from the triangulation crew directed by Michler.[34]

The Díaz triangulation of the Colorado River included preparation of a topographical sketch. Agustín Díaz carried out the survey without the help of his brother Luis, who suffered from an illness he had contracted during the previous year's fieldwork. Luis was left behind in the frontier town of Altar, Sonora, where he continued drawing maps from

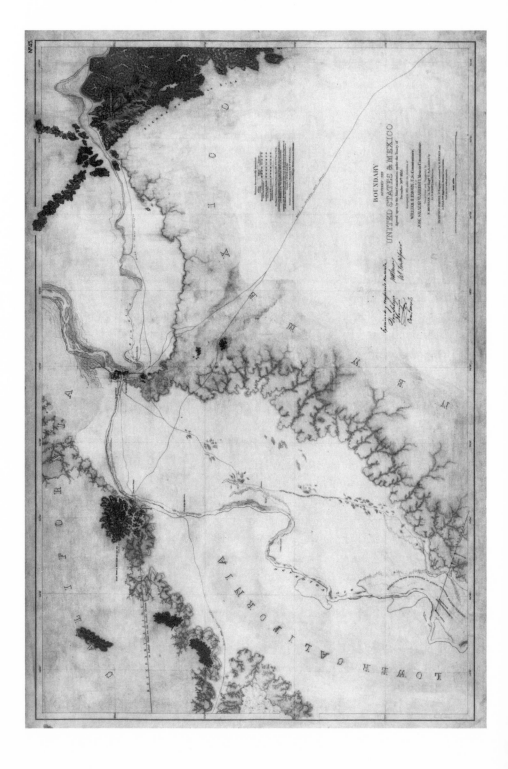

earlier surveys, while Agustín spent about six weeks on the Colorado, assisted by several soldiers of the escort. A report he presented to Jiménez included the data he collected and a description of his operations. He noted that his orders, in addition to specifying a triangulation and topographical survey, required him to compile the information into a rough map at the scale of 1:50,000.

Díaz extended his survey from a short distance above the confluence of the Gila and Colorado Rivers, on both rivers, to a short distance below the initial point on the Colorado, as Salazar had directed. At the confluence, it was necessary to measure a baseline for the triangulation. The Mexican commission had three measuring instruments in its equipment, among which Díaz had his choice: a steel tape, a chain, or simple wooden rules. Díaz and Alemán compared the instruments with the iron bars the U.S. commission had used in its triangulation, and judging that the wooden rules gave the most uniform results, Alemán assisted Díaz in using them to measure a baseline. Díaz then worked with his military assistants to carry out the triangulation, marking the vertices of triangles with signals and measuring angles with a Troughton theodolite.[35]

Díaz identified three classes of triangles that he used to construct the triangulation. The three types served different purposes and were fixed with different levels of accuracy. Those he called *los triángulos de la cadena* (the triangles of the chain) were the triangles that directly connected the monument at the confluence with the initial point on the Colorado. In nearly all the triangles of the chain, all three angles of each triangle were measured. Triangles that Díaz called *de rectificacion del rio* (of rectification of the river) were those used to check the details of the topographical survey of the river, while triangles labeled *ausiliares* (auxiliaries) located topographical features in general. In the majority of the triangles of rectification and the auxiliary triangles, Díaz resigned himself to measuring only two angles, but they were done with the same care as the angles in the triangles of the chain. The course of the river was determined by means of what Díaz, mixing French and Spanish terms, called a *canevas topográfico*. He described it as a scrupulous measurement of rhumbs and distances, in which he sighted the directions

FIG. 3-3. U.S. map "No. 45." (National Archives)

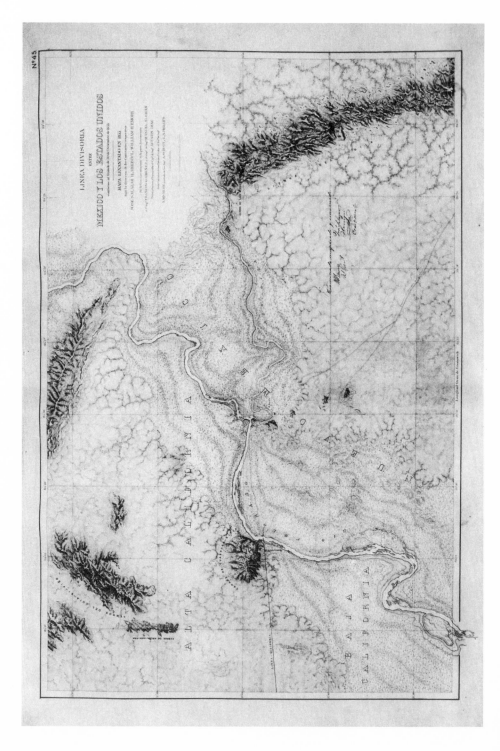

LINEA DIVISORIA
ENTRE
MEXICO Y LOS ESTADOS UNIDOS

ALTA CALIFORNIA

BAJA CALIFORNIA

and angles with another, smaller theodolite made by Troughton. The drawing of the *canevas topográfico* was corrected by the triangulation.[36]

Maps "No. 44" and "No. 45" recorded the boundary on the Colorado River (figs. 3-3, 3-4, 3-5, and 3-6). The maps combined information about the junction of the Gila and Colorado Rivers, surveyed according to the Treaty of Guadalupe Hidalgo, and the course of the Colorado River, surveyed under the Treaty of 1853. The maps also depicted the course of the Gila River, surveyed by the two commissions in 1852, but made obsolete as the international boundary by the Treaty of 1853.

Mexican and U.S. maps "No. 45" differed from most pairs of maps by the two commissions in showing differing extents of territory. In Mexican map "No. 45," the Gila River ran across the middle of the sheet to its confluence with the Colorado; nearly half of the map image was occupied with the land north of the Gila. The map reached far enough to the south to show about sixteen of the twenty miles of the Colorado River boundary. Mexican map "No. 44" was a continuation of map "No. 45," reaching to the initial point on the Colorado River and the boundary running east. U.S. map "No. 45," on the other hand, placed the confluence near the top of the sheet, so the entire Colorado River boundary from the confluence to the initial point was included in the image, while U.S. map "No. 44" presented an image similar to Mexican map "No. 44" and thus repeated the representation of the initial point shown on U.S. map "No. 45." Nowhere else in the U.S. map series was a section of the boundary repeated on two maps.

The attention that each party was able to grant to different surveying tasks was reflected in the finished maps. The U.S. maps emphasized the astronomical determinations and geodetic calculations to which the U.S. section devoted so much care. U.S. map "No. 45" carried a lengthy legend giving the latitude and longitude of various points and monuments, the azimuth bearings of the California and Sonora lines, and magnetic variation. Mexican map "No. 45" bore no such legend, and the large area that corresponded to the legend and surrounding blank space on the U.S. map was filled with renderings of topography on the Mexican map. The only astronomical determination provided in a legend on Mexico's maps was given on "No. 44" and contained the latitude and

FIG. 3-4. Mexican map "No. 45." (Mapoteca Manuel Orozco y Berra)

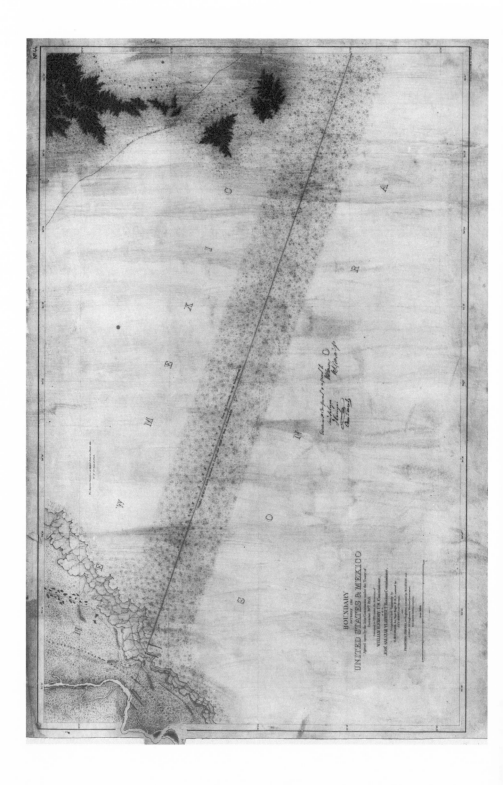

BOUNDARY
BETWEEN THE
UNITED STATES & MEXICO
Surveyed under the direction of the Joint Commission under the Treaty of
Guadalupe Hidalgo
WILLIAM H. EMORY U.S. Commissioner.
JOSE SALAZAR YLARREGUI Mexican Commissioner.

longitude of the initial point on the Colorado, as agreed upon by Jiménez and Michler. Both U.S. maps "No. 44" and "No. 45" showed and
labeled the initial point in the middle of the river and also marked with
a star and label "Lt. Michler's Observatory." Mexican map "No. 44"
showed the initial point but neither Michler's nor Jiménez's observatory.

Although the same large landforms appeared on the maps of both
commissions, the Mexican maps showed greater concern with the details of topography, such as land surface and land cover, and the complexities of the river channel. Compared to U.S. map "No. 45," the
Mexican map conveyed more of the nature of the landscape: the entire
sheet was filled in, the areas between the hachured hills and mountain
ranges covered almost completely with symbols that indicated mesas,
arroyos, and expanses of sand, where the U.S. mapmakers were frequently satisfied to leave blank spaces. The Mexican picture of the Río
Colorado was intricate in its side channels, islands, and sandbars. The
course of the Río Gila as shown on the Mexican and U.S. maps varied
considerably, possibly resulting from changes in the river that occurred
between surveys made at separate times.

U.S. map "No. 45" was unusual in being one of only three U.S. sectional maps that did not bear the name of the person who drew it. Maps
"No. 41" and "No. 42" also lacked a drafter's credit. All three of the maps
preserved evidence of the drawing process, showing extensive annotations and underdrawing in pencil (in marks too fine and faint to be seen
on photographs of the maps). On map "No. 45," for example, a penciled
registration mark just inside the neatline may have been used with tracing sheet overlays. A penciled, mechanically drawn oval separated the
title block from the image elements, and freely drawn pencil lines
bounded the image areas of stipple patterns. Pencil guidelines were provided for much of the lettering on the map, including curved guidelines
for the widely spaced, shaded block letters of the state names. The place
name Vicente, for an Indian village that was called after its leader, was
lettered in ink, but the name written in pencil appeared above it as a
guide. At the northeastern corner and central western edge of the map,
where the rendering of topographical features was allowed to flow
through the neatlines, pencil lines marked the breaks in the neatlines.

FIG. 3-5. U.S. map "No. 44." (National Archives)

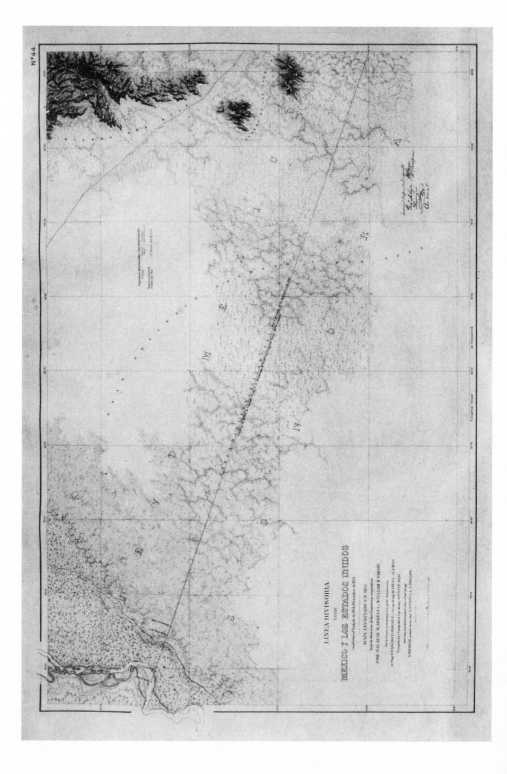

LINEA DIVISORIA
ENTRE
MEXICO Y LOS ESTADOS UNIDOS
conforme al Tratado de 30 de Diciembre de 1853.

MAPA LEVANTADO EN 1855,
bajo la dirección de los Comisarios respectivos
JOSE SALAZAR YLARREGUI y WILLIAM H. EMORY

De la Linea, se encuentran en la parte delineamos
el Plag FRANCISCO JIMENEZ ... etc. ... el ing MANUEL ALEMAN
Levantamos y Topografía al cargo de ing AGUSTO DIAZ
Y DIBUJO á cuenta de los ing A. SCHOTT y J. E. WELLER.

The unsigned map "No. 45," like maps "No. 41" and "No. 42," in which the penciled notes and guidelines were similar to those described for map "No. 45," had an appearance of being not quite finished. All three of these sheets were among the last for which the data were available to the drafters in the office.

The survey of the other boundary river between the United States and Mexico, the Río Bravo or Rio Grande, was organized under the Treaty of Guadalupe Hidalgo and was designed to be carried out independently and agreeably by the U.S. and Mexican commissions. Shortly after completing the surveys of the California coast and the confluence of the Gila and Colorado Rivers, the joint commission moved east to begin work on the Rio Grande. A formal plan for the survey of the river was drawn up and signed by Mexican Surveyor Salazar and U.S. Astronomer Graham in November 1851.

The plan set forth the goals and methods of the survey and expressed the continuing independence of the two commissions in conducting their surveys, as well as their intention to reach agreement in their results. It was an ambitious plan for a meticulous survey, stating, among other points,

> That the course and sinuosities of the river shall be run out by means of theodolites of portable and convenient size, or by surveyors' compasses, and the measurements made with the chain or by means of portable micrometer telescopes for observing the angles of subtense of a rod of given length, placed at various distances.

> All towns, villages, and habitations in the immediate vicinity of the river, shall be surveyed and laid down upon the maps, and also the topography, as far as it can be done without too much retarding the work. . . .

> The run of the work will be corrected by determinations of latitude and longitude from astronomical observations at suitable points, to be selected as the work progresses. . . .

> Should either party be prepared to commence the survey of this river before the other, the aforesaid party may go on with it, conformably

FIG. 3-6. Mexican map "No. 44." (Mapoteca Manuel Orozco y Berra)

with the foregoing articles, and the result, on being verified and assented to by the other party, will be authenticated and agreed to by both.

The language of the agreement was Graham's. Salazar had advised Graham, however, that his instructions from his government would not permit him to make a full topographical survey of the river, so it was provided that,

> Should the commission on the part of either of the two governments . . . find it inconvenient to make this survey so minute as is above described, the said party may, at its option, confine this degree of minuteness to the inhabited and any other portions of the river that may be deemed to possess sufficient interest, and make a more rapid and more general survey of the other portions. Such party shall, however, in that case, satisfy itself as to the correctness of the more minute surveys of the other party; and when so satisfied, shall authenticate it by signing the notes of survey, and the maps projected therefrom.[37]

Despite their thorough planning, Salazar and Graham made little progress in practice. While Salazar awaited the arrival of Commissioner García Conde, Graham was removed from the survey and returned to Washington less than a month after he signed the agreement with Salazar.

In summer 1852, Graham's replacement, U.S. Surveyor Emory, and Salazar, now the Mexican commissioner, met on the Rio Grande to once again plan the survey of the river. Scattered surveys had been done by that time, and they wished to coordinate the work in order to speed its completion. They agreed that each commission would survey only specified portions of the river.

Their plan divided the Rio Grande into six portions (Location Map 2; also see Location Map 4). The first portion, "from the initial point to the colony of San Ignacio," began at the Bartlett–García Conde initial point, where the 32°22' parallel crossed the Rio Grande, and ended at San Ignacio, a town on the Mexican bank of the river about fifty miles below Paso. The second portion continued from San Ignacio to Presidio del Norte, located at the confluence of the Rio Grande and Río Conchos. From Presidio del Norte, the third section of the river ran to the military colony of Agua Verde. Agua Verde had been a Spanish presidio south of the Río Bravo, near the mouth of the Pecos River; it was no longer occupied by the time of the boundary survey. The fourth section stretched between Agua Verde and Laredo, a town that included settlements on both sides of the Rio Grande and was located about midway between the mouth of the Pecos River and the Gulf of Mexico. From Laredo to Matamoros was the fifth portion of the river. The town of Matamoros, Tamaulipas, was situated across the river from Brownsville, Texas, and had an earlier history as a rancho and a mission. The sixth and last section reached from Matamoros to the mouth of the Rio Grande. The work was to be divided so that the second and fourth sections of the river would be surveyed by the U.S. commission, the third and fifth by the Mexican commission, and the first and last portions would be surveyed in detail by both parties. The agreement further called for the establishment of astronomical stations at the mouth of the Pecos, Eagle Pass, Laredo, Matamoros, and the mouth of the Rio Grande. The plan was not ultimately executed in all its details as originally conceived, but upon reaching the agreement, each commission set out to fulfill its part.[38]

The sixth portion of the river was an important section, for here would be fixed the eastern end of the boundary, located in the Gulf of Mexico opposite the *desembocadura* (river's mouth), where the Río Bravo flowed into the sea. Both the U.S. and Mexican commissions surveyed the *desembocadura* in 1853—an uncomfortable time when the Bartlett commission had been recalled, and the negotiations for the Treaty of 1853 were not yet complete. The U.S. surveyors at the river's mouth were members of the Campbell commission; Mexico was represented by a small party appointed by Commissioner Salazar called the *sección Matamoros*.

Francisco Jiménez, leader of the *sección Matamoros*, had specific instructions regarding the *desembocadura* from the Mexican commissioner. As principal engineer of the Mexican commission, Jiménez was to meet at the mouth of the river with the appointed principal engineer of the U.S. commission to determine the deepest channel and to select the positions on each side of the channel where boundary monuments would be erected. He was also to sign a formal agreement with the U.S. principal engineer specifying the latitude and longitude of the two monuments. The choice of the deepest channel was to be based upon the

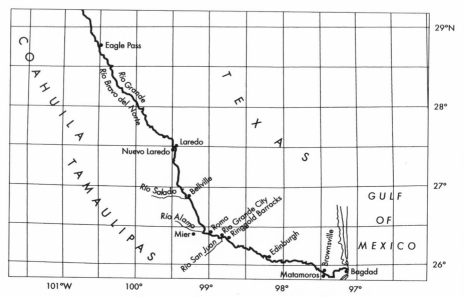

LOCATION MAP 2. Boundary between the United States and Mexico, showing the Rio Grande between the Gulf of Mexico and Eagle Pass. Source: [U.S. Boundary Commission], *Index Map No. 1.*

topographical survey that would be conducted by members of the *sección Matamoros* Agustín and Luis Díaz. If the U.S. topographical survey were completed first, and Jiménez found it absolutely precise, he was to accept the U.S. survey as the basis for the selection of the channel, while making the necessary examinations and soundings. Jiménez's instructions were in keeping with a plan for establishing the initial point at the *desembocadura* adopted by the joint commission at an official meeting on 8 October 1852.[39]

The Mexican engineers were working at Matamoros and the *desembocadura* when U.S. Chief Astronomer and Surveyor Emory arrived at Brownsville in May 1853. Jiménez and Emory presently became involved in a contention over the wording of the agreement that was to be formed between the principal engineers. Jiménez insisted on stating that the authority of the engineers was derived from the resolution of the joint commission, while Emory, with motives unrelated to the demarcation of the boundary at the *desembocadura*, refused to recognize the proceedings of the joint commission. Because at that time negotiations to settle the southern boundary of New Mexico were about to begin, Emory did not want to participate in a declaration that would lend authority to the joint commission, whose support of the Bartlett–García Conde compromise Emory hoped to see overturned in the new treaty.[40] To avoid an extended controversy, Jiménez did not press Emory to name a principal engineer to represent the United States and sign an agreement with him on the river boundary. To Jiménez's consternation, Emory eventually decided that two individuals would represent the United States. Since the U.S. commission had not yet made a topographical survey of the lower river, the selection of the deepest channel would be postponed until later, when Radziminski, as principal engineer for the United States, would agree on the channel through an exchange of official notes with Jiménez. Emory himself would agree with Jiménez upon the placement of the two monuments at the mouth of the river.

Subject to flooding, and bordered on both sides by shifting sand dunes, the *desembocadura* was not well suited for the location of marble pillars. "On this unsuitable ground, the points least poor had to be selected," Jiménez wrote, explaining his choice of the highest dune on the Mexican side of the river as a site for a monument.[41] Emory set up his telescope on the dune he selected on the U.S. side. Emory's transit was used to align a position on the Mexican dune in the same meridian as the telescope on the U.S. side, and the determined point was marked with a great log.

The Díaz survey of the *desembocadura* was relied upon to determine the location of the deepest channel and its relationship to the monument sites. Shortly after the places for the monuments had been chosen, the Díaz brothers presented field maps of the river between Matamoros and the mouth to Jiménez. Emory viewed the plans and agreed with Jiménez that they should measure the distance from each of the monuments to the deepest channel and also the distance between the U.S. and Mexican observatories at the river's mouth. Jiménez and his assistant astronomer, Alemán, measured the required distances at once.

The Mexican commission prepared an agreement describing the location of the monuments and the boundary. The Mexican statement said that, as authorized by one of the resolutions of the joint commission of 8 October 1852, U.S. Chief Astronomer and Surveyor Emory and Mexican Principal Engineer Jiménez agreed that the river had only one channel at its mouth and that the two monuments should stand in the same astronomical meridian. The distance of the U.S. monument from the channel was given as 450 feet in the direction of the meridian, and the distance of the Mexican monument from the channel as 1,560 feet in the same direction. Emory refused to sign the Mexican document. Instead he prepared an official statement of his own that consented to the measurements presented in the Mexican agreement but did not acknowledge the authority of the joint commission.[42]

The U.S. topographical survey of the river's mouth was not completed for another three months. Radziminski reached the *desembocadura* with his assistants early in November. By that time, Emory had returned to Washington, and Jiménez and Alemán had carried their astronomical work upriver to Mier. At Mier, Jiménez received an official note from Radziminski advising him that the U.S. survey was finished from Brownsville to the mouth of the river. Radziminski wrote that he had compared his surveys with the Mexican maps and found them in agreement, so that the determination of the principal channel presented no difficulty. He proposed that they agree that the deepest section of the Rio Grande as surveyed by the two parties be designated the principal channel. "As a result of the comparison made between the maps surveyed by both commissions," Jiménez responded, "I agree with your proposal"; and so through a comparison of maps and an exchange of notes, Radziminski and Jiménez concluded consultations at the *desembocadura*.[43]

The sixth portion of the river, from Matamoros to the mouth, was shown on U.S. and Mexican maps "No. 1." The map titles named the astronomers and topographers who provided the map information: Emory, Radziminski, and Schott for the U.S. map; and Jiménez, Alemán, and Agustín and Luis Díaz for the Mexican map. The U.S. and Mexican sheets were both designed with the same layout, the right-hand side of the sheet containing only the title and the commissioners' signatures, the coastline drawn north to south through about the center of the sheet, and the river surrounded by a band of topographical drawing. The Mexican map depicted a slightly greater extent of the country south of the river than the U.S. map, while the U.S. map pictured much more of the Texan side of the river than the Mexican sheet.

In details of the *desembocadura* from maps "No. 1," the same topographic information was provided on the U.S. and Mexican maps, yet differences were evident (figs. 3-7 and 3-8). The outlines of the coast

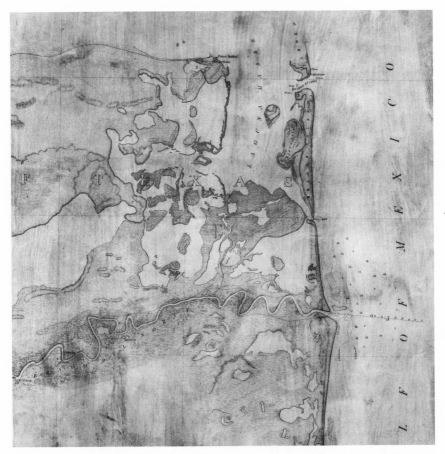

FIG. 3-7. Detail of U.S. map "No. 1," showing the mouth of the Rio Grande (this map is especially heavily varnished). (National Archives)

and the meanders of the Río Bravo, while recognizable when compared between the U.S. and Mexican maps, were generally more smoothed on the U.S. map. The coastal lagoons appeared to be definite lakes on the U.S. map, while the same areas looked like swampy wetlands on the Mexican map. The sand dunes along the coast were more prominent features on the Mexican map than on the U.S. map. What appeared to be an abandoned channel of the Río Bravo, the Arroyo de la Placeta, located to the south of the river, was shown on the Mexican map, suggesting the changeable geographical position of the *desembocadura;* it was not shown on the U.S. map. The U.S. map emphasized the delineation of the Laguna Madre and barrier islands north of the Río Bravo

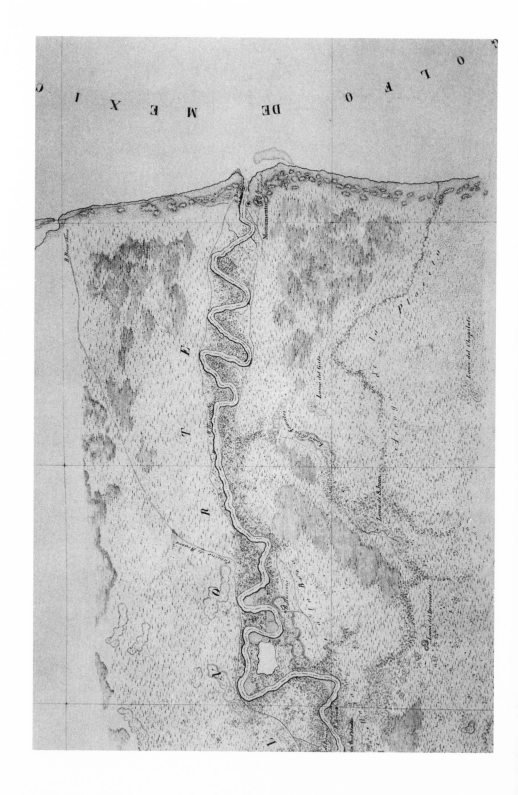

that the Mexican map left out. The Mexican map included more toponyms, principally names of ranches and hills.

Maps "No. 1" mirror the descriptions of the lower Río Bravo found in the writings of a famous mid-nineteenth-century traveler, Dr. Frederick Adolphus Wislizenus, who told of his journey to Santa Fe and Chihuahua during the U.S.-Mexican War in his *Memoir of a Tour to Northern Mexico*.[44] Traveling downriver, Wislizenus related, "from Matamoros we passed by *Fort Brown*, where the star-spangled banner was flying, and the battle-fields of *Palo Alto* and *Resaca de la Palma* were pointed out to us in the distant chaparráls towards the north. The river was here in a very navigable state, but continued to be as crooked as ever." Matamoros, Fort Brown, and the crooked river were evident in Mexican map "No. 1" in a detail from the southwest corner of the sheet (fig. 3-9). U.S. map "No. 1" showed the same features and also marked the battlefields, sites of U.S. victories in the recent war, but the Mexican map did not represent territory that far north into Texas. Wislizenus continued: "I saw many palm trees of small size; more settlements along the banks; sugar and cotton plantations among them, but chaparrál always in the back ground." The plantations along the riverbanks and the chaparral in the background were conspicuous in both the U.S. and Mexican maps.

Camped at the *desembocadura*, Wislizenus found some commissaries and private stores on the U.S. side at a hamlet called Mouth of Rio Grande; opposite, on the Mexican side, he saw another small village named Bagdad. Bagdad appeared on U.S. map "No. 1," while the Mexican map showed both of the villages with their names (figs. 3-7 and 3-8). Wislizenus noted that "in the river lay some smaller steamboats and schooners, but no larger crafts, which have a better anchorage nine miles from here, in Brazos Santiago." Mexican map "No. 1" showed details of the coastal topography north of the Río Bravo as far as Boca Chica, the southernmost opening between the Gulf of Mexico and the Laguna Madre, around the tip of the coastal barrier islands. The U.S. map continued the representation northward to Brazos Santiago (labeled Brazos St. Iago), the inlet past the barrier islands used by commercial shipping.

FIG. 3-8. Detail of Mexican map "No. 1," showing the *desembocadura*. (Mapoteca Manuel Orozco y Berra)

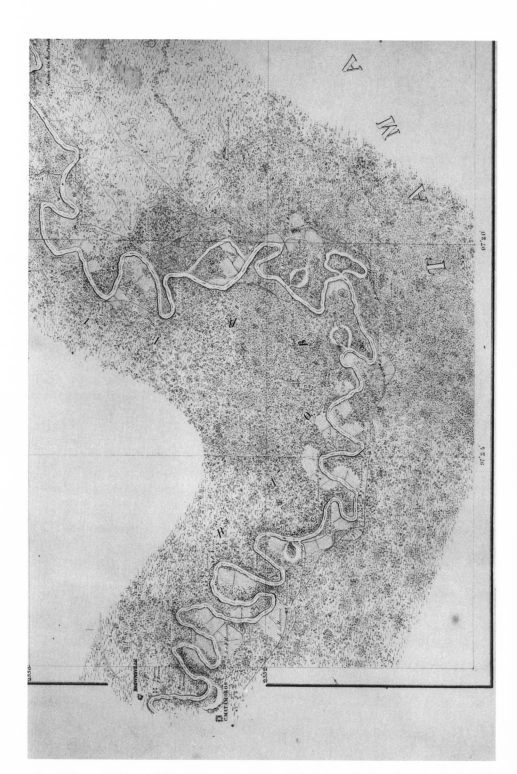

Each commission showed on its maps only its own astronomical station at the *desembocadura*. Jiménez and Alemán's station was marked on the Mexican map by a star on the banks of the river north of the village of Bagdad. A legend elsewhere on the map gave the latitude and longitude observations for the point. U.S. map "No. 1" showed Emory's astronomical station at the mouth of the river, marked by a star, with the latitude and longitude determinations also given elsewhere in a legend. Jiménez's records of his transactions with the U.S. commission did not include an agreement on the latitude and longitude of stations at the *desembocadura,* as Salazar originally instructed Jiménez to obtain. The final latitude and longitude determinations for the mouth of the Río Bravo, derived by calculations made in the office by the U.S. and Mexican commissions, differed slightly.[45] Although at the scale of the maps the small discrepancy was not apparent, it may have hinted at the nature of the shifting river's mouth and the possibility of future problems.

Features at the *desembocadura* that were subjects of formal agreements between Jiménez and the U.S. engineers were important details of Mexican map "No. 1." The position of the Mexican boundary monument at the mouth of the river, agreed upon by Jiménez and Emory, was marked on the map of the Comisión de Límites and boldly labeled "Monumento." A continuous dashed-and-dotted line symbolized, according to the map legend, the boundary in the Río Bravo. The line followed the approximate center of the river, although the true deepest channel agreed upon by Jiménez and Radziminski may have traced a wandering course in the river that would have been difficult to depict at the small scale of the map. U.S. map "No. 1" neglected to recognize the engineers' field agreements, showing neither the monument at the *desembocadura* nor the boundary in the river.

Although on Mexican map "No. 1" the boundary line in the Río Bravo ended at the *desembocadura,* on the U.S. map a boundary line began at the river's mouth and extended into the Gulf of Mexico. An offshore survey was first planned as part of the agreement signed by Graham and Salazar in November 1851. As ambitious as the rest of the plan, it stated:

FIG. 3-9. Detail of Mexican map "No. 1," showing Matamoros and Brownsville at the western edge of the sheet. (Mapoteca Manuel Orozco y Berra)

Should the Rio Grande or Bravo del Norte be found to flow into the Gulf of Mexico by more than one channel, all shall be sounded, so that the boundary line may be laid down along the middle of the deepest one. Soundings shall then be carried out from the mouth of this deepest channel to a distance of three leagues into the Gulf of Mexico, in order to show the best entrance for vessels into the river. Either party desiring it may extend these soundings to the said distance of three leagues out from the entrance of all the said channels, the result to be considered as for the benefit of the navigation of both countries, and to be rendered for that object in duplicate to the commissioners of the two governments.[46]

The U.S. Boundary Commission afterward arranged for a hydrographic survey in the Gulf of Mexico to be done by the U.S. Coast Survey, but the Mexican commission did not provide for soundings in the Gulf. Perhaps if Commissioner García Conde, who was charged with overseeing the development of Mexican harbor charts at the same time he headed the Comisión de Límites, had lived, the project might have been attempted.

The U.S. Boundary Commission's contract with the Coast Survey was managed by Commissioner Campbell, although Surveyor Emory conducted much of the communication between the two agencies. The kinds of hydrographic data needed for the boundary survey—measurements of water depths, latitude and longitude positions for coastal locations, and coastal topography—were regularly acquired by the Coast Survey in its chart-making operations. The superintendent of the Coast Survey, Alexander Dallas Bache, was interested in avoiding duplication of effort on the Gulf Coast and was willing to arrange a contract with Campbell, who in turn was pleased that the contract spared the boundary commission a much larger expense.[47]

The Coast Survey examined the entrance to the Rio Grande as part of its regular operations on the Gulf Coast. Emory summarized the work of the Coast Survey briefly in his final *Report*, saying that, "Lieut. Wilkinson, in command of the brig Morris, repaired at the appointed time to the mouth of the river and made soundings, marked on sheet No. 1, by which we were enabled to trace the boundary, as the treaty required, 'three leagues out to sea.'"[48] John Wilkinson was chief of a hydrographic party that had been working southward from Galveston

Bay along the Texas coast in spring 1853; it was typical that the work was directed by a lieutenant of the U.S. Navy, as the Coast Survey commonly employed naval officers for its hydrographic surveys. Wilkinson completed over five thousand soundings at the entrance to the Rio Grande in August 1853, at the same time that the boundary commission surveyors were in the field. Also at that time, Gustavus Würdemann of the Coast Survey performed hourly tidal observations at the mouth of the Rio Grande.[49] Wilkinson's survey was not acknowledged on U.S. map "No. 1," but the U.S. commission's engraved plate for *No. 1*, from which a number of proof prints were made, stated that "the soundings were made in 1853 by Lt. Wilkinson U.S. Navy, assistant U.S. Coast Survey."[50]

With a concern for the facilities for navigation, the Coast Survey also investigated the lower Texas coast. From November 1853 to April 1854, Assistant W. E. Greenwell, aided by P. C. F. West, carried out a triangulation and topographical survey of the entrance to the Rio Grande and for four miles up the river, encompassing an area north and south of the river of sixty-three square miles. The results of Greenwell's survey were sent to the boundary commission and contributed to the detailed representation of coastal topography on U.S. map "No. 1." Both the printed U.S. map *No. 1* and manuscript map "No. 1" credited Greenwell's survey. In addition, the results were promptly published by the Coast Survey in a map titled *Preliminary Survey of the Entrance to the Rio Grande, Texas*, displaying the hydrography completed by Wilkinson and the topography by Greenwell.[51]

Although Emory's final *Report* suggested that the offshore boundary was fully surveyed, the bathymetry for the entire distance of three marine leagues was not actually accomplished. According to a Coast Survey report, another party in 1854 attempted to carry out additional hydrographic observations at the Rio Grande but was defeated by bad weather.[52] A search for records of the original offshore survey, needed as evidence in a U.S. Supreme Court case decided in 1960 regarding the maritime boundaries of the states bordering on the Gulf of Mexico, revealed the incompleteness of the Campbell commission's soundings. Coast Survey documents brought forward in the case showed that the actual survey, completed in August 1853, extended for a distance of two nautical miles, or two-thirds of a marine league, from the coast.[53]

The manuscript and printed versions of U.S. map "No. 1" portrayed the results of the hydrographic survey (fig. 3-7). Around the river's mouth, a scattering of spot soundings, given in fathoms and fractions of fathoms, was shown. Contour lines connected the soundings at depths of one, two, and three fathoms. The three bathymetric lines, drawn before the mouth of the Rio Grande through the Gulf of Mexico for a distance equivalent to about four land miles, were the only instance of contour lines used to depict a physical feature in either the U.S. or Mexican boundary map series, as hachures were used everywhere in the maps to represent relief. A dashed line, labeled "boundary," extended from the mouth of the river toward the southeast. It was drawn as a straight line exiting the mouth of the river through the deepest channel, as indicated by the bathymetric contours, and continued out to sea in the direction established as it exited the mouth. Spot soundings also placed the line in what appeared to be the middle of the area of deepest water. Seaward of the three-fathoms bathymetric line, however, the soundings were so scattered that the deepest channel was not unambiguously defined. The boundary line was drawn only slightly farther into the Gulf than the most seaward soundings. The boundary required by the Treaty of Guadalupe Hidalgo, "in the Gulf of Mexico, three leagues from land," was therefore not fully delineated on the final boundary maps of either commission.

The finished boundary maps of the Pacific Coast, the Colorado River, and the mouth of the Rio Grande, containing important turning points on the line, offer ample evidence of the independent work performed by the U.S. and Mexican Boundary Commissions and of consultation between the commissions during the survey. Map evidence conforms with the descriptions of independent work and consultation given in the manuscript and published reports of the two commissions. Through counsel in the field, representatives of two sovereign nations attempted to interpret the boundary treaties in relation to particular geographical situations. The commissions found that geographical features and positions named in the treaties required definition and selection; that standards of measurement and other mathematical elements had to be chosen in order to carry out computations; that conformity between astronomical determinations made by each commission was necessary; and that the final demarcation had to be agreed upon. The U.S. and Mexican engineers had in common a scientific training that enabled them to reach consensus in the methods and standards to be used, usually based on the latest European developments in surveying and geodesy. Each commission attempted both to serve the interests of its country and to apply the best possible scientific information. Cooperation between the commissions continued to develop as they took up the surveys of the land boundary.

CHAPTER FOUR

COOPERATION IN SURVEYING AND MAPPING

The Land Boundary

To the success of the operations in tracing the line . . . the
harmony we had among all the individuals of both parties
contributed much, for in a country so lacking in resources as
that one, nothing would have been done without that harmony.

Second Engineer Agustín Díaz, "Memoria sobre los trabajos topográficos"

THE LAND BOUNDARY BETWEEN THE UNITED STATES AND
Mexico extended nearly seven hundred miles from the Rio Grande
to the Pacific Coast, continuous except for the twenty-mile stretch
where the line was interrupted to follow the Colorado River. The joint
commission divided the survey of the land boundary into three sections: the California azimuth line, from the coast at San Diego to
the Colorado River, delimited in the Treaty of Guadalupe Hidalgo; the
United States–Sonora azimuth line, from the Colorado River to the
111° meridian, delimited in the Treaty of 1853; and the parallels between
the 111° meridian and the Rio Grande, including the 31°20′ parallel, the
31°47′ parallel, and the meridian connecting them, also defined in the
Treaty of 1853. Each section consisted of one or more straight lines, connected at turning points (Location Map 3; also see Location Map 1).

Delimited by mathematical definitions rather than by topographical
features or map interpretation, the land boundary was congenial to

cooperation between the U.S. and Mexican commissions. The land boundary depended upon three mathematical concepts: the azimuth line, the meridian line, and the line of latitude; thus the object of the surveys was to realize an ideal line upon the land. In tracing the ideal line, the U.S. and Mexican commissions often found that they were able to unite their efforts in a single survey.

On the California azimuth line, the U.S. and Mexican commissions first attempted to work together. In spring 1851, after most of the members of the joint commission had moved from San Diego to the Rio Grande, U.S. and Mexican surveying teams completed the demarcation of the California boundary. Rather than conducting separate surveys and comparing results, U.S. and Mexican engineers worked conjointly to locate geographical positions, run the azimuth line, erect cast-iron monuments, and measure distances along the boundary.

Once the end points of the California boundary had been established, the joint commission had treated the demarcation of the connecting line as a rather perfunctory task. Before departing from California, the commission decided that seven marble or cast-iron monuments were to be erected between the coast and the Colorado River, and positions were fixed for four of them, two at each end of the line. Of the remaining three monuments, one was to be constructed as near as possible to the New River, which flowed across the Colorado Desert and the boundary line midway between the Colorado River and the Peninsular Ranges, and the other two "at such points on the intervening mountains as may be most visible and of greatest interest." The members of the joint commission were satisfied that seven monuments would be "amply sufficient," supposing that "a very large portion of the territory on both sides of the line, for many miles between the Pacific and Colorado, is barren and never can be cultivated by either party." The U.S. commissioner appointed E. L. F. Hardcastle, and the Mexican commissioner appointed Francisco Jiménez for the task of erecting the monuments.[1]

In summer and fall of 1850, Hardcastle remained alone at work on the California azimuth line. Salazar and Chavero, having completed their station on Tecate Peak, followed the rest of the Mexican commission to Mexico City. The U.S. commission meanwhile gradually disbanded under Emory's direction as acting commissioner. Emory assigned Hardcastle to carry on the topographical survey of the boundary, working eastward from the vicinity of Tecate Peak. After some time spent at that task, Hardcastle and his party reversed the survey, skipping over the desert country to the Colorado River and attempting to work westward, but succeeded in completing only a reconnaissance. Reconnaissance observations led Hardcastle to believe that the boundary would cross Signal Mountain (Cerro Centinela), and he planned to use it as a signal station to locate the azimuth line eastward and westward from the peak.[2]

Hardcastle returned to San Diego and was awaiting the Mexican engineer when Ricardo Ramírez, in Jiménez's place, arrived in March 1851. Together the two engineers inspected the cast-iron monuments, which had been fabricated and delivered at San Diego, and formed a plan for marking the California boundary. The plan consisted of four operations. First, they would locate the designated positions near the Colorado River and place the monuments there. Then, they would run the line westward and place monuments at two locations to be selected: one near the emigrant trail and the other near the New River. As the third step, they would return to San Diego and set up permanent monuments on the coast and on the main road from San Diego to Baja California at the positions established by the joint commission. East of the main road, where the boundary crossed the road from Rancho Otay to Rancho Jesús María, they would choose a position for the final permanent monument. The fourth and last step would be to extend the line eastward from Tecate Peak to New River. The engineers' main tasks would thus be to locate the course of the azimuth line as well as to erect permanent markers at the designated positions.[3]

Ramírez and Hardcastle established monuments at the previously determined positions without complications but found it necessary to form an additional plan for locating the azimuth line. Upon commencing work at the eastern end of the line, close inspection of Signal Mountain revealed to Hardcastle that the line would not pass over it, as he had earlier mistakenly inferred—"from the magnetic bearing taken, on a windy day, with a pocket compass." The mountain therefore could not be used as a signal station, so that the only alternative remaining was to prolong the line continuously, an undertaking that Hardcastle saw as opposing "many and serious obstacles." The U.S. and Mexican engineers agreed that Hardcastle should "run the line" while Ramírez would measure the distance along the line, working westward. "It was not in my power," Hardcastle reported, "to fit out a party sufficient to run + [and] measure the line at the same time."[4]

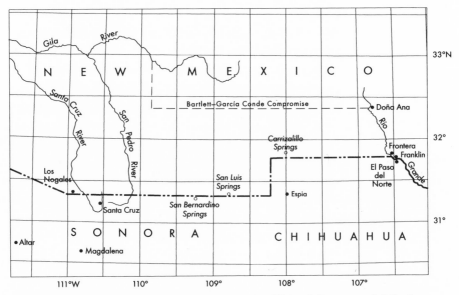

LOCATION MAP 3. Boundary between the United States and Mexico, showing the land boundary west of the Rio Grande, including the turning point at the III° meridian. Source: [U.S. Boundary Commission], *Index Map No. 3.*

In the intense heat and long waterless stretches of the Colorado Desert, running and measuring the line was an arduous task, and the results of the survey were not as certain as Hardcastle and Ramírez might have hoped. Following their original plan, the two engineers first placed the four monuments at the eastern end of the line, working westward from the Colorado River to New River, and then returned to San Diego to work eastward. When they arrived at New River with the line they had run from the Pacific, it struck south of the monument they had earlier placed there by 1864 feet. In order to connect the lines from east and west, Hardcastle and Ramírez agreed to move the monuments they had established on the New River and the emigrant trail so they would be positioned on the line run from the west. Hardcastle considered that the line from the Pacific had been determined with a superior instrument and was more accurate than the line run from the Colorado River.[5] In their report, Hardcastle and Ramírez did not mention the adjustment to the line, stating simply that the direction of the azimuth had been satisfactorily verified. The distance measurements between the monuments, recorded in the engineers' report and represented on the final maps, were found to be in need of correction by the International Boundary Commission that later resurveyed the boundary and made more accurate measurements.[6]

Working together harmoniously, Ramírez and Hardcastle ran, measured, and marked the California line. At the end of July 1851, the engineers approved the marble monument erected at the initial point on the Pacific and closed the California survey. Their achievement went largely unnoticed, as attention was then focused on Paso and the unfolding dispute over the Bartlett–García Conde compromise. U.S. Surveyor Gray, who had moved on to Paso with the rest of the U.S. commission, made representations to the secretary of the interior that he had run, marked, and taken the topography of the line all the way from the Pacific to the Colorado River, a claim to which Hardcastle strenuously objected.[7] Proper recognition was accorded to Hardcastle, however, in the final boundary maps; and Ramírez was remembered in the Mexican maps.

The California azimuth line located by Hardcastle and Ramírez was shown on U.S. and Mexican maps "No. 45" through "No. 54." Maps "No. 45" also included information from work on the Colorado River done later under the Treaty of 1853, while maps "No. 53" depended partially on Emory's and Salazar's surveys eastward from the coast. Maps "No. 54" were based on the earlier work of the joint commission but included the monument erected by Ramírez and Hardcastle on the road from Rancho Otay to Rancho Jesús María (see figs. 3-1 and 3-2).

Emory began to prepare the final maps of the California boundary before Hardcastle returned to Washington from the survey. After projecting the azimuth line from mathematical calculations on each map sheet, Emory left instructions for Hardcastle to fill in the topography from his reconnaissance observations. Emory also made up the title for each sheet, which Hardcastle was to have lettered on the final maps. The titles for U.S. maps "No. 46" through "No. 53" all stated that they were surveyed in 1850 by Captain Hardcastle and thus acknowledged the reconnaissances made by Hardcastle while Emory was still in California. Gray's claims to have surveyed the entire California line were wholly rejected, but Emory did not prepare or authorize a title that recognized the Hardcastle-Ramírez survey.[8]

Although the Mexican engineers probably drew field maps of the

California boundary during the course of the survey, the Mexican commission did not attempt to compile its own finished maps.[9] Maps "No. 46" through "No. 52" of the Comisión de Límites bore the legend, "Copia hecha en 1857 de orden de José Salazar Ilarregui, Comisionado mexicano" (Copy made in 1857 by order of José Salazar Ylarregui, Mexican Commissioner). The map images were copied from the U.S. sheets, although the Mexican titles were original and acknowledged the efforts of Ramírez and Hardcastle, stating that the line had been run, traced, and marked by them in 1851. Map "No. 53," based on the surveys of Salazar and Chavero and credited to them, also included topography credited to Hardcastle. Why the Mexican commission did not compile more of its own maps of the California line is not clear. An array of data collected by Mexican engineers was available to the mapmakers, including the azimuth agreed upon by the joint commission; the stations established by Salazar and Chavero; the locations fixed astronomically by Jiménez, Chavero, and García Conde in their traverse of the line; and Ramírez's measurements of the line. Apparently, only extensive topographical information was lacking.

Some of the U.S. maps of the California azimuth line depicted the topography in detail, but others illustrated no topography at all. Topographical information depended largely on what Hardcastle was able to accomplish in his reconnaissances of 1850. Pushing eastward from Tecate Peak, where Emory and Salazar had determined the last of their stations, Hardcastle acquired the topography for sheets "No. 53" through "No. 50." For maps "No. 49" through "No. 46," approaching the Colorado River, the only landscape features shown were Signal Mountain on "No. 49" and a section of New River on "No. 48." Ramírez and Hardcastle must not have attempted to gather topographical data in their survey of 1851, for much of the country they traversed was represented in the maps simply as a line bordered by a narrow band of sand-and-gravel pattern crossing the graticule.

Maps "No. 48" were representative of the maps that resulted from the Ramírez-Hardcastle survey (figs. 4-1 and 4-2). The U.S. map and the Mexican map copied from it showed the azimuth line, a part of New River, and monuments four and five (labeled with arabic numerals on the Mexican map and roman on the U.S. map) at the sites selected by the engineers near New River and the emigrant trail. The topographical representation was limited to a strip close to the azimuth line. Like all

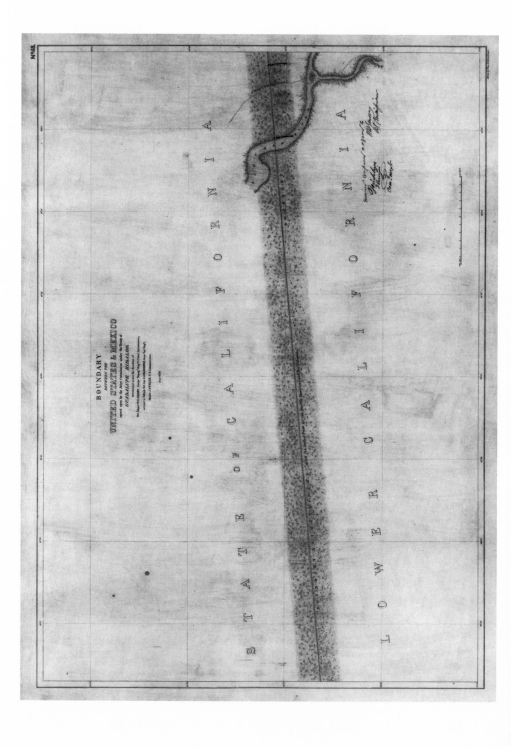

BOUNDARY
BETWEEN THE
UNITED STATES & MEXICO
agreed upon by the Joint Commission under the Treaty of
GUADALUPE HIDALGO

STATE OF CALIFORNIA

LOWER CALIFORNIA

the maps of the California boundary, maps "No. 48" were drawn at a scale of 1:30,000, a larger scale than most of the boundary maps, and the map area inside the neatline was slightly smaller than on sheets from the rest of the boundary. The U.S. map included a graphic scale, but the Mexican map did not. The graticule was the same on both maps.

Because of the joint commission's decision that only seven monuments should be established on the California boundary, long stretches of the azimuth line were unmarked. Between Hardcastle and Ramírez's monument number three on the road to Rancho Jesús María, shown on map "No. 54," and monument number four at New River, shown on "No. 48," no monuments were located in an expanse that covered five map sheets. Ramírez and Hardcastle reported that they marked the boundary between cast-iron monuments three and four with monuments of loose stone, producing the long line by means of signal fires between Tecate Peak and New River.[10] By the time of the resurvey of 1891–96, the International Boundary Commission found only that "a long interval, including the whole mountain region, occurs before reaching No. IV on the west side of New River, in the middle of the Colorado Desert, distant from No. III about 82.2 miles."[11]

New River was not a permanent stream but flowed only at times of extraordinarily high water in the Colorado River. Overflow from the Colorado filled the lagoons of the river's delta, and the water then flowed outward by the channel of the New River, in a northwest direction, emptying into the Salton Sea. When the U.S. commission first arrived in California, the New River was a dry streambed, but soon afterward it filled with water. Emory wrote an excited description of its discovery by parties of immigrants:

> A very remarkable circumstance has occurred in that portion of the country between the mouth of the Gila River and the mountains, usually called the "desert" sometimes the "jornada."
>
> A river forty feet wide and more than waist deep has appeared in the middle of this desert affording delicious water to drink, making an oasis at the most convenient spot for the traveler. . . .

FIG. 4-1. U.S. map "No. 48." (National Archives)

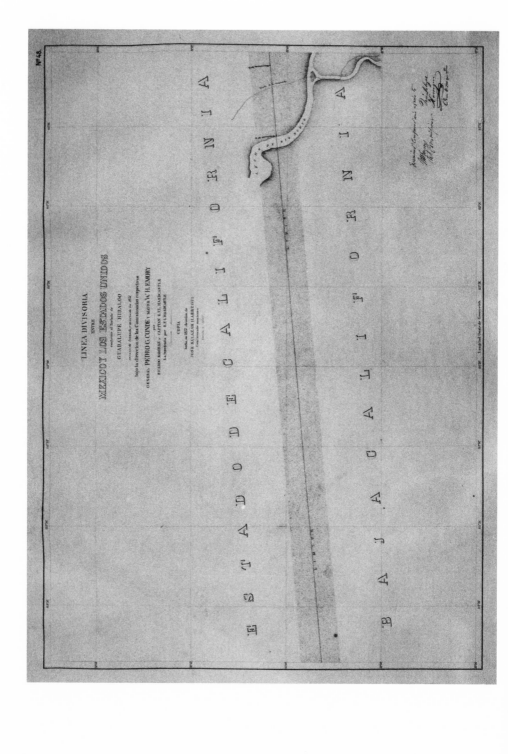

. . . Where it comes, and where it goes is a matter yet to be determined. I will take an opportunity to detach a party to examine it.[12]

Hardcastle and Ramírez also found water at New River, where they established a camp after a difficult crossing from the Colorado.

An anomaly in maps "No. 48" was the location of Ramírez and Hardcastle's monument at New River, which did not agree with the position reported by the engineers. Ramírez and Hardcastle described the placement of the monument and the selection of the monument site at the emigrant trail as follows:

> The undersigned having met at the camp on New River, and having run and measured the line, as previously agreed upon, from the point situated on the right bank of the Colorado and south of the mountain called by the Yuma Indians "Ariculatl" and by Emory "Pilot-Knob," to where it intersects the emigrant trail, they placed a third monument at this point, a distance of 61640.7 metres from the second monument [where the boundary crossed the Colorado River]; on the same day a fourth monument was placed on the left bank of New River, at the distance of 2785.8 metres from the preceding or third monument.[13]

According to common usage, the left bank of New River would have been the west bank, the bank to the left when facing downstream, which, in the case of New River, was to the northwest. Boundary commission reports often employed the terms "left bank" and "right bank," but the usage was prone to confusion; in the case of New River, the direction of flow might easily be misconstrued. Whatever meaning Ramírez and Hardcastle intended, it was interpreted in the boundary office in maps that placed monument number four, the New River monument, on the east bank of the river (fig. 4-3). The International Boundary Commission that later recovered the original monuments, however, described Monument No. IV as being located on the west side of New River, as stated in the quotation above.

While Hardcastle and Ramírez were at work in California, the impasse over the interpretation of Disturnell's map halted the survey of the land boundary westward from the Rio Grande. After the Treaty of 1853

FIG. 4-2. Mexican map "No. 48." (Mapoteca Manuel Orozco y Berra)

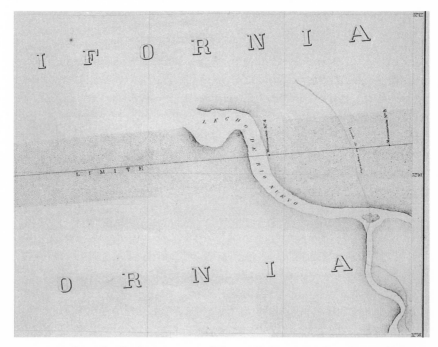

FIG. 4-3. Detail of Mexican map "No. 48," showing New River. (Mapoteca Manuel Orozco y Berra)

had been settled, the survey of the newly delimited line offered an opportunity for the U.S. and Mexican commissions to work together—an opportunity that was not immediately realized, although the commissions found a different way to cooperate in marking the parallels west from Paso.

The U.S. Boundary Commission, reorganized under the Treaty of 1853, was a well-financed and highly efficient corps, but the new Comisión de Límites Mexicana had little government support. U.S. Commissioner Emory's advance scout in Paso del Norte reported before the survey got under way:

> The Seven Millions received by Santa Anna of the United States
> [from the Gadsden Purchase] has already been exhausted, the new
> Commissioner is endeavoring to raise funds to transport his party
> to the field of operations with little prospect of success. . . .

> I am furthermore assured, Major: that the best informed persons
> in Chihuahua very much doubt the arrival of any commission at all.

The finances of the Government are now in a most deplorable condition, and the General Government arrangements in a more confused state than they have ever been since Santa Anna's accession to power.[14]

Nevertheless, Commissioner Salazar and two assistants succeeded in reaching Paso early in November 1854, shortly before Emory's arrival. Both commissions set to work as speedily as their resources would allow, but the government in Mexico City, no doubt experiencing financial pressures, agitated for more rapid progress in the survey. Emory, with some irritation, reminded Salazar that a U.S. force of one astronomical party, "two surveying parties, seventy hired men and an escort of sixty soldiers commanded by three officers" was "actively and efficiently engaged," and he challenged Salazar to place an equal force on the line. "When this is done," he further suggested, "we can if it meets your views divide the work by taking alternate sections, and I doubt not we can finish it in time even sooner than contemplated."[15] Salazar, of course, could not hope to match the U.S. commission in the size of his field parties. He replied that he had no escort and could not move at the time proposed; but since he would be remaining at Paso, he offered to take charge of erecting the permanent monuments at that place.[16]

U.S. surveyors, ahead of Emory, meanwhile had begun to work westward from the Rio Grande. The negotiators of the Treaty of 1853, however, had not contemplated that only one commission would demarcate the new boundary; the treaty required that "that line shall be alone established upon which the Commissioners may fix, their consent in this particular being considered decisive and an integral part of this Treaty."[17] Emory became concerned that the positions on the line established by the U.S. party might be found invalid, should the Mexican commissioner later be unable to visit and verify the points. Salazar, not wishing to hold back the survey, therefore reached an agreement with Emory and consented to adopt, in his own name, all the points on the treaty line west from Paso that the U.S. commissioner might establish in his absence.[18]

From the initial point on the Rio Grande, the line was to run west on the 31°47′ parallel for one hundred miles. Emory sent Assistant Astronomer Clark to establish an observatory at the western end of the parallel, near Carrizalillo Springs, with a party that included Campbell as computer, Chandler as surveyor and magnetic observer, and Wheaton as reconnaissance surveyor. Emory calculated the distance in degrees between the Rio Grande and the one-hundred-mile point and furnished the results to Clark, along with the following instructions:

> You will proceed without delay to establish an observatory at the point on parallel of 31°47' most convenient near the western extremity of the one hundred mile line, which point (using Besel [*sic*] Elements) is 1°.41'.57".55 west of the Initial Point on the Rio Grande.

> Get your approximate position in Longitude by the transmission of chronometer. Satisfied you are near the point, erect an observatory and commence observations for Longitude by Moon Culm[inations]: and for Latitude with the Zenith Telescope.[19]

While Clark worked at Carrizalillo, Assistant Surveyors Hippel and Weyss conducted a triangulation of the line from the initial point.[20]

One hundred miles west of the Rio Grande, the boundary turned southward on a meridian line. Emory set up camp at Espia, near the southern end of the meridian, where it intersected with the 31°20' parallel. Hippel ran the meridian line connecting the two parallels while both Emory and Clark made astronomical observations at Espia.[21] Turning west, the boundary followed the 31°20' parallel to the intersection with the 111° meridian, where the party for the Pacific side, working eastward, was to meet Emory's party. Clark went ahead from Espia to determine the position of the next astronomical station at San Luis Springs, while Hippel produced the line from Espia and Chandler and Wheaton erected stone mounds as monuments on the line. Weyss was directed to make sketches of the country, in order to "perpetuate the evidences of the location of the boundary, in the event of the Indians removing the monuments erected on the ground."[22] The survey continued with a similar organization beyond San Luis Springs to San Bernardino Springs, the San Pedro River, the Santa Cruz River, and Río los Nogales.[23]

The U.S. commission's line from the Rio Grande to the 111° meridian was adopted by Salazar, as he had officially agreed to do. Throughout the survey, Emory, having little knowledge of Salazar's continuing financial difficulties or news of Salazar's imprisonment, complained about the Mexican commission's lack of assistance. Emory returned from the field to Paso to find the Mexican commissioner missing, a prisoner in Chihuahua.[24] When Salazar was released and restored to his position, he met with Emory to confirm the U.S. survey. Emory turned over to Salazar the astronomical and geodetic data and the field maps of the U.S. survey, which the Mexican commissioner studied for two days before a formal agreement of the joint commission was drawn up. Emory agreed to adopt the three permanent monuments that Salazar had established west of the Rio Grande (see figs. 5-11 and 5-12). Salazar in turn agreed to adopt all the "monuments, mounds, lines, and points" fixed by the U.S. commission, reserving the right to erect additional monuments on the 31°47' parallel. Thereupon the two commissioners officially declared the boundary "surveyed, marked, and established as far as the 111th meridian of longitude."[25]

Salazar then organized the Mexican commission for a resurvey of the line west from Paso—despite grumbling from Emory, who considered the fieldwork closed. Salazar's goals were to improve the monumentation of the 31°47' parallel and to verify or correct the U.S. positions on the line. The U.S. commission had constructed two types of monuments during its survey: some monuments were simply mounds of stone, whose locations may or may not have been kept track of; others, more substantial, were built of dressed stone, laid without mortar, and their positions were noted for mapping. The more permanent monuments were ten in number, and all except one were located on the 31°20' parallel. One of the ten monuments, placed at the intersection of the 31°20' parallel with the meridian connecting it to the 31°47' parallel, established the position of the meridian. The only monuments on the 31°47' parallel, other than unsubstantial mounds of stones, were the three permanent monuments that Salazar had established near the Río Bravo and a single monument of dressed stone erected by the U.S. commission.[26]

Salazar assigned his assistants, Molina and Contreras, to execute a triangulation of the 31°47' parallel, and Engineers Fernández and Herrera to triangulate the meridian between the parallels. Molina and Contreras would be accompanied by craftsmen and laborers who were to construct permanent monuments on the line. Engineer Iglesias would assist Salazar in making astronomical determinations on the parallels. The 31°20' parallel was to be located by astronomical reconnaissance, without attempting triangulation.

The Mexican field parties carried out their separate assignments simultaneously. Molina and Contreras began work in the Carrizalillo

Hills, about eighty-five miles west of the Río Bravo, where the U.S. commission had constructed its durable monument on the 31°47′ parallel. Molina recounted that he had the monument, built "only of superposed rock," torn down, and a new one built of stone and mortar.[27] Salazar arrived at the site and designated a baseline that Molina and Contreras would measure, beginning from the center of the monument. Salazar also established the tangent to the parallel at the monument and then continued to the west with it. Molina and Contreras worked eastward, performing several operations: measurement of the baseline, alignment of the tangent, triangulation, and construction of monuments. In addition to the monument in the Carrizalillo Hills, Molina expected to find two more monuments between Carrizalillo and Paso del Norte that the U.S. engineers had reported. An assiduous search, however, turned up no additional monuments, so Molina and Contreras proceeded to erect four more monuments on the line. The positions for the monuments were obtained, according to Molina, by measuring the direction and distance from the tangent to the parallel, employing the formulas of Francoeur. Meanwhile, Fernández and Herrera carried out the triangulation of the meridian, beginning from a baseline located midway between the 31°47′ and 31°20′ parallels and linking up with the triangulation executed by Molina and Contreras. Salazar and Iglesias observed for longitude at the southern end of the meridian and then traversed the 31°20′ parallel, locating a number of points and directing the construction of several monuments. At the end of December 1855, the Mexican engineers were reunited and closed the fieldwork.[28]

The boundary from the Rio Grande to the 111° meridian was shown on maps "No. 30" through "No. 37" in each commission's series. Of those made by the Mexican commission, maps "No. 30" through "No. 33," representing the 31°47′ parallel and the meridian line, were drawn from the commission's own surveys, and sheets "No. 34" through "No. 37," showing the boundary on the 31°20′ parallel, were copied from the U.S. maps. Whether compiled independently or copied from U.S. sheets, the Mexican maps agreed with the U.S. maps in boundary location and landscape portrayal. The two commissions differed, however, in their inventories of the monuments on the line.

The U.S. and Mexican commissions each used their own numbering system for the boundary monuments and disagreed in the total number of monuments. Upon completion of the Mexican resurvey, Salazar gave official notice that the 31°47′ parallel had been marked with ten monuments, and Emory recorded his "entire satisfaction" with the results.[29] The final Mexican maps, however, showed only nine monuments on the 31°47′ parallel, and the final U.S. maps depicted only eight monuments. The Mexican maps identified the monuments as Monumento N. I on the west bank of the Rio Grande through Monumento N. IX at the meridian one hundred miles west, while the U.S. monuments were numbered 1 through 8 from the Rio Grande to the meridian. Most of the eight monuments documented by the two map series were the same monuments, shown in approximately the same positions in both series, but not all monuments could be matched. The boundary commission that attempted to relocate the original monuments some forty years later found that "considerable confusion and uncertainty was occasioned by these differences."[30]

Maps "No. 32" were among the sheets that were compiled independently by each commission (figs. 4-4 and 4-5). The maps showed the western end of the 31°47′ parallel, the intersection of the parallel with the meridian one hundred miles west of the Rio Grande, and approximately one-half of the length of the meridian line. The U.S. map stated that it was made under the direction of William H. Emory and named M. von Hippel and J. E. Weyss for triangulation and topography. Although he was not credited in the title, much of the astronomical work on which the map was based was done by Assistant Astronomer Clark. The Mexican map named Surveyors Fernández, Herrera, Molina, and Contreras and attributed the astronomy to Salazar.

The topographical portrayals by the two commissions were nearly alike. The Carrizalillo Hills, or Sierra del Carrizalillo, straddled the boundary at the eastern edges of the maps. On the northern slopes of the hills, both commissions showed the Carrizalillo Springs (Ojo del Carrizalillo), the source of water that made Carrizalillo a significant place on the boundary. A large range of mountains to the south of the Carrizalillo Hills, unidentified on the U.S. sheet, was labeled "Sierra de la Boca Grande" on the Mexican map. The boundary turned the corner in the Apache Hills, a mass of hachured relief drawn at the center of each sheet but unnamed in either map, and the meridian line was flanked to the west by the Big Hatchet Mountains, also shown but unnamed on the maps of both commissions. In the northeast area of the sheet, the U.S. map noted no landscape features surrounding the

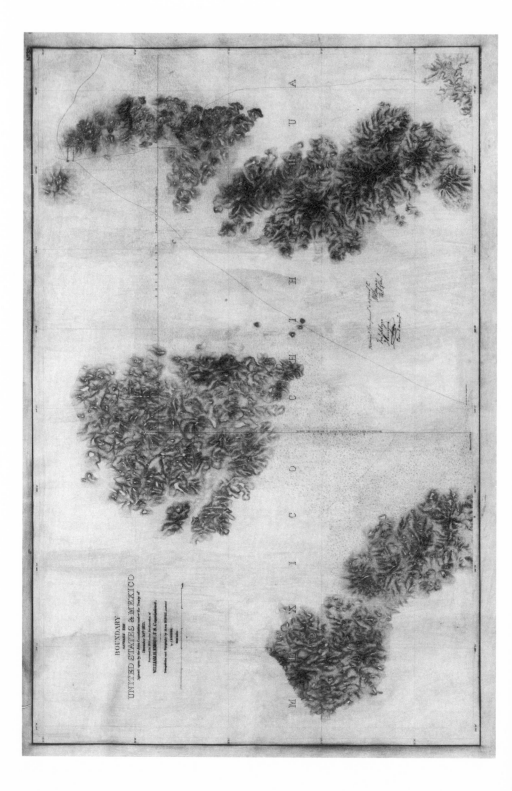

BOUNDARY
between the
UNITED STATES & MEXICO
agreed upon by the Joint Commission under the Treaty of
Guadalupe Hidalgo 1853.
Surveyed under the direction of
WILLIAM H. EMORY U.S. Commissioner,
Completed and Drawn by John ROSS assisted
by J. SEIBER.

Carrizalillo Hills, while on the Mexican map, many details of topography were shown (fig. 4-6). The drawing was very sketchy, the hachuring unfinished, as though the Mexican surveyors had collected more topographical information than the drafter had time to render.

Three boundary monuments were symbolized on U.S. map "No. 32," and two on the Mexican map. The difference in number was accounted for by the monument on the meridian line, shown on the U.S. map as Monument No. 9 at the very southern edge of the sheet; the Mexican commission showed the same monument at the very northern edge of map "No. 33." Both maps "No. 32" portrayed two monuments on the 31°47′ parallel, but they were numbered inconsistently. The U.S. map showed Monument No. 7 on the parallel south of Carrizalillo Springs, in the same position as Monumento N. VIII on the Mexican map. The identification numbers did not agree, even though it was the same monument that was symbolized on both maps, because on the preceding sheet, map "No. 31," the Mexican commission showed one monument that was not included in the U.S. inventory and, thereby, advanced its number series. The monument at the intersection of the 31°47′ parallel and the meridian was Monument No. 8 on the U.S. map, but Monumento N. IX on the Mexican map.

The U.S. and Mexican surveys of the meridian line were combined uniformly. The Mexican commission confirmed and reconstructed the U.S. monuments at the extreme points of the meridian and constructed an additional monument midway along the line, which became U.S. Monument No. 9 and Mexican Monumento N. X. When the boundary commission of 1891–96 rediscovered the original monuments, its observations on the meridian line "showed that the 3 original monuments were in the same straight line, and that this line was a true meridian."[31]

Neither commission actually measured the length of the 31°47′ parallel, supposedly one hundred miles from the Rio Grande to the meridian line. Molina and Contreras, whose purpose in triangulation was to find the distances between monuments, did not extend their measurements beyond the easternmost monument they constructed, and they did not reach the Rio Grande. The extent of the U.S. triangulation is not known, as the U.S. commission did not publish its triangulation

FIG. 4-4. U.S. map "No. 32." (National Archives)

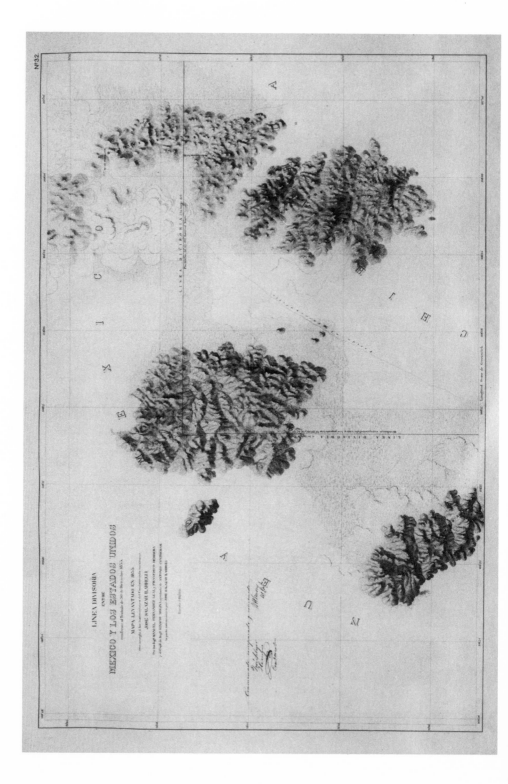

LÍNEA DIVISORIA
ENTRE
MEXICO Y LOS ESTADOS UNIDOS

MAPA LEVANTADO EN 1855

data. Emory did not clearly explain how the U.S. commission determined the end of the one-hundred-mile line but included in his final *Report* only an abridged statement: "The 100 miles was obtained by combining the observed longitude at Carrizalillo, and the distance actually measured."[32] In reestablishing the line, the boundary commission of 1891–96 measured the distance between the Rio Grande and Monument No. 8 (Monumento N. IX) as 159,193 meters (about 98.9 miles) and, seeking to discover the method used in the original survey to arrive at that distance, could find no explanation in the records. At present, the distance is given as 158,995.81 meters or 98.8 miles.[33]

Mexican map "No. 36" was an example of a map of the parallels that was copied from a U.S. map, even though information for compilation was available from Salazar's reconnaissance (figs. 4-7 and 4-8). The representations were the same except for variations in drawing style, and the Mexican map's translation of legends and toponyms from English into Spanish. The terrain depicted included the San Pedro River and the mountains of the Sierra San José, an area where there is no doubt that Salazar made observations, for he discussed the monument on the Río San Pedro at a meeting of the joint commission. Salazar stated that he had observed for latitude on the Río San Pedro but had been unable to find the monument that Hippel and Weyss were supposed to have erected there; the Mexican commissioner, therefore, established a monument on the river based on his own latitude determination. Emory speculated that if the U.S. monument at the San Pedro River were still standing, there might be some discrepancy between its latitude and that of Salazar's monument, which could produce confusion in the future. Considering the consequences of the possibility pointed out by Emory, Salazar agreed that if both monuments existed, he would take the monument erected by the U.S. commission as the true boundary.[34] Salazar's approval of the U.S. monument was demonstrated by its portrayal in Mexican map "No. 36," where Monumento No. 21 was located on the west bank of the river in the same position as Monument No. 20 on the U.S. map.

The monument established by Salazar, not shown on the Mexican map, was constructed on the east bank of the Río San Pedro. It was later

---

FIG. 4-5. Mexican map "No. 32." (Mapoteca Manuel Orozco y Berra)

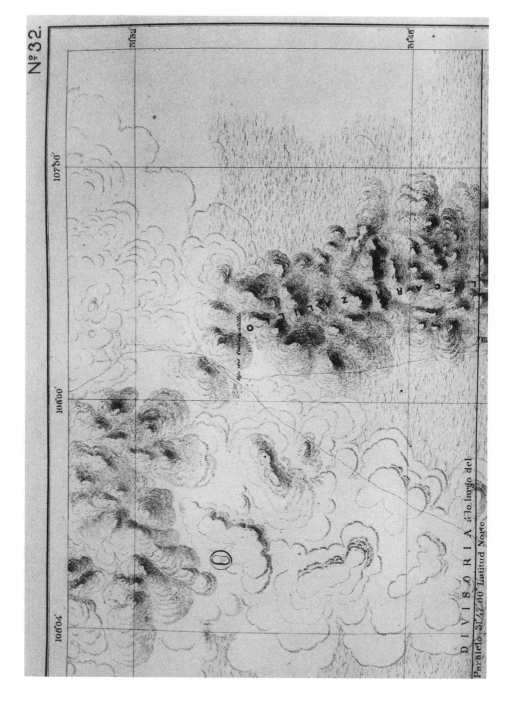

discovered by the boundary commission of 1891–96 and described as follows:

> A monument of dressed stone was found on the east bank of the San Pedro River. . . . Afterwards another monument, consisting only of a pile of loose stones, was found on the west bank of the river and was recognized as the one erected by Emory. It was evident that the monument found on the east bank of the river was the one erected by Salazar, who did not find the one erected by Emory on the west bank.[35]

The 1891–96 commission made a triangulation connecting the monuments and found a difference in latitude between the two monuments of 29.67″ (about one-half mile); Salazar's monument was located well to the south and Emory's monument slightly to the north of the 31°20′ parallel.

With the land boundary run and marked at its eastern and western ends, only the azimuth line across the Sonoran Desert remained to be done. In the difficult desert country, the U.S. and Mexican commissions found it most efficient to cooperate in a single survey. The work was assigned to the Mexican *sección de Sonora* and the U.S. party for the Pacific side, who had surveyed the Colorado River and planned to run the azimuth line eastward. Members of the *sección de Sonora,* directed by Jiménez, included Alemán and Agustín Díaz. The U.S. party, led by Michler, included Assistants Schott and Phillips; Computer O'Donoghue dropped out of the group after completing the Colorado River survey.[36]

Michler and Jiménez had received instructions from the U.S. and Mexican commissioners that differed in their emphasis on the operations to be performed. Michler's instructions stressed the computation of the azimuth line and its demarcation with monuments. Emory enclosed an elaborate set of formulas and constants for computing geodetic azimuth and distance between two points of known latitude and longitude—the same, he said, as had been used in California. Michler was to extend the azimuth line to the 111° meridian, placing monuments at intervals of not more than five miles. When the party approached the

FIG. 4-6. Detail of Mexican map "No. 32," showing the area of the Carrizalillo Hills. (Mapoteca Manuel Orozco y Berra)

LINEA DIVISORIA
ENTRE
MEXICO Y LOS ESTADOS UNIDOS

MAPA

JOSÉ SALAZAR ILARREGUI

Longitud Oeste de Greenwich.

intersection of the 31°20′ parallel with the 111° meridian, a point that would be identified by direct measurement, Michler should commence astronomical observations to determine the intersection. The intersection was to be marked by a suitable monument. No reference was included in the U.S. commissioner's instructions to working or consulting with the Mexican engineers.[37]

The Mexican section was prepared to work in union with the U.S. engineers and expected to extend the line by triangulation. For figuring the direction the line was to follow, Salazar noted simply that, knowing the latitude and longitude of the initial point on the Colorado, Jiménez would have the elements to trace the line and compute its length. Salazar directed Jiménez to locate and connect essential points in a triangulation, which, "though not geodetic, will be of sufficient value, striving to make the most complete topography of the terrain possible, principally with more extent toward the Mexican side."[38] Upon arriving at the 111° meridian, which would be predicted from calculation of the length of the line and subsequent measurement by triangulation, Jiménez was to make astronomical observations and correct the terminal position of the line.

During the Colorado River survey, Jiménez and Michler had become accustomed to a great deal of conferral, and they began to work together to extend the line eastward from the initial point. The two engineers erected a monument on the bank of the river and designated it "monument I." Its latitude and longitude were deduced from its distance from the initial point in the middle of the river, and the azimuth of the line, originally calculated from the initial point, was recalculated from the monument. Both commissions prepared computations. Michler set up his theodolite at monument I and aligned point II, where he placed the iron monument that the party for the Pacific side had removed from the confluence of the Gila and Colorado Rivers.

Before continuing the alignment to monument III, Michler and Jiménez drew up a plan for the survey of the azimuth line. The plan affirmed,

> That the line be traced by both parties at the same time, each alternating with the other at the successive stations; that the distance of the line be measured by triangulation, one party operating from the

---

FIG. 4-7. Mexican map "No. 36." (Mapoteca Manuel Orozco y Berra)

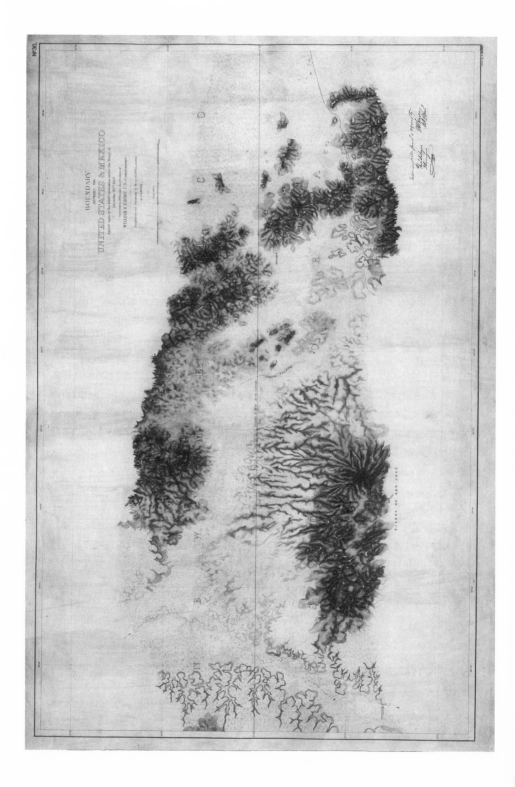

BOUNDARY
BETWEEN THE
UNITED STATES & MEXICO
Agreed upon by the Joint Commission under the Treaty of
December 30th 1853
Surveyed in Atlantic the Journey of
WILLIAM H. EMORY, U.S. Commissioner
Jurisdiction and Sovereignty by M. on SCHOTT, control
on 1 EMORY.

SIERRA DE SAN JOSE

initial point to the environs of Sonoyta, the other thence to the termination of the line; and that the results be mutually exchanged.

. . . That at all prominent points of the line which are deemed proper, suitable monuments, from such materials as are at hand, be erected to mark it.[39]

The engineers also agreed to continue the numbering of stations by Roman numerals, eastward from monument I on the bank of the Colorado River.

Michler and Jiménez's plan proved unworkable because of the scarcity of water in the desert east of the Colorado River. The alignment of the boundary had been continued only as far as station III when the joint section was forced to abandon the survey and retreat to the river. Deciding to attempt the survey by working in a westward direction, both parties traveled up the Gila River and then, by way of Tucson, joined Emory in camp at Los Nogales. There they found that the U.S. commission had already determined the intersection of the 31°20′ parallel with the 111° meridian and had erected a monument at the point.[40]

Jiménez and Emory met at Los Nogales to discuss the survey of the azimuth line. Emory advised Jiménez of his agreement with Salazar empowering the U.S. commission to establish the boundary in the Mexican commissioner's absence and explained that Salazar had agreed to adopt all the points that would be fixed by the U.S. party, including the position of the 111° meridian. According to Emory's account, Jiménez was invited to inspect the instruments, still in position, the data, and the computations, "the result of that inspection being satisfactory."[41] According to Jiménez's report, however, the Mexican engineer proposed that he be allowed sufficient time to make astronomical observations, and that the average of his results and Emory's be taken as the point in question. Emory rejected Jiménez's proposal, insisting that the position at the 111° meridian had been officially approved and that the monument could not be moved. He proposed in compensation that Jiménez determine a position on the azimuth line that Emory would agree to adopt. Jiménez, considering his party's lack of funds and the news he had recently received of Salazar's imprisonment, decided to accept Emory's suggestion and to proceed with the azimuth survey.[42]

FIG. 4-8. U.S. map "No. 36." (National Archives)

Jiménez and Emory drew up a new agreement. Emory pledged to adopt a point to be determined by Jiménez, who selected a position on the line near Quitovaquita (Quitobaquito), a spring about halfway between the Colorado River and the 111° meridian. For travelers going west, the spring was the last permanent watering place on the line and was near the village of Sonoita, a midpoint that had been named in the agreement between Jiménez and Michler. Emory and Jiménez agreed that the U.S. and Mexican parties would work conjointly but changed some of the terms that Jiménez had agreed upon with Michler. The modifications proposed:

> That the plan of triangulation is impracticable; that the American and Mexican surveying party shall proceed forthwith to run the unfinished portion of the line; take the topography near the line; erect monuments at points where the line crosses a mine, a settlement, a road, or water.

> It is agreed if either party break down, the other is not to suspend or delay operations in consequence of it.[43]

The new plan for the survey of the azimuth line was acceptable to Michler, who observed that the changes required him to assume the correctness of the point at the 111° meridian and to abandon all attempt at triangulation.[44]

Jiménez remained at Nogales long enough to join Michler in establishing the first point west of the 111° meridian. "Our instrument being placed in position," Michler reported, "the azimuth of the new line (69°19′45.9″ northwest) was measured from a meridian established by Assistant Clark; a large live-oak growing on the adjoining ridge was found to be in the direction of the line, and answered the purpose of a monument, (No. XIX from the Rio Colorado.)"[45] Jiménez noted that the measured azimuth was the same that he and Michler had calculated and agreed upon in their camp on the Colorado River. Jiménez and Alemán then traveled to Quitovaquita, making astronomical observations along the way.

It was left to Agustín Díaz to devise a method of delineating the topography of the boundary. Díaz understood that he would not have time or resources for topographical operations separate from the running of the line. He therefore proposed a survey by the method of intersection, which would not break the terms of the agreement, but would produce results equal to those of a well-formed triangulation. Natural objects to the north and south of the line, which by their form or surroundings could not be confused with others, would be selected as vertices, but would not be occupied. The angles between stations on the line and the selected natural features would be read without leaving the line. All the angles at each station would be taken by the same person, members of the two commissions alternating in stations on the alignment. Díaz's proposal was approved by Michler, although Michler later said nothing of the plan in his report, revealing only that "Señor A. Diaz, with a party, operated conjointly with us in the prolongation of this line." [46]

The line was run according to the Díaz plan. With two soldiers and two servants to assist him, Díaz occupied stations on the line in alternation with the U.S. surveyors, Michler, Schott, and Phillips. The parties at two adjacent stations aligned the points by means of signals observed through a telescope; sometimes the stations were aligned at night, using fires as signals. As they ran the line, the surveyors observed angles from the stations to principal features in the terrain. Arthur Schott sketched the views to each side of the line. The surveyors had planned to make a barometric profile of the azimuth line, but the Mexican commission's boiling-point thermometer, the instrument that was to be used for that purpose, was broken early in the survey. Elevations were obtained only at the 111° meridian and monument XIX because the U.S. commission's barometer had already been broken. [47]

The surveyors reached Quitovaquita as Jiménez and Alemán were completing their astronomical observations. The two astronomers had set up an observatory, installing the large astronomical instruments that Jiménez had favored at Paso and Matamoros, after transporting them across the desert in carts. Michler and Díaz proceeded to align monuments VIII and VII to the east and west of the observatory. While the surveyors then extended the line to the Colorado River, Jiménez and Alemán moved to Sonoita, where they furthered Díaz's plan for the topography by measuring a baseline. Díaz and Michler had informally agreed that a base would be measured in the direction of the astronomical meridian at Sonoita, to be related to the nearby stations. The measurement would allow approximate distances to be derived between all the stations along the line. When Michler and Díaz returned from the west, together they tied the measured base to the neighboring stations.[48]

At Jiménez's suggestion, the U.S. and Mexican parties left Sonoita for the town of Magdalena, Sonora, where they remained for a month working on their survey data. Jiménez and Alemán related the positions of the two monuments at Quitovaquita, monuments VII and VIII, to the position determined for the observatory and used Puissant's geodetic formulas to derive the distance from monument VIII to the intersection of the 31°20' parallel with the 111° meridian. Díaz, meanwhile, constructed a chain of triangles, selecting vertices from among the angles that had been measured from stations on the line and defining the principal and auxiliary triangles. He used the astronomers' geodetically calculated distance to proportionally adjust the lengths within his chain of triangles. The triangulated distances between monument VII at Quitovaquita and monument V to the west were used without correction, and the remaining distances were taken from the triangulation made eastward from the Colorado River. Michler and Díaz agreed upon the final results and presented tables of distances between the monuments in their final reports.[49]

Jiménez's latitude and longitude determinations at Quitovaquita were used in plotting the positions of the monuments and verifying their placement in the true azimuth. Jiménez explained that the geographical position for monument VIII that he had calculated from the astronomical observations at Quitovaquita revealed the azimuth line to be too far to the north. When the corresponding observations at Greenwich became available, however, the longitude would be recalculated using Greenwich data as a correction. "The points to which this correction is applied turn out to be generally 16 seconds of time or 4 minutes of arc more to the West," he said, which would then place the line in its correct latitude, or nearly so—"at least only the small difference originating from the scant errors of direction, alignment, and position of points inherent to this class of operations, practiced in a terrain that opposed every type of obstacle."[50] The small errors of direction and position that Jiménez expected to be found in the line were, in fact, disclosed by the resurvey of 1891–96. The resurvey showed that the boundary was partly broken and stepped rather than straight.[51]

Jiménez's comments on the Greenwich corrections also suggested the possibility of the major error in the azimuth line that was uncovered by the commission of 1891–96. The monument at the intersection of the

31°20' parallel and the 111° meridian, whose position Emory had insisted upon, was found to be located slightly to the south of the parallel and approximately four minutes, or over four miles, west of the 111° meridian. At present, the location of the reconstructed monument on the site of the original monument is given as 111°04'27.600"W longitude, 31°19'56.070"N latitude. The azimuth line, therefore, did not comply with the treaty delimitation but began from a point too far to the south; between the 111° meridian and the Colorado River, it cut off from Mexico a triangle of land of about 77,000 hectares in area and misplaced it in the United States.[52]

The error arose in spite of the U.S. commission's careful field methods. The position of the observatory at Los Nogales was determined from 120 observations with the zenith instrument for latitude and observations during two lunations with the transit instrument for longitude. By direct measurement and triangulation, the longitude was transferred to the intersection of the 31°20' parallel with the 111° meridian. When Emory presented the results to Salazar for inspection, he explained that the methods employed had been the familiar ones used by both commissions. On the subject of longitude, however, Emory reminded Salazar of an earlier discussion, in which they had reached the following agreement:

> In all determinations of longitude by the moon and moon-culminating stars they should take the Greenwich ephemeris, and not await the publication of the corresponding observations made at Greenwich, as at this distance it would necessarily involve a delay of eighteen months or two years—a result clearly not contemplated by either government. The correction due from corresponding observations cannot be foretold, but is small, and as likely to be to the advantage of one as the other.[53]

Although he had originally planned for Jiménez to participate in the determination of the 111° meridian, Salazar accepted Emory's monument as one of the U.S. commission's points that he had agreed beforehand to adopt. When the error was discovered in the resurvey of 1891–96, the governments of the United States and Mexico decided to maintain the line that had already been established rather than negotiate a treaty of rectification.[54]

In addition to performing calculations, the other purpose of the stay in Magdalena, not mentioned by Michler but promoted as a matter of importance by Jiménez, was the preparation of field maps. Jiménez believed it was the duty of the two sections to produce maps, compare the copies, and agree on them, for "although the topographical maps of the line drawn up and agreed on by the two [would be] in rough draft," he explained, "upon making fair copies and comparing them, they would prevent the least difference from arising, and they would spare our commissions any disagreement in the future."[55] Michler and Agustín Díaz planned the format for the field maps—a set of ten sheets at a scale of 1:100,000, five sheets showing the topography north of the line and five sheets showing the south side of the line. Luis Díaz, who had been too ill to participate in the fieldwork, was reunited with the *sección de Sonora* and assisted Agustín in preparing the Mexican commission's maps; Michler named Schott to draw the maps for the U.S. section. Díaz reported that he made two sets of maps of the azimuth line, using the data obtained by the two sections, and that he kept the original maps and gave the copies to the U.S. section. Díaz also compiled maps of the triangulation he had done on the Colorado, of which he gave the original copy to Michler. When all the maps had been completed, Michler and Jiménez signed them, each of the engineers keeping a set.[56]

The final maps consisted of seven sheets in the U.S. and Mexican series, beginning with map "No. 38" at the 111° meridian and ending with map "No. 44" at the Colorado River. The legends on each nation's maps named members of both commissions, and the same credits were given consistently throughout the series. The seven U.S. maps stated that they were surveyed under the direction of U.S. Commissioner Emory and Mexican Commissioner Salazar, with triangulation and topography done by Michler, assisted by Schott, and by Jiménez, assisted by Alemán and Díaz, "both parties working conjointly." Map "No. 38" gave, in addition, the name of Chandler as another assistant in the triangulation and topography and attributed "Latitude and Longitude of Observatory" to Clark, assisted by Campbell. The Mexican maps stated that the survey was directed by Salazar and Emory and named Jiménez and Alemán "for the Mexican Commission, in the astronomical part," while triangulation and topography were credited to Díaz. "For the U.S. Commission," Michler and Assistant Schott were named. On maps "No. 38," "No. 43," and "No. 44," Phillips, whose name did not appear on the U.S. maps, was cited as an additional assistant to Michler. In their reports, the Mexican engineers mentioned that Phillips assisted in

the alignment of stations at the eastern and western ends of the azimuth
line, but dropped out of the survey because of an inflammation of the
eyes, an affliction from which several of the surveyors suffered.[57] Mexican map "No. 38" also included Chandler's name and specifically credited Clark and Campbell with "the astronomical determination of the
intersection of the 111°00′ meridian and 31°20′ parallel."

The monument at the 111° meridian may be seen in a detail from U.S.
map "No. 38" (fig. 4-9). Labeled "Monument No. 27 from the Rio Bravo
del Norte," it was plotted precisely at the intersection of the meridian
with the 31°20′ parallel. The mountainous landscape surrounding the
monument was shown in great detail, and dense hachuring enveloped
the boundary line, the monument symbol, and its label. The unap-
proachable location of the monument was described by the engineer
who recovered it in the resurvey at the end of the century:

> Knowing the difficulty of finding it I made efforts to meet with
> somebody who had seen it or could tell me where it was. I could only
> find one man who laid claim to having seen it, and all the informa-
> tion I received from him turned out in the end to be worse than val-
> ueless, as it misled rather than guided. Three days of the most ardu-
> ous labor were spent in searching for this monument, over one of the
> roughest and most cut-up mountainous countries that can be imag-
> ined. It is impossible to travel in the deep and rocky cañons, and the
> hills are very steep and covered with live oak, manzanita, and juniper
> bushes so thick that it is difficult to penetrate them. On the third day
> of the search we were gladdened by hearing the shots that told that
> the monument was found.[58]

The detailed topographical portrayal on map "No. 38" was probably
made possible by the long encampment of Emory's party at Los Nogales, giving the surveyors ample time to work, as well as by the combined efforts of the U.S. and Mexican sections on the azimuth line west
of the 111° meridian. The map was drawn by J. E. Weyss and was one of
only two maps in the U.S. series that bore the drafter's name in the title.
Weyss drew the map from personal experience, for he was present in the
camp at Nogales and also had made landscape sketches of the area.

The surveyors spent little time at most of their stations on the azimuth line, but Díaz's intersection method enabled them to gather abundant topographical information for the final maps. The landscape portrayal in a detail of Mexican map "No. 39" was typical of the azimuth

line sheets (fig. 4-10). The map showed Monumento No. XVI near the "Aguaje del Granizo" (Waterhole of the Hail), where Díaz and his party camped during a hailstorm, and Monumento No. XV in the Sierra Pozo Verde. A dotted line near the boundary, labeled "Camino seguido por la Comision de Limites" (Path followed by the Boundary Commission), indicated the route taken by the Mexican section. Monument XVI was aligned by Díaz and Phillips, and Monument XV was aligned by Díaz and Schott, in the week of 12–18 July 1855. During that short time, the surveyors experienced not only a hailstorm, but also rain that caused flooding in the arroyos, washed away some of their equipment, and caught Díaz and Schott in the hills for a night without food or sleep.[59] In spite of the hardship and the rapidity with which they worked, they were able to record many landscape details. How well their method worked may be appreciated by comparing the maps of the Sonoran azimuth line to the maps of the California azimuth line, where the survey team had no plan for observing topography (see figs. 4-1 and 4-2).

U.S. and Mexican maps "No. 41" exemplified the use of the same data by the two commissions for independent map compilation (figs. 4-11 and 4-12). Maps "No. 41" showed Quitovaquita, where Jiménez established an astronomical observatory, and Sonoita, where the baseline was measured. The spring at Quitovaquita is now part of Organ Pipe National Monument; at the time of the boundary survey, it was an oasis inhabited by the Papago. The town of Sonoita was described by Michler as a "resort for smugglers, and a den for a number of low, abandoned Americans," and he contrasted the poverty of the place with "the comparative comfort of an Indian village of Papagos within sight."[60] The U.S. and Mexican maps presented the same general features, but in addition to having different drawing styles, the two maps interpreted the data somewhat differently. Some of the conical hills on the U.S. map, for example, appeared as flat-topped mesas in the Mexican map, or alluvial fans were placed on the U.S. map where arroyos occurred on the Mexican map. The usual greater interest of the U.S. commission in astronomy was shown in its representation of the Quitovaquita observatory, symbolized by a star and labeled "Observatory," while the Mexican map showed its own commission's observatory only as an unidentified rectangle.

FIG. 4-9. Detail of U.S. map "No. 38," showing the intersection of the 111° meridian and the 31°20' parallel. (National Archives)

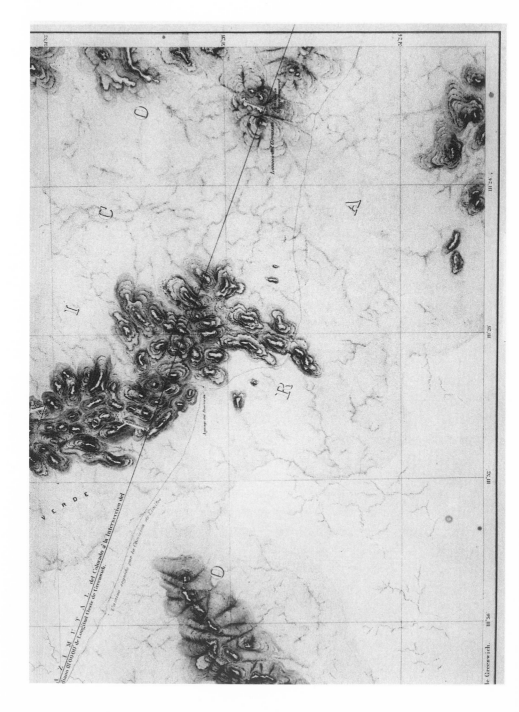

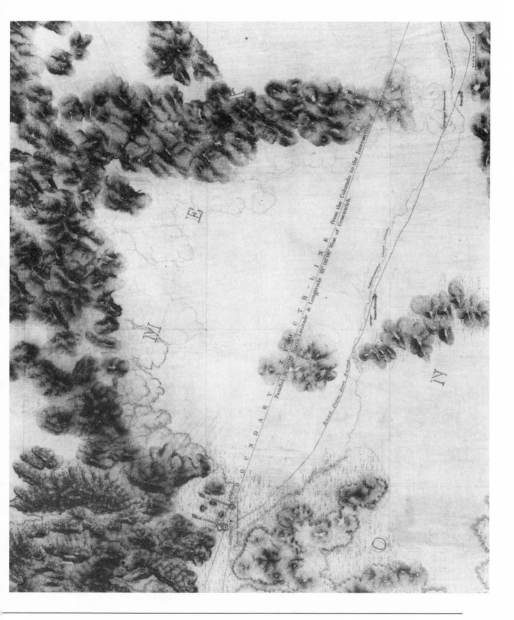

FIG. 4-10. (*opposite*) Detail of Mexican map "No. 39," showing the boundary across the Sierra Pozo Verde. (Mapoteca Manuel Orozco y Berra)

FIG. 4-11. (*above*) Detail of U.S. map "No. 41." (National Archives)

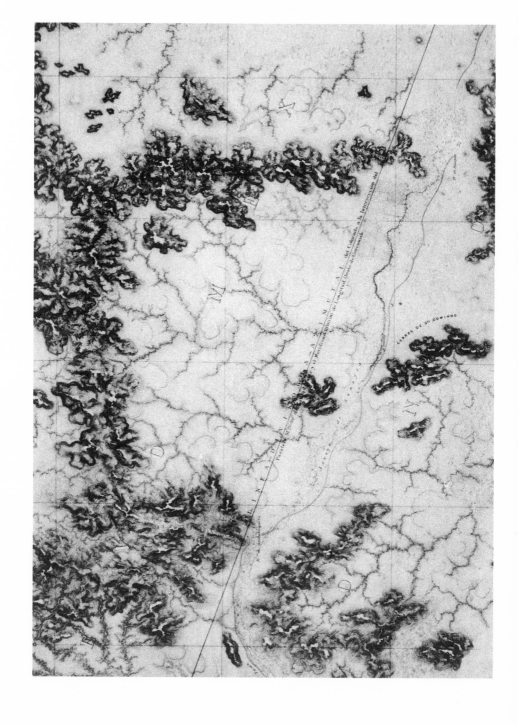

U.S. map "No. 41" was one of three maps of the Sonoran azimuth line, along with maps "No. 42" and "No. 45," that was apparently left unfinished. The central area of the sheet contains penciled sketches of hills or arroyos that have not been inked, and penciled outlines surrounding areas of hills and plains appear throughout the map. Many lines of lettering still have penciled guidelines. There is no drafter's name at the bottom of the sheet. On Mexican map "No. 41," however, no pencil marks remain to suggest that the map was unfinished. An artifact of the compilation process is evident in the extension of the boundary beyond the map's neatlines, displaying its construction as a calculated angle across the graticule of the map; the same feature may also be seen in Mexican map "No. 39" (fig. 4-10).

The U.S. and Mexican commissions discovered different modes of cooperation in each of the three sections of the land boundary. On the California azimuth line, U.S. and Mexican engineers first ventured, in a rather tentative effort, to work together in a single survey. Entire operations were divided between the sections, and the compilation of maps was attempted only by the United States. The survey of the parallels was proposed as a combined effort of the two commissions, but the political and financial difficulties of the Mexican commission prevented its fulfillment. Instead, the Mexican commission adopted the U.S. survey and later repeated much of it, combining additional monuments with the U.S. demarcation. Mexico and the United States each drafted maps based on its own surveys, which resulted in some confusion, as full coordination was lacking. The final leg of the boundary survey, the United States–Sonora azimuth line, summoned a fully developed alliance between the two commissions. The U.S. and Mexican sections worked as equals, alternating in performing the same operations. The one essential procedure in which collaboration was lacking, that of determining the intersection of the 31°20′ parallel with the 111° meridian, resulted in the only serious error in the survey. While each commission's maps, compiled from the common bank of data, were distinctive, they presented a consistent picture of the boundary and the borderlands. Such model cooperation, however, did not characterize the survey of the longest section of the boundary, the Rio Grande.

FIG. 4-12. Detail of Mexican map "No. 41." (Mapoteca Manuel Orozco y Berra)

CHAPTER FIVE

CONTROVERSY ON THE BOUNDARY

Surveys of the Rio Grande

It is the course that any geographer would have pursued,
if unbiased by any sinister motive.

*U.S. Commissioner John R. Bartlett to Secretary of the Interior
Alexander H. H. Stuart, 8 August 1851*

*T*HE STEADY PROGRESS OF THE UNITED STATES–MEXICO
boundary survey was interrupted at Paso del Norte. Consultation
and cooperation between the commissions dissolved in controversy over
the position of the line west from Paso and led finally to suspension of
the survey and negotiation of a new treaty that redefined the boundary.
While dissent ripened, the U.S. and Mexican commissions attempted
to continue work under the Treaty of Guadalupe Hidalgo. Seeking to
pursue the survey in a section of geography that was not involved in the
controversy, U.S. and Mexican parties turned their attention to the Rio
Grande below Paso (Location Map 4).

No problems were expected in the survey of a boundary so self-
evident as the Rio Grande. The U.S. commission went on to survey the
entire river, while the Mexican commission surveyed several portions of
it, despite having expended most of its resources in locating the compromise land boundary that was later nullified. Nearly all of the surveys
of the Rio Grande were carried out during the prolonged debate over
the New Mexico boundary. But even on the river, the commissions
could not escape the climate of disagreement; lack of a working associa-

tion between the U.S. and Mexican field parties made the discord manifest. Separate surveys, without consultation or cooperation between the commissions in the field, produced most of the final maps of the boundary on the Rio Grande.

In December 1851, following the death of Mexican Commissioner García Conde and the recall to Washington of U.S. Astronomer Graham, the activities of the Mexican and U.S. commissions were in disarray. The survey of the Rio Grande was supposed to be regulated by the Graham-Salazar agreement, but the commissions' problems overwhelmed the aspirations of the plan. Upon his arrival at Paso, newly appointed U.S. Astronomer and Surveyor Emory was more concerned about reorganizing the disorderly U.S. commission than in discussions with the Mexican surveyor.

As part of the reorganization, Emory found it necessary to perform repeat surveys of sections of the Rio Grande that had been surveyed inadequately by Bartlett's unskilled appointees. One resurvey had already been set in motion by Graham after the deficiencies of the original survey had been uncovered by Draftsman Hippel, who had been ordered to make a map of the Rio Grande between Doña Ana and San Elizario from the survey notes. Of the errors in the survey notes, Hippel "spoke generally" as follows:

> The topography of the country on the United States side is very deficient, and on the Mexican side not given at all; not one course of the compass to the tops of the mountains is given, neither their forms, heights, nor characteristics.

> Nowhere is mentioned the position of a road to the line; very seldom from where it comes, or to where it leads. All acequias in appearance cross the line by right-angles, which in reality is not the case.

> The distance of the Rio Grande from the line is so seldom mentioned that it is impossible to give its true course on paper. Those places passed by the surveyor are merely mentioned by name, without giving their position.[1]

Graham had responded to Hippel's criticism by assigning him to survey the Rio Grande himself. He was to start from Frontera, an outpost constructed by a U.S. citizen at the supposed location of the boundary, eight miles above Paso, and continue downriver as far as possible. In order

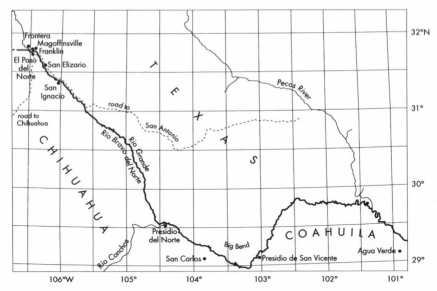

LOCATION MAP 4. Boundary between the United States and Mexico, showing the Rio Grande between Agua Verde near the Pecos River and Paso del Norte. Source: [U.S. Boundary Commission], *Index Map No. 2.*

that the results might be adequate for mapping, Graham instructed Hippel as follows:

> Mountain-ranges may be laid down, with sufficient accuracy for the accomplishment of the object in view, by observing, from a sufficient number of stations, as your work progresses, the bearings of remarkable summits, or other points, and then sketching between these points the general contour of these ranges. In order that your survey may be connected with the astronomical points that may hereafter be established, you will lay down with care the positions of all churches and other remarkable buildings in the vicinity of your line; and you will also for the same purpose, occasionally designate your survey-stations by stakes driven firmly into the ground and properly numbered.[2]

Hippel had worked downriver from Frontera to Paso when he was met by Emory, arriving to take over from Graham. Emory reequipped the party and instructed Hippel to push the survey as rapidly as possible. By the middle of May, he reached Presidio del Norte, a fort at the junction of the Río Conchos and Río Bravo that had been occupied since 1760. Hippel's party was the first topographical or astronomical party of either commission to arrive there. They had hoped to proceed further but were unable to do so; the party's outfit was too broken down to continue.[3]

Not long after Emory's arrival, Salazar received his appointment as interim commissioner, but he was left with little financial support for the work. At length, in March 1852, he assigned Agustín Díaz, and Luis Díaz as assistant, to begin a survey from the town of San Ignacio, some fifty miles below Paso. They were to work upriver until they met Augustus de Vaudricourt, who would be surveying downstream from the Bartlett–García Conde initial point on the 32°22′ parallel. Vaudricourt, originally a Bartlett employee, had left the U.S. commission to work for the Mexican commission.[4] Salazar directed Díaz to prepare a map and emphasized that it would be a *topographic* map, meaning, he said, that it should be surveyed with exactness but not that it should render details of the landscape that were useless to the survey's purpose. He required that the map should show the course of the Rio Grande as the engineers found it; the river's abandoned channels; the Rio Grande valley as far as the hills that bordered it on the Mexican side; and, if possible, the valley up to the bordering hills on the U.S. side. Other features to be included were towns, roads, acequias, arroyos, and dams; and the trend of the hills was to be noted.

Salazar gave general instructions for carrying out a triangulation. Díaz was to measure a baseline and then link together the principal points that would be shown on the map, including a number of positions on the banks of the river, with well-formed triangles. Where triangulation did not suit the terrain, Díaz could "zigzag, taking bearings with the theodolite" and measuring distances.[5] Salazar also gave special instructions to investigate the river near Socorro, Isleta, and San Elizario, where the villages stood on an island between the migrating channels of the Rio Grande. At the time of the survey, the river flowed southwest of the towns, while the old channels of the river, the Río Viejo del Bracito and the more recently abandoned Río Viejo de San Elizario, encircled the towns to the northeast. Salazar expected that water would be found in more than one branch of the river, so Díaz was to make soundings to determine which channel was deepest, in order to demarcate the deepest branch as the boundary river. A boat was constructed for his use.

From a baseline measured near San Ignacio at the end of March,

Agustín and Luis Díaz progressed upriver and reached the mouth of the Río Viejo del Bracito at the end of April. Although the flood season had begun by then, they found that there was not enough water in the abandoned channels to require soundings. The Rio Grande poured through the southwestern branch, and in fact no island existed. In the middle of June, they received a second theodolite that Vaudricourt had been using, enabling Luis and Agustín to work separately and rapidly carry the survey to Paso, where they arrived on 31 July. Finally, above Frontera, the Díaz brothers related their survey to the last side of Vaudricourt's triangulation from the initial point.

In the diary that he was directed to keep for the survey, Díaz described the operations. He constructed a network of principal triangles, as well as measuring angles for the rectification of details, auxiliary triangles, and triangles marking points on the roads. He also traced the courses of the river, the abandoned channels, and the acequias by taking bearings and distances between points in the network. Agustín and Luis kept up the projection and drafting of field maps, and twice during the survey, in late June and at the beginning of August, Agustín delivered maps to the commissioner. With the final report completed on 31 October 1852, Díaz submitted the finished field maps, drawn in scales of 1:20,000 and 1:50,000, and considered his instructions fulfilled. He noted that the maps showed the banks of the Rio Grande in the positions in which he found them, but that the river underwent changes in its course annually during the flood season.[6]

While U.S. and Mexican surveys proceeded in spring 1852 without coordination, Salazar and Emory met in Frontera to renew plans. They retained the working methods for the Rio Grande survey, which had previously been formulated by Salazar and Graham, and agreed to meet again at Presidio del Norte on the first of August. That meeting, "for the purpose of signing and marking a red line shewing the Boundary on all the maps of surveys now unfinished from the Initial point to that Presidio," would bring concord to their separate surveys. Salazar and Emory also approved the boundary "as far as the maps have been finished, that is to say from Frontera to the point where the San Antonio road leaves the River," marking the boundary with a red line on the finished maps and signing them.[7]

The maps that Emory and Salazar agreed upon in the spring meeting were probably the work of Hippel's rapid survey. They would have been used in the compilation of sheets 27, 28, and 29 of the finished map series, since Frontera appeared on map "No. 29" and the San Antonio road, which followed the eastern bank of the Rio Grande downriver from Paso, turned east on map "No. 27." In U.S. and Mexican maps "No. 28," Hippel's results may be compared to the results of the Díaz survey completed later that year (figs. 5-1 and 5-2). The finished maps showed that the Díaz brothers conducted a more detailed topographical survey than that made by Hippel; land cover and cultural symbols, including roads, buildings, acequias, and cultivated fields, were more dense on the Díaz map. Since the Graham-Salazar agreement allowed considerable leeway in the "minuteness" of the surveys to be made, however, the maps of both commissions fulfilled the requirements.

The course of the Rio Grande and its abandoned channels were thoroughly explored in the maps of both commissions. A note on the U.S. map emphasized that the Río Viejo del Bracito was "dry or low water," forestalling any question that the northeastern channel might be the boundary river. The Díaz brothers had discovered the low water of the Río Viejo when they first made a reconnaissance from its junction with the Rio Grande to the Arroyo del Canutillo (see fig. 5-1); the survey that resulted in the detailed map depiction was made later when the acquisition of a second theodolite allowed Agustín and Luis to work separately. The course of the Rio Grande itself was portrayed differently in the U.S. and Mexican maps. Above and below the junction of the Rio Grande with the Río Viejo, for example, the two maps presented different patterns of meanders in the boundary river. The annual changes in the course of the river that Díaz had noted evidently had occurred between the times of the two surveys.

With the important meeting at Presidio del Norte a few months ahead, Emory pursued the astronomical survey of the Rio Grande. After establishing the positions of Frontera, Paso del Norte, and San Elizario, he continued downriver to the mouth of the canyon where the San Antonio road left the river, where, with John O'Donoghue as computer, he determined the latitude by astronomical observation and the longitude by signal flashes from San Elizario. Emory and O'Donoghue then moved to Presidio del Norte, where they completed the determination of latitude and longitude by early August. Meanwhile, Salazar traveled to the city of Chihuahua, possibly to obtain resources.[8]

Except for observations at Paso, a Mexican astronomical survey could

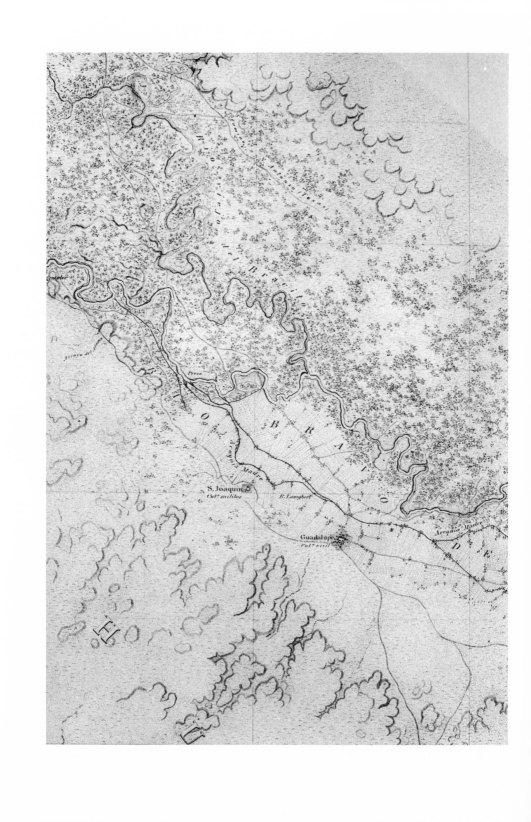

not be sustained in the months before the meeting at Presidio del Norte. In early 1853, planning to carry out the survey to Presidio himself, without assistants or funding, Salazar worked his way downriver from Paso. At Presidio in May 1853, writing to First Engineer Jiménez, Salazar told that he had suffered many upsets due to the political movements in the Republic, that he had received not one peso, and that he had been entirely alone without Señores Ramírez or Sherges, whom he must have expected to arrive as assistants. He described some operations he had practiced from Paso to Presidio, including astronomical location of points and observation of chronometric longitudes. Some months later, Emory reported that the Mexican commissioner had been robbed near Presidio and forced to return to Paso.[9]

The meetings at Presidio in August 1852 were polite contentions in which Salazar tried to pressure Emory into perfecting the Bartlett–García Conde agreement, and Emory, in spite of his instructions, attempted to avoid doing so. In his appointment as U.S. surveyor, Emory had been directed to support the survey based on the Bartlett–García Conde compromise that former Surveyor Gray had refused to approve. Although Emory, too, believed that the compromise was an erroneous interpretation of the treaty, he acted according to his instructions, seeking at the same time not to commit himself or his government to the Bartlett–García Conde agreement.

As planned in the meeting at Frontera, Salazar and Emory intended to sign and mark the boundary on all the maps of surveys between the 32°22′ initial point and Presidio del Norte. The engineers working on the river were to send their maps to Presidio by the first of August. According to the plan, if one party only were to send maps, Emory and Salazar would proceed as if the maps of both parties had been sent and agree upon the boundary, subject to the action of the joint commission.

Emory opened the meeting by declaring he had not yet been sent any maps by his engineers, although he had received a letter from Principal Assistant Radziminski, who was at work on the survey between the initial point and Frontera and expected to be finished soon. Radziminski

FIG. 5-1. Detail of Mexican map "No. 28," showing the junction of the Río Viejo del Bracito and the Río Bravo del Norte (Rio Grande). (Mapoteca Manuel Orozco y Berra)

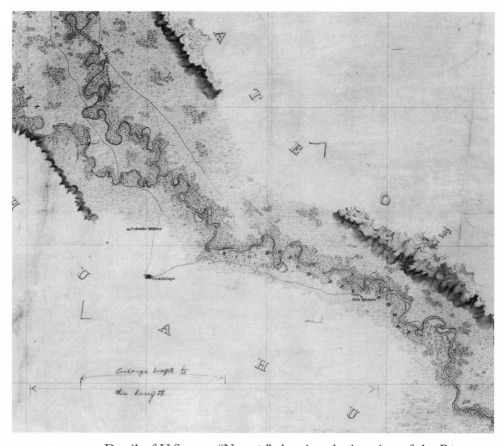

FIG. 5-2. Detail of U.S. map "No. 28," showing the junction of the Río Viejo [del Bracito] and the Río Bravo del Norte (Rio Grande). (National Archives)

was carrying out another repeat survey like that done by Hippel, necessary because of errors in the work of Bartlett's appointees. Emory was not eager to receive the maps of Radziminski's survey, for as he later explained,

> I ordered the resurvey with reluctance, knowing that I was touching on disputed ground with which I desired in its then condition not to touch; but it occurred to me, and I think the judgment sound, that if any weight or consideration could be attached to commencing the survey at that point, the consequences, if any had already been incurred, and that it was to the best interest of the Government, if it made any survey at all, to make a correct one.[10]

In fact, Radziminski did not complete his survey maps and send them to Emory until October. He described the maps as "drawn to a scale of four inches to the mile" and plotted on "a dozen sheets of protracting paper." Years later, the Radziminski maps were sought as evidence in a boundary case between New Mexico and Texas before the United States Supreme Court, but the maps apparently were not preserved.[11]

Salazar, in turn, announced that he had received maps of the survey from the initial point to Frontera—field maps sent to him by Díaz. Emory proposed that the accuracy of the maps be tested by astronomical determinations, to which Salazar acquiesced and suggested that U.S. Assistant Gardner be assigned to make the measurements and calculations, although Salazar also did so himself.

Gardner submitted a comparison of distances measured on the maps with distances ascertained by geodetic calculations from known positions of latitude and longitude. He measured the north-south distance between the initial point, where the latitude had been determined by Salazar, and Frontera, where the latitude had been determined by Emory, and then measured the east-west distance between the two places, where Salazar and Emory had also made longitude determinations. Gardner found that the survey maps placed too great a distance between the initial point and Frontera—that they were too far apart by .53 mile in latitude and by 2.99 miles in longitude.[12]

Emory offered the opinion that because the differences were very great, the maps should not be signed. Salazar was not happy with the results and objected that his longitude at the initial point had been only approximate, as he did not have the books and tables necessary for an exact determination, and that field maps could not be drawn with the exactness of maps being submitted to the governments. The surveys, he said, had been done with all the scientific exactness possible. Emory acquiesced, although he could not withhold "from observing Mr. Salazar's anxiety to have his signature affixed to the first sheet of the series of maps presented to him for signature, which map contains incidentally the initial point." Emory signed the maps with a statement of qualification, to be set forth on the maps: "boundary line as agreed upon by the two commissioners April 24, 1851."[13] He thus fulfilled his obligation to sign the maps but declined to certify their correctness, leaving the Bartlett–García Conde compromise open to repudiation.

The debate over the field maps brought up another issue for negotiation. Emory proposed an agreement forbidding the attempt to make finished maps in the field. "It has never been attempted before, on a large scale," he said, "except on this survey, where the facilities are necessarily less than elsewhere."[14] Salazar said he agreed with Emory's proposition. Since Emory and Salazar were about to endorse their grand plan for dividing the survey of the Rio Grande into six portions, they added an article to the plan stating that finished maps of the surveys would not be made for signature in the field; but they provided no method for comparing and checking the surveys of the two commissions before construction of the final maps.

Information from the surveys between Paso and Presidio del Norte was compiled on maps "No. 22" through "No. 29" in each commission's final map series. Even though the field maps for the Rio Grande above Paso to the Bartlett–García Conde initial point played an important role in the controversy over the commissioners' compromise, the new initial point delimited by the Treaty of 1853 made those surveys irrelevant in the compilation of the final maps. Because of the new boundary delimitation, the Díaz survey of 1852 was useful only for final maps "No. 28" and "No. 29." Salazar halted work near Paso soon after the meeting at Presidio and sent his engineers, including the Díaz brothers, to carry out what he considered a more important survey at the river's mouth. As a result, Mexican mapmakers had to rely on U.S. surveys to produce most of the final maps in the Paso-to-Presidio section of the boundary.

Mexican maps "No. 23" through "No. 27" offered evidence of Salazar's effort to complete the survey between Paso and Presidio, even though the maps in general were copied from those made by the U.S. commission. Emory's astronomical observations and Hippel's topographical data had been remitted to Thom in Washington, and work on the U.S. maps probably had begun in 1853. The title blocks for all five Mexican maps stated that they were "copied in 1857 by order of José Salazar Ylarregui, Mexican Commissioner," and credited Hippel's 1852 survey. The titles also declared, however, that the maps were "reconnoitered astronomically and topographically in 1853 by José Salazar Ylarregui, Surveyor and Interim Commissioner of Mexico," and all five maps were labeled with special notes that gave "determinations by Salazar," specifying positions of latitude for stations marked on the maps.

The dissociation of Salazar's survey from the compilation of the U.S.

maps resulted in some anomalies in the Mexican maps, but the circumstances elucidate some annotations on the U.S. maps. Six U.S. maps,
"No. 23" through "No. 28," contained handwritten notes, some of them
signed with Emory's initials, W. H. E., specifying changes needed in
the final maps. The annotation on map "No. 23" stated, "These plls
[parallels] should be all shifted South to correspond with the Lat [lati-
tude] of Vado de Piedras (29°52′36″8.) W. H. E." On map "No. 24" the
note read, "The plls of Lat on this Map should be shifted to bring IX in
Lat: 30°.5′.24″ W. H. E."; and "No. 25" stated, "The parallels on this
map should be shifted to bring Pilares in Lat 30°.25′.9″ W. H. E." Additional notations indicating parallels and their latitudes, written in
pencil and not initialed, appeared on maps "No. 26" and "No. 27." Map
"No. 28" contained a penciled instruction, also unsigned, to elongate a
certain portion of the map.[15]

The annotations on the six U.S. maps appear to have been made as
records of Salazar's survey, although the source of the information can
be appreciated only by reference to the Mexican maps. On the section
of the Rio Grande covered by the maps, the U.S. commission astronomically determined only one position, the mouth of the canyon
where the San Antonio road left the river, shown on map "No. 27."
There, Emory found both latitude and longitude. In the same section
of the river, Salazar made astronomical observations, for latitude only, at
eight stations. The determinations for Salazar's stations probably located those places more accurately than had the rapid topographic survey carried out by Hippel. The final U.S. maps "No. 23" through
"No. 28," however, must have been drawn before the boundary office in
Washington had knowledge of Salazar's survey. The annotations, therefore, were added later to the finished maps, after the locations for Salazar's stations had already been drawn on the basis of Hippel's survey,
with which Salazar's determinations were not in agreement.

The dislocation was revealed on map "No. 23." There were no U.S.
observatories on this sheet, but Salazar established astronomical station X at Vado de Piedra (fig. 5-3). A legend lettered on the Mexican
map stated, "NOTA Determinacion de Salazar N° X 29°52′36″.87 Lat.
Norte," and a star and a large "X" near the river marked the station. A
cluster of buildings identified as "Vado de Piedras" [*sic*] was shown on
the U.S. map "No. 23," but it was located on the map grid at about
29°50′N (fig. 5-4). In addition to the annotation written in ink in

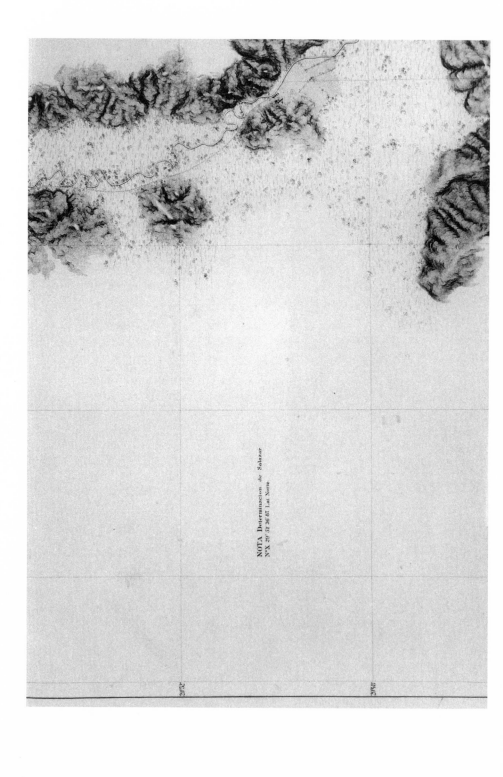

NOTA Determinacion de Salazar
N°X 29°3′ 36′ 6″ Lat Norte

Emory's handwriting, stating that the parallels should be shifted south, there was a pencil line drawn as a parallel through Vado de Piedra and labeled, "29°52'36".87 N° X Vado de Piedra." The penciled parallel indicated about a two-minute shift southward. The Mexican map, although having the formal legend presenting Salazar's determination, had no annotations about moving the parallels. Yet, because it was copied from the U.S. map, it showed station X in latitude 29°50'.

The same type of error was repeated on maps "No. 24" and "No. 25." Mexican map "No. 24" showed a stretch of wilderness where the Arroyo de San Antonio, the only named feature, was the site of Salazar's station IX. Mexican map "No. 25" showed the presidio of Pilares, where Salazar established station VIII. On both maps, there was about a two-minute difference between Salazar's latitude determination and the station's position relative to the graticule, again requiring the parallels to be shifted southward. The U.S. maps, with no astronomical stations in this stretch of the river, were labeled in pencil at the appropriate locations with Salazar's determinations. Mexico's map "No. 26," another wilderness sheet with an Indian trail as the only cultural feature, included three of Salazar's astronomical stations. Only one of them was out of position relative to the graticule, however. On the U.S. map, all three of the stations were marked by a penciled parallel, each with Salazar's station number and latitude determination written above it.

U.S. and Mexican astronomical positions were combined on maps "No. 27." The site of Emory's observatory at the mouth of the canyon was placed in longitude 105°37'15.0"W and latitude 31°02'26.35"N and so labeled on both the U.S. and Mexican maps. Salazar's station IV, shown in the Mexican map on the west bank of the Río Bravo and south of the canyon, was fixed in 31°01'1.34"N. On the U.S. map, Salazar's station was marked by a dot without a label and had a penciled parallel drawn through it. The parallel was labeled, but the number varied slightly from Salazar's determination: "31°1'1".32 N° IV." There was a similar slight discrepancy between Salazar's determination for station III at Presidio Viejo, given in a legend on the Mexican map, and the latitude added in

FIG. 5-3. Detail of Mexican map "No. 23," showing Salazar's station X at Vado de Piedra, on the river opposite the "*Nota.*" (Mapoteca Manuel Orozco y Berra)

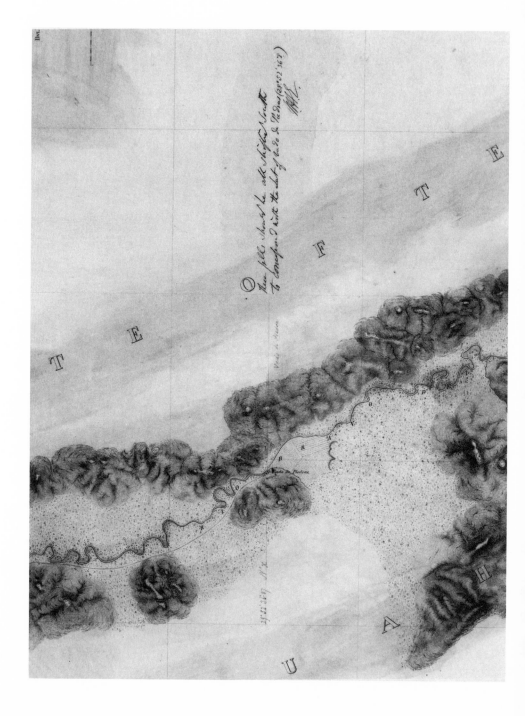

pencil to the U.S. map. Perhaps the incongruence of the pencil notes on the U.S. map with Salazar's determinations were due to adjustments to the calculations for Salazar's positions, made in accordance with the observations at Emory's observatory on the same map sheet.

The final sheet marked with annotations was U.S. map "No. 28." Mexican map "No. 28," drawn from the Díaz survey of 1852, contained no determinations by Salazar but, nevertheless, differed from the U.S. map in the placement of the geographical grid. Differences were most noticeable in the positions of the settlements (see figs. 5-1 and 5-2). The *colonia militar* (military colony) of San Joaquín, for example, was located on the Mexican map at approximately 31°24′N and 106°08′W, while the U.S. map placed it at about 31°25′N and 106°09′W. Guadalupe and San Ignacio were similarly displaced. On the U.S. map, corners were drawn in pencil around the general area of the settlements and two arrows, a shorter arrow and a longer one, were roughly sketched beneath the box corners, and a note in Emory's handwriting indicated that the area should be elongated from the length of the short arrow to that of the long arrow (see fig. 5-2). Since the river flowed from northwest to southeast through the boxed area, the indicated elongation would have the effect of moving the positions of longitude eastward and positions of latitude southward, bringing the area into alignment with the Mexican map. There were no annotations on Mexican map "No. 28," so the Díaz survey may have been regarded as the more accurate of the two topographical surveys, and U.S. map "No. 28" as the source of the displacements on the sheets below.

From Presidio del Norte, the boundary commissions looked downstream toward the most difficult portion of the Rio Grande survey—the formidable canyons of the Big Bend and beyond. The remote region was known only through a few reconnaissance reports. Mexican Army Colonel Emilio Langberg, who had campaigned through the area against the Comanches in 1851, presented a reconnaissance map to the U.S. commission to guide a survey from Presidio to the mouth of the Pecos River.[16] The expedition was led by Assistant Surveyor Chandler, with an escort commanded by Lieutenant Green to accompany the party. In

FIG. 5-4. Detail of U.S. map "No. 23," showing Vado de Piedra. (National Archives)

LINEA DIVISORIA
ENTRE
MEXICO Y LOS ESTADOS UNIDOS
conforme al Tratado de Guadalupe Hidalgo

MAPA
levantado en 18xx con arreglo á las instrucciones
del Comisionado Mexicano

por
JOSE SALAZAR YLARREGUI

Y
MANUEL FERNANDEZ
Y
FRANCISCO HERRERA MIGUEL YGLESIAS

La parte astronomica á
por
JOSE SALAZAR YLARREGUI
Jefe é Id.m

SIERRA DE LA LUZ

SIERRA DE SAN JOSE

fall 1852, Chandler and Green traversed much of the canyon country but were able to execute surveys only as far as San Vicente, the ruins of a Spanish fort located about halfway between Presidio and the Pecos. Their boats lost in the rapids of the Rio Grande and their provisions failing, the party marched to Fort Duncan, near Eagle Pass. There they received news that the U.S. survey had been suspended.[17]

Chandler's and Green's reports testified to the character of the survey as "one of great difficulty and danger," as Chandler described it, and celebrated the grandeur of the country.[18] They gave little account of the scientific work, however. Chandler mentioned only that the peak for which he proposed the name Mount Emory (now Emory Peak) was, "from many places on the line . . . taken as a prominent point on which to direct the instrument," and that in the canyons, "it was impossible to carry the line nearer the bed of the river than the summits of the adjoining hills."[19]

In 1855, when the U.S. commission regarded its survey of the Rio Grande complete, the Mexican commission attempted again to finish work on the river below Paso. Fernández, Herrera, and Iglesias were named as the *sección del Río Bravo* and given the heroic assignment of mapping the course of the river from Paso to the town of Laredo. They actually began their survey at Presidio del Norte, where Salazar had stopped in 1853, and they traveled downriver only as far as the town of San Carlos before their supplies were exhausted and they returned to Paso, where they were reassigned to the more pressing survey of the land boundary. The three engineers received little attention in the records of either commission, although the results of their survey became the bases of the Mexican commission's final boundary maps "No. 21" and "No. 22." Their triangulation data were later published, and these, together with several field maps that have survived, summarized the engineers' scientific work.[20]

Mexican and U.S. maps "No. 22" documented the commissions' separate surveys (figs. 5-5 and 5-6). The maps were clearly based on different sets of data, varying in the selection, form, and placement of features. The section of the Río Bravo above Presidio on Mexican map "No. 22," for example, which was reconnoitered by Salazar in 1853 but not included in the survey by Fernández, Herrera, and Iglesias, was shown

FIG. 5-5. Mexican map "No. 22." (Mapoteca Manuel Orozco y Berra)

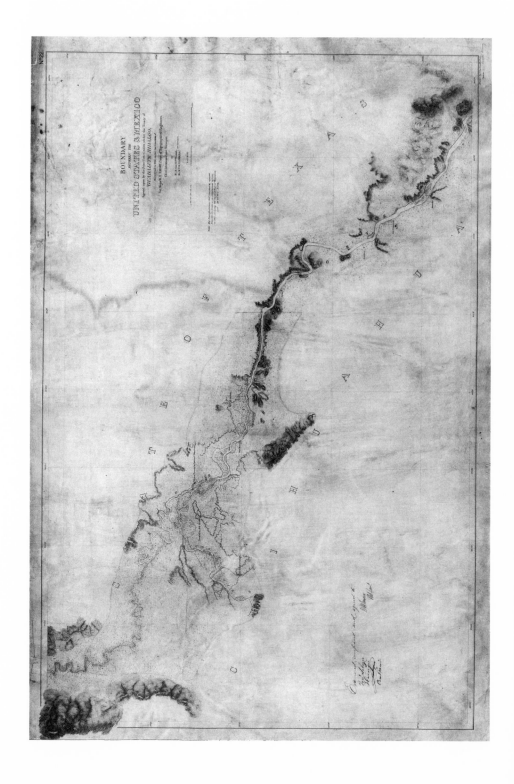

BOUNDARY
BETWEEN THE
UNITED STATES & MEXICO

TAMAULIPAS

TEXAS

COAHUILA

CHIHUAHUA

devoid of any surrounding topography other than a sandy plain. In the same area of the U.S. map, surveyed by Hippel in 1852, the river valley was shown enclosed by hills. Below Presidio, however, in the area traversed by Fernández, Herrera, and Iglesias, the Mexican map encompassed terrain far from the river, on both sides. The distant peaks of the Sierra de Bofecillos in Texas and the Sierra de San José in Chihuahua surrounded the Río Bravo in Mexico's representation; but the U.S. map, based on Chandler's survey below Presidio, did not show the mountains. The area around Presidio del Norte and the complexities of the confluence of the Río Bravo and Río Conchos received the most attention from both commissions, with the U.S. map including more islands in the boundary river. The meanders of the Rio Grande as well as the configurations of islands varied between the two commissions' maps.

There were also small differences between Mexican and U.S. maps "No. 21," arising from separate surveys, but all of the remaining maps of the canyon country made by the two commissions matched, as the Mexican maps were copied from U.S. originals. The Rio Grande between San Carlos and Laredo, which included most of the third and fourth portions of the river as designated in Emory and Salazar's agreement, was surveyed by the U.S. commission alone, resulting in final maps "No. 9" through "No. 20." Maps "No. 18" through "No. 20" were based on the Chandler expedition, and "No. 9" through "No. 17" were surveyed by Lieutenant Michler or Assistant Surveyor Schott. The Mexican copies of maps "No. 9" through "No. 20" were finely drawn and conformed to the specifications for the final map series but acknowledged the U.S. surveys as their sources. All of them stated in the titles that they were copied in 1857 by order of Commissioner Salazar.

Before the Bartlett commission was withdrawn from the field late in 1852, U.S. parties had surveyed the Rio Grande from the Bartlett–García Conde initial point to Laredo, except for the stretch of river between San Vicente and the mouth of the Pecos. Emory had also completed astronomical observations between the initial point and Presidio del Norte and had moved downriver. "The position of Loredo was determined by me (nearly)," he recounted, "and observatories erected at Ringgold barracks [near Rio Grande City], ready to set up the great

FIG. 5-6. U.S. map "No. 22." (National Archives)

instruments when the work was suspended."[21] In April 1853, the Camp-bell commission arrived on the Rio Grande to conclude the survey of the river. Mexican engineers of the *sección Matamoros*, meanwhile, had begun work at the *desembocadura*. After initial consultations at the river's mouth, members of the U.S. and Mexican commissions sepa-rated to pursue surveys of the fifth portion of the river, from Matamoros to Laredo, and did not meet again on the lower Rio Grande (see Loca-tion Map 2).

Several U.S. parties worked concurrently on topographical surveys. Michler, assisted by Ingraham and Phillips, completed the section of the river from near San Vicente to the mouth of the Pecos. Schott, aided by Seaton and Weyss, directed the survey from Laredo as far as Ring-gold Barracks. The section from Ringgold Barracks to the *desemboca-dura* was assigned to Principal Assistant Surveyor Radziminski, assisted by Houston and Jones. Radziminski's group was first assailed with yel-low fever and then beset with tragedy, when a boat overturned in the river and Jones was drowned. Assistant Prioleau transferred from duty with Emory's astronomical party to take Jones's place, and when Schott, Seaton, and Weyss had completed the section of the river above Ring-gold Barracks, they joined Radziminski near Brownsville to assist in completing the survey to the river's mouth.[22]

U.S. topographical work on the lower Rio Grande was not well docu-mented. Chief Astronomer and Surveyor Emory, who took charge of the technical work, commented to Radziminski that the experienced surveyors of the Campbell commission did not require detailed written instructions, so the surveyors' assignments were therefore general. The data that survived in the final *Report* were largely astronomical obser-vations and calculations based upon them.[23]

Emory's destination on the Rio Grande was Ringgold Barracks, where he had stored the surveying and astronomical instruments when the Bartlett commission folded. There he set up an astronomical obser-vatory, with the assistance of Gardner, Clark, and Prioleau. From Ring-gold Barracks, the astronomical party made expeditions to other loca-tions on the lower river to observe for latitude and longitude. Emory returned to Washington in September, leaving Gardner in charge of a small group at the river's mouth. Gardner and Clark continued to make astronomical observations through November 1853.[24]

The observatories at Ringgold Barracks and the mouth of the Rio

Grande became the most well-determined U.S. positions on the lower river. At Ringgold Barracks, Emory determined the latitude and longitude by a series of observations "nearly approximate to a first class determination."[25] The observatory at the river's mouth was set up with a zenith telescope and a large transit instrument, which Gardner and Clark used for their extensive observations. Stations for determining what Emory called "minor points of latitude and longitude" were established at Fort McIntosh near Laredo, Bellville (also called Redmond's ranch), Roma, Edinburgh, and Old Fort Brown near Brownsville.[26]

The Mexican commission turned to the survey of the lower river as a vital interest. Before the Bartlett commission was recalled, Salazar had already dispatched the *sección Matamoros*, made up of astronomers Jiménez and Alemán and topographers Agustín and Luis Díaz, to work on the fifth and sixth portions of the river, from Laredo to Matamoros and from Matamoros to the mouth. Felipe de Iturbide, who was to accompany the section as interpreter and translator, died at Matamoros of yellow fever. The engineers were to begin at the *desembocadura* and work upriver until meeting Salazar and his assistants carrying the survey downriver. Traveling from Paso by way of Mexico City, where they obtained some financial resources from the collapsing government of President Mariano Arista, Jiménez and his party arrived at Matamoros about a month ahead of the Campbell commission.[27]

Jiménez and Alemán erected an observatory at Matamoros and determined its position, afterward moving on to observations at the *desembocadura*. The astronomers then departed for Laredo to work downriver from that point, as the Díaz party had already done with the topographical survey. After making extensive observations at Nuevo Laredo, on the Mexican side of the Río Bravo, the astronomers progressed to other stations on the river, catching up with the topographical party at the town of Mier. Although Luis Díaz had fallen ill, he and Agustín were slowly persevering with the survey. Jiménez and Alemán, struggling with bad weather that made travel difficult and cut short their observations at two stations, continued with the astronomical work ahead of the topographers.[28]

The Mexican commission's most well-determined position on the lower Río Bravo was Matamoros, where Jiménez and Alemán extended observations for two months (see fig. 3-9). Jiménez considered the Matamoros observations the most dependable of all those made on the river by the Mexican commission. The observatory at Matamoros, constructed of brick to withstand the strong winds, offered better conditions for observation than even the observatory at Paso del Norte. The instruments set up at Matamoros included a zenith telescope and a portable transit, both made by Troughton and Simms. At the *desembocadura*, Salazar had instructed Jiménez and Alemán to observe for a month and then to connect the observatories at Matamoros and the river's mouth by signal fires or flashes in order to transfer the longitude from Matamoros. The engineers found it impractical to use signal fires, however, because of the lack of prominent points between the two stations from which to send signals, and so carried out observations at the *desembocadura*, as at Matamoros, for two months. In other places where they had only a few days to work, they used a repeating circle to find the latitude and a chronometer for the longitude. Secondary positions that they located included Rancho de los Fresnos, at the mouth of the Río San Juan, and Guerrero, on the Río Salado, as well as several others that were determined less meticulously.[29]

Jiménez had been directed by Salazar not to intervene in the Díaz brothers' work, so that his only instructions to them were for relating the topographical survey to the astronomical observations. He charged them to prepare foundations of rocks or tree trunks in places that would be suitable for setting up astronomical instruments and to relate the places by triangulation to the channel of the river. In this way, Jiménez explained, the observatories would be connected to the boundary, and the absolute longitudes observed at various points could be referred to a single longitude determination by means of the geodetic calculation of the triangulation. The instruments available to the Díaz party consisted of one theodolite with compass, two chains, a case of drawing instruments, and supplies for drafting. Agustín and Luis had four assistants and a small escort of soldiers, who were to double as laborers in such tasks as clearing trees. Jiménez provided a cart and mules and a boat for the survey.[30]

The Díaz party conducted a triangulation between Laredo and the *desembocadura*, recording the network of triangles on field maps of their survey. The field maps also noted topographical features, including islands in the Río Bravo, cultural features, such as roads, ranchos, and forts, and many place names. Published tables of triangulation data named the vertices of the triangles, giving their calculated latitudes and

longitudes, and recorded the azimuths and lengths of the sides of the
triangles used in calculation.[31] Some triangles were connected with the
astronomical observatories as Jiménez had directed. At Nuevo Laredo,
for example, a post that the topographers had prepared was used as a
station where Jiménez and Alemán observed for a month.

Jiménez and Alemán returned to Matamoros from their astronomical
reconnaissance at the end of December 1853. The U.S. Boundary Commission had departed the river by that time, and—expecting that the
joint commission would be meeting in Mexico City to begin work on
the final maps within a few months—the Mexican astronomers decided
to retire to the capital. Luis Díaz's condition had required him also to
return to Mexico, leaving Agustín alone to complete the topographical
survey. Agustín arrived in Mexico City some seven months after the rest
of the *sección Matamoros*, just in time to join the new commission
formed under the Treaty of 1853.[32]

The fifth portion of the river, the section between Laredo and Matamoros, was shown on final maps "No. 2" through "No. 8" of both
commissions. Although the plan for the Rio Grande had assigned the
survey of the fifth portion to the Mexican commission, both commissions, in fact, surveyed it separately in its entirety. The U.S. and
Mexican maps agreed in the general delineation of the river and its environs, but they also showed many variations derived from their separate
sources. The most striking difference between the maps of the two commissions was the much more extensive topographical information on
the Mexican maps, which not only covered a wider band of territory to
either side of the Río Bravo but also presented more details in the area
close to the river. The U.S. maps, on the other hand, recorded a larger
number of astronomical stations.

The Mexican emphasis on topographical representation was best
demonstrated in map "No. 8," the Laredo sheet (fig. 5-7). Like the other
maps of the lower river, the title credited astronomical determinations
to Jiménez and Alemán and triangulation and topography to Agustín
and Luis Díaz. The Mexican engineers reported, however, that they
carried their surveys only as high as Laredo, which was located approximately in the center of the sheet. The map presented an extensive and
detailed image of the environs of the Río Bravo below Laredo, where
the *sección Matamoros* reported working, while above Laredo the topographical information was abruptly reduced to a narrow strip on either

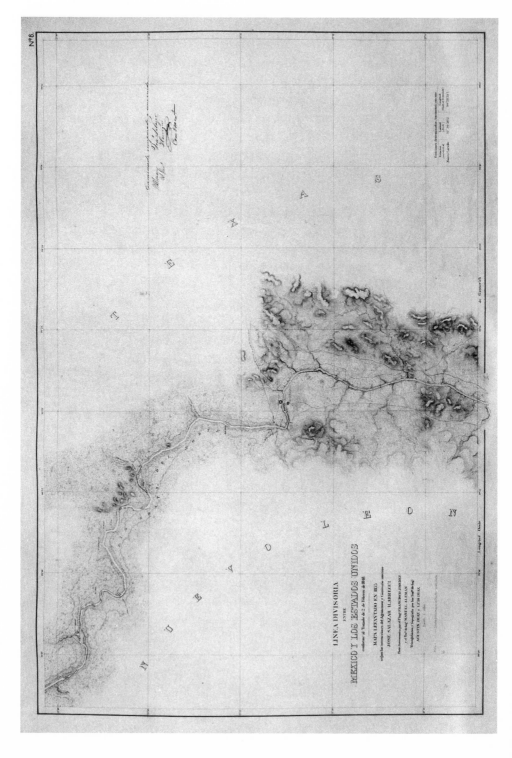

T E X A S

N U E V O L E O N

LINEA DIVISORIA
ENTRE
MEXICO Y LOS ESTADOS UNIDOS
conforme al Tratado de 2 de Febrero de 1848

MAPA LEVANTADO EN 1855
según las instrucciones del Agrimensor y Comisario americano
JOSE SALAZAR ILARREGUI

Este instrumento por el Ing.ᵒ FRANCISCO JIMENEZ
y el Encᵒ de Ingᵒ MANUEL ALEMAN
Triangulaciones y topografía por los Ings.ᵒˢ de 1ᵃ
AGUSTIN DIAZ y LUIS DIAZ

side of the river. In comparison, U.S. map "No. 8" restricted the topography to a narrow band throughout the length of the river, and the drawing contained little information, consisting for the most part of a generalized sand and gravel pattern (fig. 5-8). Below Laredo, the U.S. and Mexican maps were very different; above Laredo, the two images were nearly identical.

The succeeding sheets in the final map series explained the images presented in maps "No. 8." Mexican map "No. 9" and maps ascending the Río Bravo through "No. 20" were copies of U.S. maps. Although the title of map "No 8" did not acknowledge a copied source, Mexican copying actually began with that sheet in the section above Laredo. The scanty topographical representation above Laredo was taken from U.S. map "No. 8," based on the Schott survey, while the Díaz survey contributed the luxuriant topographical rendering below Laredo. Where the U.S. map provided little information, the Mexican map showed details of the physical geography, such as hills, cliffs, and streambeds, and cultural features, including roads, towns, and cultivated fields, as well as the string of deserted ranchos included on the U.S. map (fig. 5-9).

Topographical features of special concern to both commissions were the islands of the lower Rio Grande. Each of the many islands and its situation in the river had to be explored in order to assign its ownership to either the U.S. or Mexico. The islands were not officially demarcated during the fieldwork, however. Field maps were not exchanged for signature, and the engineers did not engage in formal agreements regarding the islands. The partitioning of islands was officially established in the final boundary maps, where the commissioners' signatures indicated their approval.

Because the Treaty of Guadalupe Hidalgo stated that the boundary in the Rio Grande should follow the deepest channel, the award of an island to either Mexico or the United States depended in general upon which side of the deepest channel the island was located. Soundings to locate the deepest channel to one side or other of the islands were carried out by both commissions. The U.S. commission produced a set of five large-scale maps that assigned a number to each island and showed survey results. The island maps were included in the final map series,

FIG. 5-7. Mexican map "No. 8." (Mapoteca Manuel Orozco y Berra)

and their numbering system for the islands was reproduced on the sectional maps. The Mexican commission did not create a distinct series of island maps, but Agustín Díaz prepared a report on his survey of the islands, in which he described all of the islands between Laredo and the mouth of the Río San Juan and designated the deepest channel in each case.[33] The islands, not numbered, were shown on the Mexican sectional maps, and the deepest channels were marked.

U.S. "Sheet No. 4, Islands in the Rio Bravo del Norte" was correlated with three of the U.S. sectional maps and was typical of the island maps (fig. 5-10). It exhibited a number of discrete sections of the river with the islands they contained. Each section was shown in its correct orientation, relative to the north arrow placed at the bottom center of the sheet, and was drawn on a scale of 1:6,000. Islands number 36 through 39, located below Laredo, were shown in the lower left quarter of "Sheet No. 4" and in the lower half of map "No. 8." The other islands on "Sheet No. 4," numbers 27 through 35, appeared on sectional maps "No. 6" and "No. 7." Islands in the Rio Grande above Laredo were not assigned numbers. Although they were shown on map "No. 8" and other sectional maps, they were not depicted on special island maps. Thus island sheets "No. 1" through "No. 4" displayed islands number 1 through 39, from the *desembocadura* to Laredo; the fifth island sheet presented a large-scale view of the islands in the confluence of the Río Conchos and the Rio Grande.

The purpose of the U.S. island maps was to show the topographic and hydrographic details of the islands and to exhibit the data used for their assignment to the United States or Mexico. Important data on the island sheets that were not given in the sectional maps were the depths of the channels around each island. In some places, the suitability of a channel for navigation was noted, and hazards such as rocks and rapids were charted. A dashed line labeled "Main Channel," separating each island from the country that did not own it, represented the boundary line. Where several islets were grouped together, the dashed line followed the main channel among them. Each island or islet was designated United States or Mexico. The dashed lines symbolizing the boundary were repeated in the island representations on the U.S. sectional maps. The Mexican sectional maps also showed dashed lines in

FIG. 5-8. U.S. map "No. 8." (National Archives)

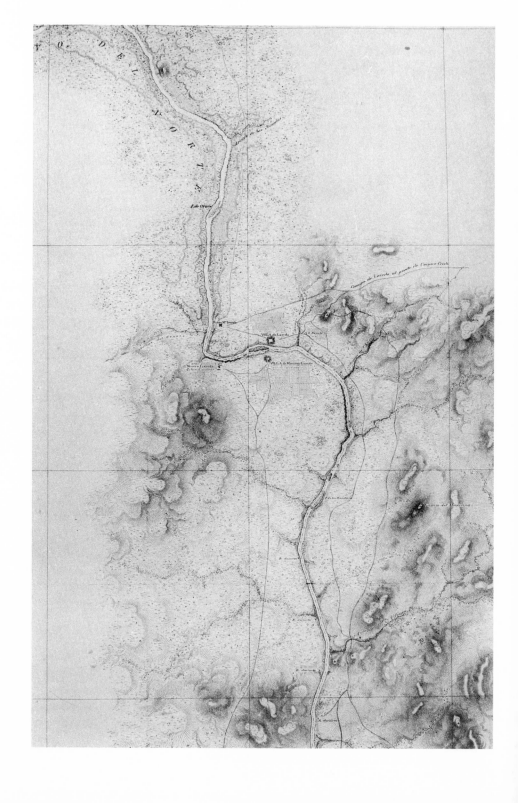

the Rio Grande that assigned the islands to the United States or Mexico and agreed with the island allotments shown on the U.S. maps (see fig. 5-9).

Near Laredo, the Rio Grande was relatively stable, but in much of the river, dry seasons and floods alternately built up and eroded away the islands, strands, and sandbars. A deeper channel might be scoured first on one side of an island, then the other. The problems of the changeable river and the islands within it were evident to all who worked on the survey. Díaz found the river so volatile that at a certain point he felt it was futile to continue the report on his survey, as he explained: "The frequent change that the Río Bravo undergoes below its confluence with the San Juan makes it fruitless to give a detailed account of all the strands or banks of sand that, as the maps demonstrate, are found in the center of the river."[34] Emory summarized the situation as the commissioners understood it: "The allotment of all the islands was made upon the condition of things as they existed when the boundary was agreed upon. The channel of the river may change and throw an island once on the Mexican side to the American, and vice versa, but neither the Mexican commissioner nor myself could provide against such a contingency, none having been anticipated in the treaty."[35]

At the center of the great boundary debate initiated by the Bartlett–García Conde compromise were U.S. and Mexican maps "No. 29," for these were the maps that located the "town called Paso." Even though surveys began soon after the joint commission first met in Paso del Norte in 1850, maps "No. 29" could not be completed until the boundary dispute was resolved by the Treaty of 1853. In the final "No. 29" maps, the Rio Grande boundary was shown as delimited in the Treaty of Guadalupe Hidalgo, and the boundary running westward from the river as defined by the Treaty of 1853 (see figs. 5-11 and 5-12). Data collected in independent U.S. and Mexican surveys, however, resulted in maps that differed so much that the commissioners could not consent that the U.S. and Mexican maps agreed. Eventually, questions about the boundary portrayals in maps "No. 29" led to new debates about the boundary

---

FIG. 5-9. Detail of Mexican map "No. 8," showing the area around Laredo. (Mapoteca Manuel Orozco y Berra)

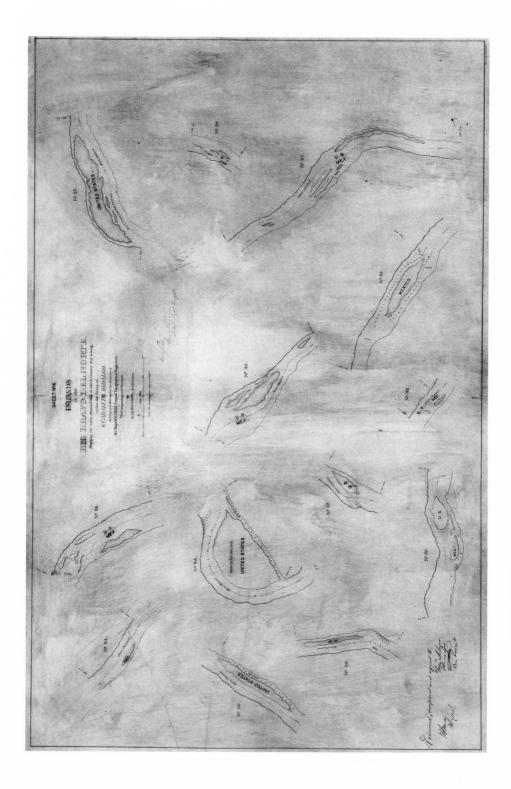

treaties. Created in an atmosphere of contention, the finished maps themselves became enmeshed in yet another controversy.

The Paso del Norte area was a natural headquarters for the joint boundary commission, for both the survey of the Rio Grande and the survey westward. The U.S. commission had its primary astronomical station at Frontera. Established as a supply depot and repository of scientific equipment by Commissioner Bartlett, the site was then used as an astronomical station by Lieutenant Whipple when he was appointed temporary chief astronomer. James Duncan Graham, Whipple's replacement as chief astronomer, began construction of an observatory at Frontera. The observatory was eventually completed under the direction of William H. Emory, who, meanwhile, assigned Graham's assistant, W. F. Smith, to set up an observatory south of Paso at San Elizario. Frontera and San Elizario became two of the eighteen primary stations established by the U.S. Boundary Commission across the length of the border.[36]

Emory observed for latitude and longitude at Frontera, assisted by John O'Donoghue as computer, while Smith made longitude observations at San Elizario. Smith was assisted by John Lawson, an individual who did not stay with the commission long but who eventually took over the task of observing from Smith. Unfortunately, Lawson's observations were made with instruments that were later found deficient, and the results were rejected. Smith's observations, carried out with better instruments for about four months before Lawson took over, were sufficient for O'Donoghue to compute the longitude of San Elizario. For the latitude of San Elizario, Whipple's determination of 1851 was used.[37]

The Mexican commission began observations at Paso del Norte in January 1851. The observatory constructed near the cathedral in the town of Paso was one of the primary stations in the Mexican survey. José Salazar observed for longitude for about a month and then turned over the work to Francisco Jiménez and assistant Manuel Alemán. Among Salazar, Jiménez, and Alemán, longitude observations were carried out for three months in 1851, and later, after his return from the survey of the Río Gila in spring 1852, Jiménez made additional observations. Ji-

FIG. 5-10. U.S. "Sheet No. 4, Islands in the Río Bravo del Norte." (National Archives)

ménez was also in charge of observations for latitude. With Engineers Juan Espejo, Agustín García Conde, and Alemán as observers, one hundred observations for latitude were made at Paso; Jiménez and Alemán completed the calculations.[38]

Meanwhile, Emory and Salazar devised a plan to refine the determinations of longitude. Emory explained: "It is agreed between Mr. Salazar and myself, to connect the Meridians of Doña Ana, Frontera, El Paso and San Elizario by Flashes, so that all the culminations and occultations observed at each may be combined. For this purpose I have undertaken to keep the local time and watch the flashes at this place [Frontera] and San Elizario and he has undertaken to do the same at Doña Ana and El Paso."[39] Appropriate sites to set off the gunpowder flashes were found by experiments with signal fires, and the observations of flashes were carried out on four nights between 14 February and 14 March 1852. For the final boundary maps, the observations at Doña Ana were not needed, but the longitudes determined from flashes at Frontera, Paso, and San Elizario were averaged with astronomical determinations for each of the places to give the final result. The adjustments were small, and the results of the gunpowder flashes were found to support the astronomical determinations.[40]

Thus the astronomical foundations for U.S. and Mexican maps "No. 29" were prepared under the Treaty of Guadalupe Hidalgo. Emory was proud of the care with which the work at Paso was done: "The positions of Frontera & San Elizario were determined in Latitude, and their positions in Longitude determined by observations running through four lunations, and the stations together with the astronomical station of Mr. Salazar at El Paso, connected together by flashes, the combined observations forming probably the best determined geographical position in the Interior of the continent."[41] Much topographical work was also completed before the boundary dispute was resolved, the Díaz and Hippel surveys of 1852 supplying most of the data for the maps.

The Treaty of 1853 demanded additional astronomical observations to determine the new initial point at the crossing of the 31°47' parallel and the Rio Grande. Soon after their return to Paso, from early December 1854 to mid-January 1855, the two commissions made observations for latitude. For the United States, the observers were Principal Assistant Astronomer Clark, assisted by Campbell, while Mexican Commissioner Salazar was assisted by Engineers Molina and Contreras. Comparing their results, the astronomers found only a small difference in their determinations, so the position of the 31°47' parallel on the ground was selected as the average of U.S. and Mexican results.[42]

The longitude of the new initial point was ascertained by triangulation from Frontera, executed by members of the U.S. commission. Hippel was in charge, aided by Weyss, Wheaton, and Houston. Located by definition in the middle of the river, the initial point was found to be in longitude 106°31'20.8"W by the U.S. triangulation, a figure assented to by the Mexican commissioner. The longitude of the initial point was not fixed, however, but was subject to change with shifts in the course of the river. Monument No. 1 was therefore erected as a permanent marker on the right (west) bank of the river, its position also found by triangulation. Over time, the distance of Monument No. 1 from the middle of the river varied with the river's meanderings; for example, when the monument was constructed in 1855, it was 71.04 meters from the middle of the river, but at the time of the boundary resurvey in 1892, Monument No. 1 was 172.6 meters from the middle of the river.[43]

Maps "No. 29" encompassed the Pass of the North, the mountain canyon of the Río Bravo where the initial point was located, and the relatively well-settled region below the pass (figs. 5-11 and 5-12). On the Mexican side of the Río Bravo, farmlands watered by an extensive system of acequias supported the inhabitants of Villa Paso del Norte, who numbered about five thousand, according to Commissioner Bartlett. A dam just above Paso controlled the water supply to the acequias. Across the river were three small U.S. settlements; the earliest was established at Franklin, although many of the buildings there were soon deserted. The principal village was Magoffinsville, founded by Santa Fe and Chihuahua trader James Magoffin, who was often a host to the officers of the U.S. Boundary Commission. Northeast of Magoffinsville was Stephenson's rancho. North of the mountains, on the U.S. side of the river, was the outpost of Frontera. To the south, maps "No. 29" extended through the settlements of Isleta, Socorro, and San Elizario. Bartlett observed that the three towns were located in "one of the most fertile spots in the whole valley . . . cultivated since the first settlement of the country." The population was mostly Mexican, for the towns had been founded in the seventeenth century and, until a recent change in the river's course, they had been located on the south bank of the Río Bravo. The three settlements and their developed agriculture were Díaz and

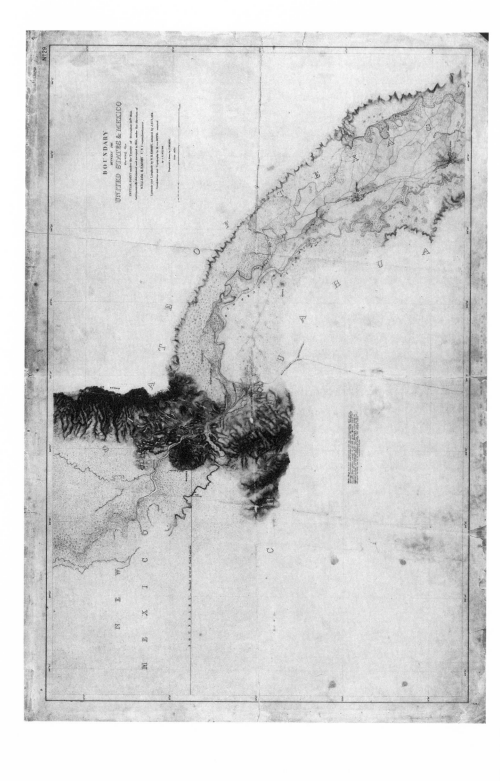

Hippel's main concerns when they surveyed the area around the Río Viejo with special care.[44]

Many of the commission members who performed the fieldwork for the maps were named in the title panels. The Mexican map stated that it was surveyed in 1852, with triangulation and topography by Agustín Díaz and Luis Díaz and "astronomical determinations of the initial point and Paso del Norte" by Salazar and Jiménez. The U.S. map was "astronomically determined and surveyed in 1855," with "latitude and longitude by W. H. Emory, assisted by J. H. Clark," and triangulation and topography by Hippel and Weyss. Only those individuals who completed the U.S. survey under the Treaty of 1853 were credited; Whipple, Smith, and O'Donoghue, whose astronomical work had been done earlier, were not named. Hippel and Weyss were a team in the 1855 triangulation of the 31°47' initial point. Weyss's role may have been recognized because he also made the landscape drawings that illustrated the engraved map *No. 29*.[45] U.S. map "No. 29" was one of only two final maps with a cartographer's credit in the title: "Projected & drawn by F. Herbst."

The Mexican map's more extensive and detailed representation of the landscape again stood out in a comparison of the maps of the two commissions. Following Salazar's instructions, Agustín and Luis Díaz surveyed the Mexican side of the river in great detail, in expectation that the U.S. party would do the same on the U.S. side, and the two sets of data together would provide a full representation of the river.[46] Hippel's topographical survey, however, was conducted very rapidly, providing a less-detailed picture of the U.S. bank of the river and representing the Mexican side of the river so sparsely that it appeared to be undeveloped relative to the U.S. side. The *acequia madre* that watered the cultivated fields on the western side of the Río Bravo between Paso and Senecu, for example, was one of the most important features on the Mexican map, but it was shown only vaguely and in part on the U.S. map. The acequia had its source at the dam north of Paso, labeled *"presa"* on the Mexican map but unlabeled and shown only by a thin line on the U.S. map. The acequia on the U.S. side—seen on the Mexican map arising from an old channel of the river and reaching from Isleta to San Elizario—was clearly drawn and labeled on the U.S. map. While Mexican

FIG. 5-11. U.S. map "No. 29." (National Archives)

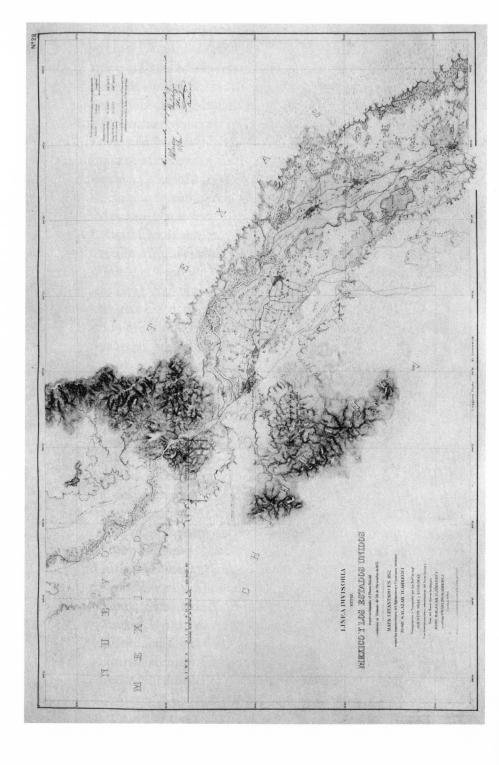

LINEA DIVISORIA
ENTRE
MEXICO Y LOS ESTADOS UNIDOS
proporcionada al Plano Social
conforme al Tratado de 30 de Diciembre de 1853

MAPA LEVANTADO EN 1852
según las instrucciones del Agrimensor y Comisario Generales
JOSÉ SALAZAR ILARREGUI

Trangulación y Topografía por los Ingenieros
AGUSTIN DIAZ y LUIS DIAZ

Bajo del Survur Survur Survur
JOSÉ SALAZAR ILARREGUI
y el Ingeniero FRANCISCO HERRERA

LINEA DIVISORIA, á lo largo del

map "No. 29" offered a relatively complete representation of the area, U.S. map "No. 29" gave the impression that the Mexicans had little at stake in locating the boundary in the region depicted.

Of greater concern were the representations of the boundary. Comparison of Mexican and U.S. maps "No. 29" revealed considerable differences in the portrayal of the boundary river. Emerging from the canyon of the Paso, where the representations were similar, the Rio Grande began to meander through different loops and turns on the two maps (figs. 5-13 and 5-14). It appeared that in the time between the U.S. and Mexican surveys, the river had wandered. Evidence of the Rio Grande's propensity for rapid and profound changes in its stretch near Paso may be found in the account of an observer a few years after the boundary survey, who described the river as follows:

> In meandering along the Texan bank of the river as a land surveyor, from the New Mexican line to a point below Fort Quitman, in 1858, 1859, and 1860, I observed that the deposit was from one-half inch to 3 inches annually, that during the floods the bed of the river was constantly changing by erosion and deposit, and that in regular cycles it shifted from one of its firm rocky or clay banks to the other, as the deposits had raised the side of the valley through which it then flowed above the level of the opposite side. Generally this change took place slowly, by erosion and deposit of matter entirely in suspension; but frequently hundreds of acres would be passed in a single day by a cut-off in a bend of one channel, and sometimes the bed would suddenly change from one firm bank to the other, a distance of perhaps 20 miles in length by 6 in width.[47]

Islands, those features that the commissions found so volatile, were presented differently on the two maps. Downriver from the dam, for example, the U.S. map showed a large island to the southeast of Franklin, with the boundary line drawn around the island to include it in the territory of the U.S. No island appeared in that location on the Mexican map. The Mexican map, on the other hand, showed a large island at the bend in the river south of Magoffinsville, with the boundary line in the river placing the island in Mexico. The U.S. map showed no islands in that part of the river. Similar discrepancies appeared further downriver.

FIG. 5-12. Mexican map "No. 29." (Mapoteca Manuel Orozco y Berra)

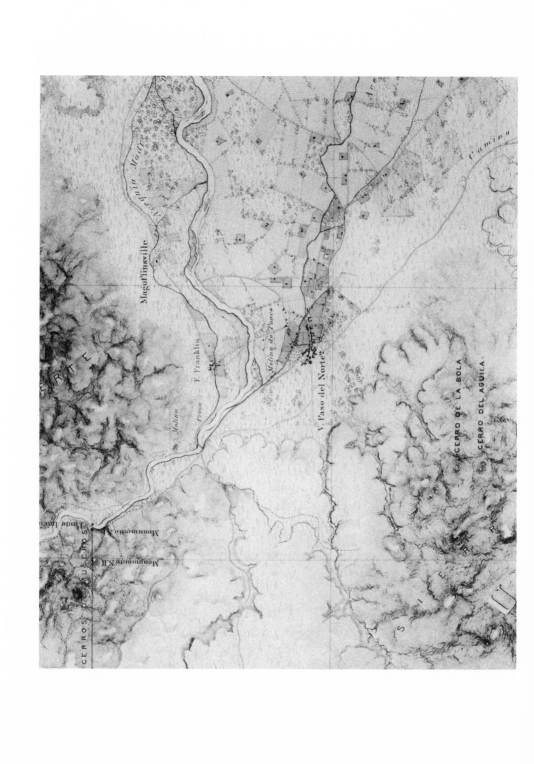

Yet another difference between Mexican and U.S. maps "No. 29" was the use of the boundary line in the river. The Mexican map designated ownership of islands with a dashed line in scattered stretches of the river. U.S. map "No. 29," however, depicted a dashed line throughout the length of the river. The line was not placed in the center of the river, but wavered from bank to bank as though following a determined channel of the river and, like the Mexican map, denoting ownership of islands. No other manuscript map of the Rio Grande by the U.S. commission delineated a continuous boundary line throughout the course of the river.

The inconsistencies in U.S. and Mexican maps "No. 29" must have disturbed the commissioners when they compared the maps for signature. A formal note was lettered on the U.S. map, stating:

This Map has been compared with the corresponding Map of the Mexican commission and is found to represent the true Boundary[.] The two Maps agree, except in the bed of the River, which circumstance is the consequence of the two Surveys being made at different periods, six months apart, during which time the River changed its bed, as it is constantly doing, but always within narrow limits.

Below the lettered note, heavy signs of erasure and faint ink marks at present appear on the map (fig. 5-14). The erasure marks have been explained as follows: "This map 29, an original, was signed by the American commissioner and verified by Captain George Thom, of the Topographical Engineers, United States Army. Probably it was signed by the Mexican commissioner also. Two signatures and the verification have been erased. Commissioner Emory's signature, written as it appears on other signed originals, is identifiable despite erasure, as is also the verification by Captain Thom. Only an erasure appears in the position where the Mexican Commissioner presumably signed."[48]

Mexican map "No. 29," however, contained no note of explanation regarding discrepancies between it and the U.S. map and was signed by both commissioners exactly as all the other maps were signed. The commissioners left no record of their discussion of maps "No. 29," nor did

FIG. 5-13. Detail of Mexican map "No. 29," showing the Chamizal area of the Rio Grande south of Magoffinsville. (Mapoteca Manuel Orozco y Berra)

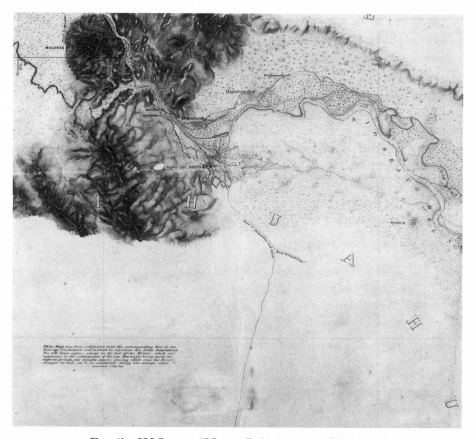

FIG. 5-14. Detail of U.S. map "No. 29," showing the Chamizal area south of Magoffinsvile. The signatures were erased from the area beneath the formal annotation at the lower left of the detail. (National Archives)

they explain their reasons for erasing their signatures from the U.S. map and retaining them on the Mexican map. The irregularities were apparently never questioned until nearly half a century later, when the maps were called upon in the legal case that was to become the most lengthy and complex dispute in the history of the United States–Mexico border, El Chamizal.

El Chamizal was a tract of land adjacent to the Rio Grande that belonged to Mexico but was cut off by a shift in the course of the river, becoming attached to south El Paso, Texas (see figs. 5-13 and 5-14). In 1895, hearings began on El Chamizal. They were held by an International Boundary Commission that had been created by treaty between the United States and Mexico and charged with investigating river changes and resolving questions of boundary location. Consulting engineers compiled maps of the land in dispute, based on Mexican and U.S. maps "No. 29," and discovered discrepancies in their compilations that were traced to the source maps. The revelations of the consulting engineers prompted the commissioners to examine the original maps "No. 29" and resulted in the U.S. commissioner's discovery, to his surprise, of the absence of signatures on the U.S. map. Investigating the matter, the U.S. commissioner was able to present only the following unconvincing findings:

> I have made diligent search and inquiry to discover if possible, when, why, and by whom the signatures were erased from this sheet, but have been unable to arrive at any conclusion entirely satisfactory. The most plausible solution is, that the erasures were made from the manuscript copy because it was not considered complete, as it was wanting in the two views shown on the lower left-hand corner of the printed copper-plate copies, in which printed copies the signatures of Major Emory seem a facsimile of that only partially erased.[49]

The Mexican commissioner held that, since the U.S. map "No. 29" did not appear to have been signed, he considered it of no legal significance.

In spite of the U.S. commissioner's efforts, the U.S. secretary of state was unwilling to support the authenticity of U.S. map "No. 29." He pointed out that even if it were possible to establish the authenticity of either the manuscript "No. 29" or the engraved *No. 29,* the differences in the representation of the boundary from the Mexican "No. 29" would entail tedious negotiations and conventional agreement to determine which map showed the true boundary. The issue was closed with the secretary's judgment that, "as matters now stand I am inclined to think that the claim of the title of the Mexican map to be regarded as authentic and paramount can not be contested by any facts or evidence in the possession of this Government."[50] The International Boundary Commission complied with the secretary of state's decision, confirming Mexico's map as the only, true "No. 29."

The commissioners' signatures on the final boundary maps were meant to certify that the U.S. and Mexican maps were in accord and that each nation held a true record of the boundary. The maps of the boundary on the Rio Grande, unlike the maps of the turning points and the maps of the land boundary, were produced with little coordination between the commissions in the fieldwork and did not always match. When comparison showed a pair of maps to be in disagreement, the commissioners dealt with the problem in one of three ways. One way was to sign the maps and add annotations regarding features that should be brought into agreement on the maps, such as was done with maps "No. 23" through "No. 27." The U.S. maps were signed with informal notes indicating corrections in positions of latitude and longitude, and the Mexican maps were corrected with formal legends.

Sometimes the commissioners signed the maps despite disagreements between them. U.S. and Mexican maps of the lower Río Bravo, as well as maps "No. 21" and "No. 22," diverged in many ways but were signed by the commissioners without explanation. The commissioners tended to accept differences in the portrayal of the course of the Rio Grande, while the actual line of the boundary was depicted only in the vicinity of islands.

The commissioners' third possible response to maps that did not agree was to refuse to sign them. That appears to be what happened with only one map, U.S. map "No. 29." With maps "No. 29," the commissioners showed a concern for consistency in the U.S. and Mexican representations of the course of the Rio Grande that did not intrude upon their evaluation of other maps of the river. The boundary problems revealed in the mapping of the Rio Grande awaited resolution.

CHAPTER SIX

AUTHORITATIVE MAPS AND THE TRUE LINE

I send you a couple of the maps with the trace of the Boundary.
The Boundary as shewn by the dotted lines on these still remains
the Boundary however much the river may have changed since,
or wherever it may now be.

*U.S. Commissioner William H. Emory to
Colonel James Magoffin, 8 November 1856*

*T*HE WANDERING RIO GRANDE INTERTWINED ITSELF
with the future of the finished boundary maps. Its changeable
channel was to become the key to interpretation of the Treaty of Guadalupe Hidalgo, the Treaty of 1853, and international law, determining
the legal status of the maps, their authority, and power. The U.S. and
Mexican commissioners intended to establish the maps as conclusive
evidence of the location of the boundary, declaring that the true line was
the line shown in the maps and views; but the usual understandings of
international law and the governments that the commissioners represented did not explicitly support their ideas. Compelled by the problem
of the wayward Rio Grande, in time the commissioners' views were
tested, and the policies of the U.S. and Mexican governments were
made clear.

One important issue in determining the status of the final maps and
the purposes they would serve was judgment of the permanence of the
demarcation. Whether the boundary line presented in the maps was to

be regarded as fixed or changeable was uncertain. The writers of the Treaty of Guadalupe Hidalgo may have contemplated a permanent line, for the treaty resolved that "the Boundary line established by this Article shall be religiously respected by each of the two Republics, and no change shall ever be made therein, except by the express and free consent of both nations, lawfully given by the General Government of each, in conformity with it's [*sic*] own constitution."[1] There were no explicit provisions, however, for the river boundaries. The Gila River and the Rio Grande were susceptible to constant change: opening new channels and abandoning others, cutting away or building up banks, developing braided channels, and swinging in and out of meanders. Without a clear treaty statement of the effects of such changes upon the location of the boundary, questions were bound to arise.

It was a problem that the boundary commission considered early in the survey. At an official meeting held while U.S. and Mexican parties were engaged in surveys of the Gila River and the Rio Grande, U.S. Surveyor Andrew B. Gray tendered the question of whether the boundary line, "after being once fixed and determined . . . would vary as the course of the several rivers might from time to time vary?" According to his own interpretation of the treaty, he asserted that the line agreed upon by the joint commission and marked with monuments would "always remain the same, however the Gila or Rio Grande might change its course." Mexican Commissioner García Conde concurred in Gray's interpretation and offered an illustration of the point:

> He represented, on a piece of paper, the Gila river with the Town of ——— situated upon its left bank; he then changed the course of the River, turning it above, and thereby cutting off the Town, or in other words throwing it on the right bank. He observed that when the Line was run and marked, the Town was in Mexico, and on the left side of the River; that now it was still in Mexico, although on the right bank, and that the River at that Place was wholly in Mexico; still, he considered the free navigation of the River secured to both Nations. The River-bed he said might change, but the Boundary Line, as marked upon the ground, in accordance with the fifth article of the Treaty, continues unchanged.[2]

The U.S. and Mexican commissions agreed that their demarcation was final and permanent.

A few years later, after the fieldwork of the survey had been completed, an alternative opinion was promulgated by U.S. Attorney General Caleb Cushing in response to further inquiry by the U.S. commission. The opinion, which included a summary of the history of legal doctrines regarding river boundaries, became the official U.S. position for many years and was often cited in disputes about the Rio Grande boundary. The attorney general submitted the following salient points:

> A portion of the boundary is formed by the Rio Bravo which is subject to change its course in two ways, first, by gradual accretion of one of its banks, followed, in many cases, by correspondent degradation of the opposite bank; and, secondly, by the more violent action of the water, leaving its actual bed and forcing for itself a new one in another direction. In case of any such changes in the bed of the river, does the boundary line shift with them, or does that line remain constant where the main course of the river ran as represented by the Maps accompanying the report of the Commissioners? . . .

> . . . whatever changes happen to either bank of the river by accretion on the one, or degradation on the other, that is by the gradual and as it were insensible accession or abstraction of mere particles, the river as it runs continues to be the boundary. One country may, in process of time lose a little of its territory, and the other gain a little, but the territorial relations cannot be reversed by such imperceptible mutations in the course of the river. The general aspect of things remains unchanged. And the convenience of allowing the river to retain its previous function notwithstanding such insensible changes in its course or in either of its banks, outweighs the inconveniences even to the injured party involved in a detriment which happening gradually is inappreciable in the successive movements of its progression.

> But, on the other hand, if, deserting its original bed, the river forces for itself a new channel in another direction, then, the nation through whose territory the river thus breaks its way suffers injury by the loss of territory greater than the benefit of retaining the natural river boundary, and that boundary remains in the middle of the deserted river bed.[3]

Cushing's remarks were based on the legal precepts of accretion and avulsion, often used to guide boundary decisions, which would permit the boundary to remain in the river when the stream changed its course by gradual processes but require it to continue in the deserted channel if the river changed its course suddenly.

Throughout the fieldwork of the survey, however, the joint commission believed that the line was being fixed permanently, regardless of river processes. While awaiting the attorney general's opinion, with production of the final boundary maps under way, Emory restated the views that Gray and García Conde had voiced several years earlier: "The Commissioners concluded and it is thought with correctness that the boundary would remain where the river fixed it, at the time of the Survey, and as shown on the Maps."[4] The Mexican government, meanwhile, continued in its official position that the boundary, once surveyed, was immovable.

By the time the maps were completed and ready for signing, the U.S. and Mexican commissioners' interpretation had become less clear. At their penultimate meeting in Washington, Emory and Salazar recorded in the journal of the joint commission the following declaration:

> The Commissioners think it proper to state that in many details
> along the Rio Bravo, in Topography, and in Latitude and Longitude,
> there are small differences, the legitimate result of scientific opera-
> tions performed under difficult circumstances. These differences are
> explained by notes on the maps, but they in no way affect the Bound-
> ary Line.[5]

At the same meeting in which they noted the discrepancies, the commissioners approved the maps as official records of the demarcation. They accepted the differences in the river shown on the U.S. and Mexican maps while continuing to affirm the stability of the surveyed line.

In addition to the permanence of the demarcation, the other important issue upon which the status of the final maps depended was their standing in international law. The commissioners valued the maps as conclusive proof of the boundary location. With his notice advising Secretary of the Interior Robert McClelland of the completion of the survey, Emory proposed that the maps would fulfill the secretary's request for official evidence of the establishment of the boundary. He advocated the maps' role as follows:

> Uninhabited as a great portion of the line is, many of the monuments
> will be removed by the Indians, and some of them will no doubt be

removed by evil-disposed white men; but the plans representing the topography of the country and views along the line of prominent natural objects, form imperishable evidence not only that the line has been actually run, but they will enable either government to settle any contested point growing out of the removal of the monuments without recourse to resurvey.[6]

Emory expected that the maps would not only attest to the completion of the survey but also verify the position of the line.

Salazar supported Emory's opinion of the importance of the final maps. In Washington, as work on the U.S. and Mexican maps began, the commissioners placed an official statement in the journal of the joint commission affirming the legal authority of the maps. They agreed that,

> Whereas Señor Salazar has stated it to be within his personal knowledge that some of the monuments erected by Mr. Emory were destroyed and others mutilated by the Indians, in the short space of time elapsing between the construction of these monuments and the final inspection of them by Mr. Salazar; and whereas it appears, from the maps and views which have been drawn, that the topographical features of the country, based upon astronomical determinations, are represented in sufficient detail to enable any intelligent person to identify the line at any required point; therefore, be it

> *Resolved,* and agreed upon in joint commission, that these maps and views, duplicate copies of which will be made—one to be deposited with the United States, the other with the Mexican government— shall be the evidence of the location of the true line, and shall be the record to which all disputes between the inhabitants on either side of the line, as to the location of that line, shall be referred; and it is further agreed that the line shown by these maps and views shall be regarded as the true line, from which there shall be no appeal or departure.[7]

The commissioners' prerogative for a ruling on the status of the boundary maps was derived from the United States–Mexico treaties, where their agreements upon the results of the survey operations were granted the same force as the articles of the treaty itself. The commissioners' agreement, it has been noted, gave "to the final maps of the Boundary Survey an all but unique significance. In effect, the maps *were* the boundary, and so remained for another generation."[8]

The maps' significance was not assured, however. Further opinions from U.S. Attorney General Cushing commented upon the commissioners' authority and their assessment of the maps. He supported the commissioners' power to establish the boundary, holding that the "establishment" of the line consisted of the official agreement of the commissioners and that their agreement was conclusive against both governments. At the same time, the attorney general depreciated the authority of the maps, maintaining that "to establish the line, it is not requisite that the maps contemplated by the treaty shall first have been made: that is not the establishment of the line, but only the record or history of its survey." Cushing continued,

> Nor is the completion of calculations or preparation of plans, which the commissioners propose to attend to hereafter, any way material. All that is but illustration or authentic statement of the acts already performed, namely, survey, marking, and establishment of the line.[9]

The attorney general, therefore, advocated the establishment of the boundary by the commissioners but not the maps by which they established it.

Cushing refined his opinion on the maps to consider the river boundaries directly. He differentiated between the status of the maps that defined geometrical lines and those that defined the river boundary, submitting that, in "parts of the boundary, which are to run in parallels of latitude or by straight-line from point to point, . . . the monuments placed by the Commissioners, or the line as otherwise fixed by descriptive words referring to natural objects, or by the drawings and maps of the Commissioners, would, it is plain, be conclusive in all time by force of the stipulations of the treaty." But in the case of the Rio Grande, he said, the boundary was a natural object rather than an astronomical or a geographical line and was, therefore, subject to the principles of public law—that is, the principles of the variability of river boundaries.[10] Since Cushing sanctioned the doctrines of accretion and avulsion rather than a fixed-line interpretation of the boundary, he could not sustain the authority with which the commissioners endowed the final maps.

Cushing's opinions reflected generally accepted readings of international law. Then, as now, international judicial proceedings relied to a great extent on documentary evidence, including materials such as contracts, opinions, letters, minutes, and decrees; but several alternatives to maps were preferred as proofs of boundary location. Unless a map was officially adopted by government representatives responsible for negotiating the boundary, or was made by a commission appointed to survey and map the boundary, the court considered that the boundary lines it portrayed were hearsay evidence. Even official maps, however, were seldom admitted as conclusive in the settlement of boundary disputes. The proofs upon which the maps were founded were regarded as better evidence than the maps.[11] The monuments that identified a boundary demarcation on the ground, or the long acceptance by one state of the possession and dominion over a territory by another, known as the doctrine of acquiescence, were conclusive evidence. Boundaries in rivers were usually understood to be located in the middle of non-navigable rivers and along the main channel of navigation in navigable rivers, and the boundary was to be adjusted and maintained in conformity with the principles of accretion and avulsion.[12]

Nevertheless, the Mexican government supported the line established by the two commissioners and the authority they assigned to the maps. In Mexico's view, the final maps, in conjunction with the commissioners' official resolution, had acquired the status of treaty documents verifying the unalterable position of the line. Mexico rarely wavered from the fixed-line interpretation of the boundary, wishing to establish the river boundaries as permanently and unequivocally as the land boundaries. The U.S. government, on the other hand, beginning with the crystallization of the principles of accretion and avulsion in Attorney General Cushing's opinion, espoused nearly consistently a variable river boundary. The commissioners' and the U.S. attorney general's conflicting interpretations of the function of the final maps coasted by until at length they were tested in the international quarrel over Chamizal.

The scene of the boundary dispute at Chamizal, near present El Paso, was documented in the controversial maps "No. 29." Over time, a greater number of boundary problems afflicted the lower valley of the Rio Grande, where changes in the course of the river disrupted towns, farms, and ranches that lined the riverbanks; but it was map "No. 29" that was premonitory in its making. In 1856 the founder of Magoffinsville, concerned about the river's effects on the boundary, wrote to Emory in Washington describing the "great injury" the river had done in the previous spring, taking "at least 500 yards of [his] land opposite

El Paso" and threatening to "take its channel—'old river' and depopulate Isletta, Socorro, and San Ylisario." [13] Recurring events such as those that had worried Magoffin even before the boundary maps had been completed led to an intractable border dispute in the Chamizal area. Hearings for the Chamizal arbitration held at El Paso in 1911 eventually opened a wider discussion of the entire Rio Grande boundary. [14]

The commissioners' resolutions, the attorney general's opinions, and the final maps became evidence in the Chamizal hearings. The case became important for the development of theory relating to the United States–Mexico boundary as representatives of the U.S. and Mexico attempted to discern the true intention of the Treaty of Guadalupe Hidalgo and debated the meaning of the original boundary survey. Mexico adhered to the fixed-line theory endorsed by Emory and Salazar, while the United States supported Attorney General Cushing's interpretation, holding that the river boundary should conform to generally accepted principles of international law. It followed from Cushing's opinion that the original survey was not meant to establish a fixed line, nor, it was argued, did the commissioners expect to do so.

Convincing evidence was provided by the final boundary maps. It was pointed out that the maps contained discrepancies noted by the commissioners, who had explained in the journal of the joint commission that differences in details of topography, latitude, and longitude shown in the maps owed to the difficult circumstances of the survey but that the differences in no way affected the boundary. The U.S. agent at the hearings made the point that it was not reasonable to suppose that Commissioners Emory and Salazar would have thought that the differences in their maps of the river could have no effect on the boundary, if the boundary were fixed and invariable. The conclusion to be drawn was that, "if it had been understood in 1857 that the boundary marked under the treaties of 1848 and 1853 was to be fixed and invariable, one or the other of the two surveys necessarily would have had to have been adopted by the two governments as the official survey." [15]

The outcome of the hearings was rejection of the fixed-line interpretation of the Treaty of Guadalupe Hidalgo. Conclusive evidence that the boundary was meant to shift with the course of the Rio Grande, it was thought, was rendered by the Treaty of 1853, which restated that the boundary was to run "as provided in the fifth article of the treaty of Guadalupe Hidalgo, thence as defined in the said article, up the middle of that river [Rio Grande]."[16] The presiding commissioner at the hearings summarized the evidence of the two treaties as follows:

During the five years which elapsed between the two treaties, notable variations of the course of the Rio Grande took place, to such an extent that surveys made in the early part of 1853, at intervals of six months, revealed discrepancies which are accounted for only by reason of the changes which the river had undergone in the meantime. Notwithstanding the existence of such changes, the Treaty of 1853 reiterates the provision that the boundary line runs up the middle of the river, which could not have been an accurate statement upon the fixed line theory.[17]

The commissioners under the Treaty of Guadalupe Hidalgo and the Treaty of 1853 had exceeded their mandate, it was held, in expressing their views that the fixed-line theory was the proper construction of the treaties.

The contradiction between the commissioners' stated approval of the invariable line and the representation of the river boundaries in the final maps remained unexplained. If the commissioners were originally proponents of the fixed-line theory, by the time they signed the finished maps the expression of their views had become equivocal. In the production of the final maps, even though the two commissions strove in many ways for agreement between their documents, they did not seek identity in the depictions of the course of the river. Moreover, in only a few special instances did the final maps draw a definite line in a determined channel of the Rio Grande: a dashed and dotted line on Mexican map "No. 1" showed the principal channel between Brownsville and the *desembocadura* agreed upon by Jiménez and Radziminski; dashed lines on both Mexican and U.S. maps partitioned the islands; and the rejected U.S. map "No. 29" displayed a dashed-line boundary all along the river. Throughout most of the Rio Grande, the surveys on which the maps were based were not done in such a way as to establish a fixed line in a determined channel. In the final maps, the commissioners did not prescribe an interpretation of the ambiguous boundary treaties.[18]

Many years after the original survey, the land boundary was also reexamined. Since the area crossed by the land boundary was largely uninhabited when the line was first run, few monuments had been erected, for it was thought that the inhospitable environment would prohibit future settlement, and no purpose was seen in demarcating the line closely. The original survey established fifty-two monuments from the Rio Grande to the Pacific, the distances between monuments varying from one-eighth of a mile to ninety miles. The quality of the monuments was highly variable, ranging from the marble monument on a pedestal at the initial point on the Pacific, to various monuments of cast iron; of cut stone, with and without cement; and of rocks piled in symmetrical heaps.[19] Many of the monuments could be easily obliterated or lost from view, and, from various motives, many were intentionally destroyed. Salazar and Emory noted that some monuments had already been destroyed or mutilated by Indians. Others may have been dismantled by local inhabitants for use as building material. A traveler through the valley of Los Nogales just eight years after the survey found one of Emory's monuments torn down and judged that "wandering bands of Sonoranians, in their hatred of every thing American, had doubtless mutilated it as an expression of national antipathy."[20] Accusations were exchanged in both directions, however, for Sonoran citizens filed complaints about boundary monuments that were destroyed or moved by American ranchers and miners in order to gain control of land and resources.[21] In order to resolve such disputes, the boundary was resurveyed and fully monumented by the International Boundary Commission of 1891–96.

The resurvey of the boundary uncovered errors in the original demarcation—a finding that was to be expected. In the forty years that had elapsed between the surveys, advances in technology had made possible more accurate measurement of angles and distances and more accurate determinations of latitude and longitude. The running of the line in 1891–96 was also aided by the country's development; the survey across the desert could be sustained without interruption by problems of simple survival. The location of the boundary was found to be in error relative to its delimitation because it had been defined mathematically—that is, in terms of parallels, meridians, and azimuth lines; positions specified in the boundary treaties, such as the intersection of the 31°20′ parallel and the 111° meridian, were not located where exact numbers would place them.

Legally, however, the boundary was not in error. Since the Treaty of Guadalupe Hidalgo and the Treaty of 1853 had empowered the commissioners to establish the line and had granted their decisions the same force as the treaties themselves, international law confirmed that the commissioners' line should supersede the treaty delimitations. The boundary established in the original survey was also supported by the doctrine of acquiescence, holding that a marked boundary line, once accepted by the interested parties, becomes the true line, whether or not it follows the written description; a monumented line on the ground has precedence over abstract lines of latitude or longitude shown on maps or determined by geodetic survey.[22] The monuments that were not in the geographical positions defined by the boundary treaties were not in error but had become correct upon their adoption by the commissioners and the two governments. The true boundary was the boundary marked on the ground.

Although Salazar and Emory agreed that the final maps would be the legal evidence of the true line and believed that their agreement was binding because of the authority conferred on them by the boundary treaties, in subsequent events the final maps did not attain the status of conclusive proof of the location of the boundary. Neither the precedents of international law nor the U.S. government's unwillingness to support a fixed-line interpretation of the boundary treaties would permit the maps to bear such decisive authority. A fixed-line interpretation might have invested the maps with greater authority: if disputes arose in relation to changes in the rivers, the original boundary maps might have provided an important reference to recover the original disposition of the meandering rivers. Instead, the application of doctrines of international law to determine the true line between the United States and Mexico resulted in both land and water boundaries that differed on the ground from the representations in the final maps.

Nevertheless, the commissioners' resolution endowed the maps with an unusual authority that was accepted for half a century. The idea of the true line expressed by the commissioners was a crucial issue debated in the Chamizal hearings. Even though in international law the proofs of maps were not valued highly, the final maps—based on original survey, signed by the commissioners representing the U.S. and Mexican governments, and accepted by the two governments—possessed the highest possible evidentiary value that legal precedents would allow. The maps became evidence in the Chamizal case for their own undoing. It was the commissioners' lack of commitment to the fixed line, demonstrated in the maps, that overthrew the maps' authority.

Cushing's principles of accretion and avulsion proved unworkable, however, in application to the boundary rivers between the United

States and Mexico. The principles were based on precedents from western Europe and the eastern United States and had been formed in response to the behavior of rivers in humid regions of the world. The actions of arid-zone rivers, commonly involving rapid and violent erosion as well as gradual avulsion processes that produce new channels, were inexplicable in terms of the classical law of fluvial boundaries.[23] One after another case of disputed sovereignty or land ownership was produced by continual change in the course of the Rio Grande, and the legal status of river processes that did not fit the classical definitions of accretion and avulsion were argued extensively. One authority commented, "It is probable that no other international boundary represents such a tangle of accretion and avulsion cases."[24]

A succession of boundary treaties between the United States and Mexico attempted to resolve the questions raised by the Treaty of Guadalupe Hidalgo. The present river boundary, established by the Treaty of 1970, continues to have its legal basis in the Treaty of 1853, which in turn retains the Rio Grande boundary surveyed under the Treaty of Guadalupe Hidalgo. The Treaty of 1970, however, abandoned the precepts of accretion and avulsion to prescribe a boundary that remains in the river. The Rio Grande boundary is mobile, always located in the middle of the channel that in normal flow has the greatest average width—a determination that is continuously maintained through surveys by the International Boundary and Water Commission. In addition, shifts in the courses of the Rio Grande and the Colorado River are now highly controlled through dams and rectified channels.[25]

The Treaty of 1970 also clarified the offshore boundaries, delimiting a boundary off the Pacific Coast and revising the boundary in the Gulf of Mexico to suit changing international concepts of maritime boundaries. The treaty allowed for the northward and southward shifting of the mouth of the Rio Grande by establishing a pivot point as the base for the seaward boundary. Maritime boundaries outside the twelve-nautical-mile extent of the territorial sea, such as boundaries of the Exclusive Economic Zone of Mexico and the Fishery Conservation Zone of the United States, continue to be developed in treaty agreements.[26]

The land boundary continues to adhere to the line of the original survey. Despite the differences between their locations and those specified in the treaties and shown on the maps, the monuments established by the survey are still recognized. After the resurvey of 1891–96, both the United States and Mexico acknowledged that if the land boundary were to be rectified, a new treaty would be needed; but the possibility was not pursued.[27]

The enduring land boundary and the mobile river boundaries maintained by the U.S. and Mexican sections of the International Boundary and Water Commission are legacies of the original boundary survey. It was significant for the development of boundary relations that the original survey was actually two surveys, one by the U.S. commission and one by the Mexican commission, both with the goal of producing authoritative maps. That both commissions succeeded in fulfilling their mission had fateful consequences.

Although the efforts of the Mexican engineers have often been overlooked, the final maps testify to the accomplishments of each of the four Mexican commissions. The first Comisión de Límites Mexicana completed surveys for Mexican final maps "No. 53" and "No. 54" on the California coast. Members of the second commission completed the demarcation of the California boundary conjointly with the U.S. commission, to produce maps "No. 46" through "No. 52," although the Mexican final maps were copied from the U.S. maps. The second commission also completed surveys for ten maps of the Río Bravo, "No. 1" through "No. 8" and "No. 28" and "No. 29," and made reconnaissance surveys for maps "No. 23" through "No. 27." In addition, the first and second commissions surveyed the junction of the Río Gila and Río Colorado, half of the Río Gila, and the boundaries of New Mexico in accordance with the Treaty of Guadalupe Hidalgo and the Bartlett–García Conde compromise. The third commission completed surveys for maps "No. 21" and "No. 22" on the Río Bravo and maps "No. 30" through "No. 33" westward from the river and made reconnaissance surveys for maps "No. 34" through "No. 36." Working with the U.S. surveyors, members of the third commission provided data for maps of the land boundary and the Río Colorado, "No. 38" through "No. 45." Mexico's remaining final maps, "No. 9" through "No. 20," showing the canyon region of the Río Bravo, and land boundary map "No. 37" were copied by the fourth commission from the U.S. final maps, with no Mexican fieldwork.

The final maps of the U.S. commission support the traditional honor given Emory as the individual who fulfilled the boundary survey, since his name appeared on all of the maps as director of the survey. The nine maps of the California line, "No. 46" through "No. 54," were based on results of the Weller commission. Surveys by the Bartlett commission resulted in eighteen maps and part of a nineteenth sheet, all depicting the Rio Grande; these were maps "No. 8" through "No. 14," part of map "No. 15," and sheets "No. 18" through "No. 28." There was also one map made of islands in the Rio Grande, "[Sheet No. 5]." None of the maps mentioned Bartlett as commissioner, however, as all of the work on the river was supervised by Emory, who saw that he received credit for the work he directed. The Bartlett commission also surveyed the entire Gila River, while the section between the headwaters of the Gila and the Rio Grande was probably never completed, although Bartlett claimed that it was.[28] The Campbell commission surveyed sections of the Rio Grande for maps "No. 1" through "No. 7," part of map "No. 15," maps "No. 16" and "No. 17," and maps of islands in the Rio Grande, "Sheet No. 1" through "Sheet No. 4." Once again the surveys were immediately directed by Emory, who was credited rather than Campbell on all fourteen maps. The Emory commission produced seventeen maps of the boundary delimited by the Treaty of 1853, maps "No. 29" through "No. 45," including maps of the United States–Sonora azimuth line surveyed conjointly with the Mexican commission.

The Mexican commission's incomplete boundary survey resulted from its lack of adequate support by the troubled Mexican government. Having fought and lost a disastrous war with the United States and suffering from continuous internal turmoil, the Mexican economy was too depleted to support a scientific project. Always short on personnel, the Mexican commission could not deploy its engineers to several, simultaneous surveys as the U.S. commission could. Mexican engineers had fewer instruments than they needed. They were often impeded by lack of supplies and protective escorts. Working more slowly, the Mexican commission did not cover as much ground during the time spent on the survey as the U.S. commission did; so that when the fieldwork was closed—under some pressure from the U.S. commission—the Mexican survey was unfinished. On the other hand, the Mexican engineers organized and executed extensive geodetic and topographic surveys, despite the difficulties they faced. They expeditiously surveyed the land boundary under the Treaty of Guadalupe Hidalgo while the U.S. commission was paralyzed in internal disagreement and debate over the Bartlett–García Conde compromise. They traversed and made observations on most of the boundary. Even if the Mexican commission did not achieve the survey of the entire boundary, its considerable accomplishment merits recognition.

Because of treaty requirements, it was necessary that both a U.S. and a Mexican commission survey the boundary. Interactions between the two commissions during the survey affected not only political events but also influenced the content of the boundary maps they produced. Over the course of the survey, the commissions found three possibilities for interaction open to them: they could carry out separate surveys in isolation from each other; conduct surveys independently and engage in field consultation; or cooperate in a single survey.[29] Each of the commissions' modes of interaction during the survey had its influences upon the resulting maps and their role in boundary history.

While the prolonged dispute over the Bartlett–García Conde compromise played out at higher levels of politics and diplomacy, the two commissions worked in disregard of each other in separate surveys of the Rio Grande. When the final maps, "No. 2" through "No. 8" and "No. 21" through "No. 29," were later drawn up and compared, many points of disagreement were to be found between the maps. Geographical positions of latitude and longitude could be inconsistent; topographical representations of both physical features and cultural features were often at variance; and the course of the Rio Grande was sometimes strikingly different on U.S. and Mexican maps. The seriousness of the discrepancies in the representation of the river was revealed at the Chamizal hearings. The commissions' isolation from each other during the surveys ultimately affected the maps' legal status and the resolution of the river boundary question.

The tendency of the commissions was to operate independently, meeting to compare data, consult in decision making, and form agreements. Cooperation was achieved while each side engaged in give-and-take in its own interests, resolving differences without great dissatisfaction on either side. Final maps based on independent operations were made of several of the boundary's turning points, including map "No. 1" at the mouth of the Rio Grande; maps "No. 53" and "No. 54" of the initial point on the Pacific and the western end of the California azimuth line; and maps "No. 44" and "No. 45" containing the eastern end of the California azimuth line and the initial point on the Colorado. The results of independent surveys with field consultations were U.S. and Mexican maps that agreed in their representations of the boundary but differed in the selection and portrayal of topographical and cultural features.

They had surveyed the same country and could agree on the location of the boundary, but the two commissions made different maps, nonetheless. Despite their own understanding of their work as the application of scientific methods to produce accurate and objective maps, the maps that resulted from the U.S. and Mexican commissions' independent surveys reflected goals and outlooks distinct to each commission. Their maps were not neutral records. Different visions of the regions presented in the maps often resulted from the commissions' different approaches to the survey.

The Mexican commission directed much of its effort into triangulation and topographical surveys, providing extensive and detailed views of the border landscape in their maps. The topographical detail offered a definitive visual record of the location of the line, demonstrating its relationship to the surrounding environment, even without reference to determinations of latitude and longitude. The Mexican engineers were eager to see the line fixed permanently in order to protect Mexican territory from further U.S. intrusion and, by pinning down the line to the landscape, intended to prevent encroachment. In addition to physical features, the maps often included a wealth of cultural information. The inventory of villages, ranchos, and cultivated fields, most of them built up by Mexican citizens, emphasized the Mexican presence in the borderlands. It may be speculated that the maps were meant to show that a country so thoroughly occupied by Mexican inhabitants must certainly be a part of the Mexican nation. The Mexican commission's maps might be interpreted as testimony to the injustice of the U.S. conquest.

During the survey, U.S. aspirations for further territorial acquisition persisted, animating the controversy over the Bartlett–García Conde agreement and perhaps endowing the U.S. commission with a flexible attitude toward the boundary delimitation. U.S. surveyors emphasized astronomical and geodetic work for rapid location of the line; their lack of interest in topography disclosed little of the Mexican occupation of the country. A more pressing priority than topographical surveying for the U.S. commission was exploration of the United States' vast new domain with its opportunities for development and exploitation. The commission's interest in gathering information was expressed in the abundant results of its scientific activities. The restricted topographical representation on many of the U.S. maps conformed to Emory's prescription for surveying the line and the countryside by measurement for one mile to each side of the boundary. For U.S. purposes, it was suitable to perceive the borderlands as empty wilderness available for settlement and development. In the U.S. maps, wilderness roads swept across great, empty expanses, inviting settlers into an open, U.S. territory.

Although the commissions preferred to conduct their surveys separately, pursuing their own methods and their own national interests, at various times they attempted to cooperate in a single survey of a section of the line. Maps "No. 46" through "No. 52" of the California line and "No. 30" through "No. 36" of the boundary west from the Rio Grande depended upon efforts at cooperative surveys that were not entirely fulfilled. A successful alliance of the commissions, "working conjointly," produced maps "No. 38" through "No. 44" of the United States–Sonora azimuth line. The U.S. and Mexican maps based on cooperative surveys, although not identical, agreed in the location of the boundary and were similar in their topographical representations. The United States–Sonora azimuth line maps combined a determination of the azimuth that depended largely on U.S. observations and calculations with a full display of topographical information gathered by techniques instigated by the Mexican commission. The collaboration between the commissions resulted in maps that were more consistent than any others for which both commissions performed surveys.

The harmony among members of the U.S. and Mexican commissions and their teamwork in the tasks of surveying made the United States–Sonora azimuth survey a model for United States–Mexico cooperation. Unmistakably, ill-feeling engendered by the U.S.-Mexican War and nationalistic pride and pain conditioned the relationship between the commissions; the tensions between them have often been emphasized. The commissions' ability to overcome enmity and cooperate as they did was, therefore, all the more impressive. The unified azimuth-line survey evolved from the commissions' earlier efforts on other sections of the land boundary and depended upon the regard for the equality of the two commissions and the sovereignty of the two nations that underlay all of the commissions' surveying and mapmaking activities. The original boundary survey offered the example of Mexican and U.S. engineers working together in an environment of mutual respect. As a foundation for a continuing relationship between the United States and Mexico in maintaining the international boundary, it extends a prospect of amicable boundary relations.

The actions of the U.S. and Mexican commissions and their interactions in surveying and mapping set the course of boundary history.

When U.S. and Mexican field parties worked in isolation on the Rio Grande, their surveys became the bases for maps that did not agree in their representations of the boundary. The maps that disagreed became keys to the construction of the boundary treaties and the maintenance of the line. Maps that agreed were made when U.S. and Mexican field parties met to compare their surveys and share results, when they cooperated in a unified survey, or when Mexican cartographers copied U.S. maps. The boundary shown in the maps that agreed became the boundary adopted by the U.S. and Mexican governments, while the processes of surveying and mapping opened opportunities for cooperation.

At the close of the survey, even the most intransigent among the members of the U.S. and Mexican commissions reflected on the harmony that had reigned between the two commissions. Said Commissioner Emory, reporting formally,

> It is proper to state that the utmost harmony has existed on this Commission between the Officers of both governments, and that all questions likely to produce the least difference have been settled harmoniously and it is believed to the entire satisfaction of both Governments.[30]

First Engineer Jiménez expressed more expansively the respect and sympathy shared among the engineers who closed the fieldwork of the survey:

> In all the time that the scientific works practiced in association with Mr. Michler continued, the best harmony reigned among all the individuals of the two Sections and between the officers of both escorts; this harmony contributed in a very effective way to the happy conclusion of the work, because we helped each other mutually in all the obstacles that we had to overcome; . . . When at last the two commissions separated for their respective destinies, it was with demonstrations of deep affection, expressing seven months of continued good will and mutual suffering in the desert.[31]

The two commissions separated in dignity, each to its own capital, bearing its own maps, documents of their common work on the distant frontier.

APPENDIX
Map Authorities

THE NAMES OF THE MAP AUTHORITIES GIVEN IN THE TITLE PANELS
and artist's credits on the manuscript boundary maps of 1857 are listed below.
Maps included are the fifty-four sectional maps, four index maps, and five island maps held in the U.S. National Archives, Washington, D.C., and the
fifty-four sectional maps and four general maps held in the Mapoteca Manuel
Orozco y Berra, Mexico City. Each person's military rank or position on the
boundary commission and his contribution to the mapmaking process are
given as stated on the maps, together with the map numbers on which the
credits appear.

Maps of the United States Boundary Commission

Alemán, Manuel, *second engineer:*
   triangulation and topography by, 38
   triangulation and topography assisted by, 39, 40, 41, 42, 43, 44, 45
Campbell, Hugh:
   latitude and longitude assisted by, 38
Chandler, M. T. W., *assistant surveyor:*
   surveyed by, 18, 19, 20, 21, 22
   triangulation and topography by, 37, 38
Clark, John H.:
   latitude and longitude assisted by, 29
   latitude and longitude by, 38
de Zeyk, A.:
   drawn by, 36
Díaz, Agustín, *second engineer:*
   triangulation and topography by, 38
   triangulation and topography assisted by, 39, 40, 41, 42, 43, 44, 45

Maps of the Comisión de Límites Mexicana

NOTES

INTRODUCTION

1. Alexander Marchant, *Boundaries of the Latin American Republics: An Annotated List of Documents, 1493–1943* (Washington, D.C.: U.S. Government Printing Office, 1944), 325, 350; David J. Weber, "Conflicts and Accommodations: Hispanic and Anglo-American Borders in Historical Perspective, 1670–1853," *Journal of the Southwest* 39 (1997): 3–14.

2. Stephen Barr Jones, *Boundary-Making: A Handbook for Statesmen, Treaty Editors and Boundary Commissioners* (Washington, D.C.: Carnegie Endowment for International Peace, 1945; reprint, New York: Johnson Reprint, 1971), 5.

3. Jones, *Boundary-Making*, 108–25, 151–55; L. J. Bouchez, "The Fixing of Boundaries in International Boundary Rivers," *International and Comparative Law Quarterly* 12 (1963): 789–817.

4. Charles I. Bevans, comp., *Treaties and Other International Agreements of the United States of America, 1776–1949* (Washington, D.C.: Department of State, 1968–76), 9:791–806, esp. 794.

5. Lassa Francis Lawrence Oppenheim, *Peace*, vol. 1 of *International Law: A Treatise*, 8th ed., ed. Herah Lauterpacht (New York: David McKay Co., 1955), 487–92; Karl M. Schmitt, "The Problem of Maritime Boundaries in U.S.-Mexican Relations," *Natural Resources Journal* 22 (1982): 139.

6. Bevans, *Treaties*, 9:794.

7. J. Disturnell, *Mapa de los Estados Unidos de Méjico, según lo organizado y definido por las varias actas del Congreso de dicha República: y construido por las mejores autoridades* [map], rev. ed. [7th], 1" = about 70 mi. (New York: J. Disturnell, 1847), Treaty series no. 207, Government Documents Having General Legal Effect, Record Group 11, National Archives, Washington, D.C.

8. Gerhard Von Glahn, *Law among Nations: An Introduction to Public International Law*, 6th ed. (New York: Macmillan Publishing Co., 1992), 399–400. On navigation of the Rio Grande, see Article VII of the Treaty of Guadalupe Hidalgo, in Bevans, *Treaties*, 9:796.

9. Jones, *Boundary-Making*, 60.

10. Bevans, *Treaties*, 9:794–95. In the English-language version of the Treaty of Guadalupe Hidalgo, the title of the map was translated into English.

11. The "editions" should properly be called "states" because they were printed from the same plates. Lawrence Martin, "Disturnell's Map," in *Treaties and Other International Acts of the United States of America,* ed. Hunter Miller (Washington, D.C.: Department of State, 1937), 5:340–45; Carl Irving Wheat, *Mapping the Transmississippi West, 1540–1861* (San Francisco: Institute of Historical Cartography, 1957–63), 2:82–87; Jack D. Rittenhouse, *Disturnell's Treaty Map: The Map That Was Part of the Guadalupe Hidalgo Treaty on Southwestern Boundaries, 1848* (Santa Fe: Stagecoach Press, 1965), 12–13.

12. Martin, "Disturnell's Map," 351.

13. William H. Goetzmann, "The United States–Mexican Boundary Survey, 1848–1853," *Southwestern Historical Quarterly* 62 (1958): 167–69; Martin, "Disturnell's Map," 362.

14. William Henry Chase Whiting, "Journal of William Henry Chase Whiting, 1849," in *Exploring Southwestern Trails, 1846–1854,* ed. Ralph P. Bieber and Averam B. Bender (Glendale, Calif.: Arthur H. Clark, 1938), 310; Joseph Richard Werne, "Pedro García Conde: El trazado de límites con Estados Unidos desde el punto de vista mexicano (1848–1853)," *Historia Mexicana* 36 (1986): 117–18.

15. John Russell Bartlett, "Official Journal," 1849–52 (Providence, R.I.: John Carter Brown Library, microfilm), 34–35, Manuscripts Division, Library of Congress, Washington, D.C.

16. Near the Initial Point opposite to Doña Ana, 24 April 1851, Proceedings, 1850–57, Entry 396, Preliminary Inventory 170, Records Relating to International Boundaries, Record Group 76, National Archives, Washington, D.C.; Whipple to Bartlett, 23 August 1852, Letters Relating to Accounts, 1850–60, Entry 437, Preliminary Inventory 170, Records Relating to International Boundaries, Record Group 76, National Archives, Washington, D.C.

17. George P. Hammond, ed., *The Treaty of Guadalupe Hidalgo, February Second 1848* (Berkeley: Friends of the Bancroft Library, 1949), 73–75.

18. Bevans, *Treaties*, 9:795.

19. Juan Pantoja, "Plano del puerto de S. Diego" [ms. tracing of map], 1802, copied n.d., Copies of Maps Filed with the Treaty of 1848, Entry 414, Preliminary Inventory 170, Records Relating to International Boundaries, Record Group 76, National Archives, Washington, D.C.; Lawrence Martin, "The Plan of the Port of San Diego," in *Treaties and Other International Acts of the United States of America,* ed. Hunter Miller (Washington, D.C.: Department of State, 1937), 5:371. The full title of the atlas from which the tracings were made is given by Martin as "Atlas para el viage de las goletas Sutil y Mexicana al reconocimiento del estrecho de Juan de Fuca en 1792, publicado en 1802" (Atlas for the voyage of the schooners *Sutil* and *Mexicana* to the reconnaissance of the Strait of Juan de Fuca in 1792, published in 1802).

20. Paul Neff Garber, *The Gadsden Treaty* (Gloucester, Mass.: Peter Smith, 1923; reprint, 1959); Josefina Zoraida Vázquez and Lorenzo Meyer, *The United States and Mexico* (Chicago: University of Chicago Press, 1985), 60–61.

21. Bevans, *Treaties,* 9:812–16, esp. 813.

22. U.S. Section, International Boundary and Water Commission, *The International Boundary and Water Commission, United States and Mexico* (El Paso: United States Section, 1990, photocopy), 1.

23. Engelmann to Emory, 8 July 1854, Copies of Letters Received by the Fourth U.S. Commissioner, 1854–57, Entry 401, Preliminary Inventory 170, Records Relating to International Boundaries, Record Group 76, National Archives, Washington, D.C.

24. William H. Goetzmann, *Army Exploration in the American West, 1803–1863* (New Haven: Yale University Press, 1959; reprint, Lincoln: University of Nebraska Press, 1979), 438; Manuel Orozco y Berra, *Apuntes para la historia de la geografía en México* (Mexico City: Francisco Diaz de Leon, 1881), 496.

25. Jorge L. Tamayo, *Geografía general de México,* 2d ed. (Mexico City: Instituto Mexicano de Investigaciones Económicas, 1962), 1:63–67; Alberto María Carreño, *México y los Estados Unidos de America: Apuntaciones para la historia del acrecentamiento territorial de los Estados Unidos a costa de México desde la epoca colonial hasta nuestros días* (Mexico City: Imprenta Victoria, 1922), facing p. 273, 273.

26. Antonio García y Cubas, *Atlas geográfico, estadístico é histórico de la República mexicana* (Mexico City: Imprenta de José Mariano Fernandez de Lara, 1858), 1.

27. Campbell to Emory, 18 February 1858, Letters Sent Concerning Boundary Surveys, 1849–1861, Entry 559, Preliminary Inventory, Records of the Office of the Secretary of the Interior, Record Group 48, National Archives, Washington, D.C.; [U.S. Boundary Commission], *Map of the United States and Their Territories between the Mississippi and the Pacific Ocean and Part of Mexico* [map], 1:6,000,000, in William H. Emory, *Report on the United States and Mexican Boundary Survey Made under the Direction of the Secretary of the Interior,* 34th Cong., 1st sess., 1857, H. Ex. Doc. 135.

28. [Office of Pacific Railroad Surveys], *Map of the Territory of the United States from the Mississippi to the Pacific Ocean* [map], comp. Gouverneur K. Warren, 1:3,000,000 ([Washington, D.C.]: Department of War, 1857); Frank N. Schubert, "A Tale of Two

Cartographers: Emory, Warren, and Their Maps of the Trans-Mississippi West," in *Exploration and Mapping of the American West*, ed. Donna P. Koepp (Chicago: Speculum Orbis Press for the Map and Geography Round Table of the American Library Association, 1986), 53; Carl Irving Wheat, *Mapping the American West, 1540–1857* (Worcester, Mass.: American Antiquarian Society, 1954), 161; Goetzmann, *Army Exploration*, 313; Seymour I. Schwartz and Ralph E. Ehrenberg, *The Mapping of America* (New York: Harry N. Abrams, 1980), 287.

29. U.S. Congress, *Report of the Boundary Commission upon the Survey and Re-Marking of the Boundary between the United States and Mexico West of the Rio Grande, 1891 to 1896*, 55th Cong., 2d sess., 1898, S. Doc. 247, 1:13–18, esp. 17, 1:53–56; United States and Mexico International Boundary Commission, 1882, *Memoria de la Sección Mexicana de la Comisión Internacional de Límites entre México y los Estados Unidos que restableció los monumentos de El Paso al Pacífico* (New York: John Polhemus and Co., 1901), 106–7.

30. Convention between the United States of America and the United States of Mexico to Facilitate the Carrying Out of the Principles Contained in the Treaty of November 12, 1884, and to Avoid the Difficulties Occasioned by Reason of the Changes Which Take Place in the Bed of the Rio Grande and That of the Colorado River, in Bevans, *Treaties*, 9:877–80.

31. Treaty between the United States of America and the United States of Mexico Respecting Utilization of Waters of the Colorado and Tijuana Rivers and of the Rio Grande, in Bevans, *Treaties*, 9:1166–92.

32. U.S. Department of State, *United States Treaties and Other International Agreements*, vol. 23, pt. 1, *1972* (Washington, D.C.: U.S. Government Printing Office, 1973), 371–445; Stephen Mumme, "Innovation and Reform in Transboundary Resource Management: A Critical Look at the International Boundary and Water Commission, United States and Mexico," *Natural Resources Journal* 33 (1993): 94–95.

33. J. Alberto Villasana and R. B. Southard, "Cartographic Cooperation along the United States–Mexico Border," *Revista Cartográfica* 32 (1977): 20–24; see, for example, U.S. Geological Survey in cooperation with the U.S. Customs Service and the Dirección General de Geografía, Mexico, *United States–Mexico Border Color Image Maps* [maps], 203 sheets, 1:25,000 (Reston, Va.: U.S. Geological Survey, 1989).

CHAPTER ONE   On the Line: Field Surveys

1. Charles I. Bevans, comp., *Treaties and Other International Agreements of the United States of America, 1776–1949* (Washington, D.C.: Department of State, 1968–76), 9:795.

2. Bevans, *Treaties*, 9:813.

3. Manuel Orozco y Berra, *Apuntes para la historia de la geografía en México* (Mexico City: Francisco Diaz de Leon, 1881), 434, 462; Harry P. Hewitt, "The Mexican Boundary Survey Team: Pedro García Conde in California," *Western Historical Quarterly* 21 (1990): 193–94. I am thankful to Héctor Mendoza Vargas for most helpfully bringing Harry Hewitt's work to my attention.

4. William H. Emory, *Report on the United States and Mexican Boundary Survey Made under the Direction of the Secretary of the Interior*, 34th Cong., 1st sess., 1857, H. Ex. Doc. 135, 1:5; José Joaquín Izquierdo, *La primera casa de las ciencias en México: El Real Seminario de Minería (1792–1811)* (Mexico City: Ediciones Ciencia, 1958), 26, 249–52; Gabriel Cuevas, *El glorioso Colegio Militar Mexicano en un siglo (1824–1924)* (Mexico City: S. Turanzas del Valle, 1937), 18, 27.

5. Lenerd E. Brown, "Survey of the United States Mexico Boundary—1849–1855: Background Study" (United States Department of the Interior, National Park Service, Division of History, Office of Archeology and Historic Preservation, 1969, photocopy), 86–94, 114–20.

6. Miguel A. Sánchez Lamego, *Generales de ingenieros del ejercito mexicano, 1821–1914* (Mexico City: N.p., 1952), 134–39; Pedro García Conde, *Ensayo estadístico sobre el estado de Chihuahua* (Chihuahua: Imprenta del gobierno a cargo de C. Ramos, 1842). On the "Carta geográfica del estado de Chihuahua" [ca. 1836], see U.S. Congress, *Report of the Secretary of the Interior, Communicating, in Compliance with a Resolution of the Senate, a Report from Mr. Bartlett on the Subject of the Boundary Line between the United States and Mexico*, 32d Cong., 2d sess., 1853, S. Ex. Doc. 41, 8–9, and copy of map.

7. Eli de Gortari, *La ciencia en la historia de México* (Mexico City: Fondo de Cultura Económica, 1963; reprint, Mexico City: Editorial Grijalbo, 1980), 257–58; Santiago Ramírez, *Datos para la historia del Colegio de Minería recogidos y compilados bajo la forma de efemérides* (Mexico City: Imprenta del Gobierno Federal, 1890), 321, 328, 396.

8. Alberto María Carreño, *México y los Estados Unidos de America: Apuntaciones para la historia del acrecentamiento territorial de los Estados Unidos a costa de México desde la epoca colonial hasta nuestros días* (Mexico City: Imprenta Victoria, 1922), 272; U.S. Congress, *Report of the Secretary of the Interior Made in Compliance with a Resolution of the Senate Calling for Information in Relation to the Commission Appointed to Run and Mark the Boundary between the United States and Mexico*, 32d Cong., 1st sess., 1852, S. Ex. Doc. 119, 56–65: his name is misspelled "F. M. de Cherero."

9. Miguel A. Sánchez Lamego, *El Colegio Militar y la defensa de Chapultepec en septiembre de 1847* (Mexico City: N.p., 1947), 44, 68; José Salazar Ylarregui, *Datos de los trabajos astronómicos y topográficos, dispuestos en forma de diario, practicados durante el año de 1849 y principios de 1850 por la Comisión de Límites Mexicana en la línea que divide esta república de la de los Estados-Unidos* (Mexico City: Imprenta de Juan R. Navarro, 1850), 8.

10. Hardcastle to Emory, 2 May 1851, Letters Received from the Fourth U.S. Commissioner, 1849–60, Entry 425, Preliminary Inventory 170, Records Relating to International Boundaries, Record Group 76, National Archives, Washington, D.C. Hardcastle referred to Ramírez's assistant as Señor Samora; Brown, *Survey of the United States Mexico Boundary*, 164, gives his name as Jose I. Tamora. Carreño, *México y los Estados Unidos*, 281; Francisco Jiménez, "Diario-memoria de los trabajos científicos practicados bajo la dirección de Francisco Jiménez, 1er Ingeniero de la Comisión de Límites Mexicana conforme a las instrucciones del Señor Comisionado Don José Salazar Ilarregui, a

quien se hace entrega de ellos," 1857, 9–35, Special Collections, University Library, University of Texas at El Paso.

11. Juan B. Espejo, "Informe de una expedición para el trazo del meridiano en el extremo occidental del paralelo 32°22′ boreal," 1852, Carpeta no. 43, no. 6, Diario del Gral. Pedro García Conde sobre los límites de las dos Californias—en relación con los trabajos astronómicos y topográficos, Expediente X-2-1, Límites y Aguas Internacionales, Archivo Histórico Genaro Estrada, Secretaría de Relaciones Exteriores, Mexico City.

12. Miguel A. Sánchez Lamego, "Agustín Díaz, ilustre cartógrafo mexicano," *Historia Mexicana* 24 (1975): 556–65; Cuevas, *Glorioso Colegio Militar*, 363; Sánchez Lamego, *Defensa de Chapultepec*, 44, 66.

13. Jiménez, "Diario-memoria," 22–24, 134–35; Orozco y Berra, *Geografía en México*, 445.

14. Jiménez, "Diario-memoria," 135–39; Orozco y Berra, *Geografía en México*, 463.

15. International Boundary Commission, United States and Mexico, 1882, *Memoria de la Sección Mexicana de la Comisión Internacional de Límites entre México y los Estados Unidos que restableció los monumentos de El Paso al Pacífico* (New York: John Polhemus and Co., 1901), Appendix no. 6; Ramírez, *Colegio de Minería*, 396, 401.

16. Wheaton to Emory, 9 November 1854, Copies of Letters Received by the Fourth U.S. Commissioner, 1854–57, Entry 401, Preliminary Inventory 170, Records Relating to International Boundaries, Record Group 76, National Archives, Washington, D.C.

17. Carreño, *México y los Estados Unidos*, 282–83; Richard A. Johnson, *The Mexican Revolution of Ayutla, 1854–1855: An Analysis of the Evolution and Destruction of Santa Anna's Last Dictatorship* (Rock Island, Ill.: Augustana College Library, 1939); Juan López de Escalera, *Diccionario biográfico y de historia de México* (Mexico City: Editorial del Magisterio, 1964), 716; Ramírez, *Colegio de Minería*, 395, 402–3.

18. George W. Cullum, *Biographical Register of the Officers and Graduates of the U.S. Military Academy, at West Point, N.Y., from Its Establishment, March 16, 1802, to the Army Re-Organization of 1866–67* (New York: D. Van Nostrand, 1868), 1:386, 2:7, 144; William H. Goetzmann, *Army Exploration in the American West, 1803–1863* (New Haven: Yale University Press, 1959; reprint, Lincoln: University of Nebraska Press, 1979), 12–17.

19. Goetzmann, *Army Exploration*, 128–30; Martha Coleman Bray, *Joseph Nicollet and His Map* (Philadelphia: American Philosophical Society, 1980), 270; Seymour I. Schwartz and Ralph E. Ehrenberg, *The Mapping of America* (New York: Harry N. Abrams, 1980), 265–69; James C. Martin and Robert S. Martin, *Maps of Texas and the Southwest, 1513–1900* (Albuquerque: University of New Mexico Press for the Amon Carter Museum, 1984), 128–29; Norman J. W. Thrower, "William H. Emory and the Mapping of the American Southwest Borderlands," *Terrae Incognitae* 22 (1990): 70–87.

20. U.S. Engineer School, United States Army, *Historical Sketch of the Corps of Engineers, U.S. Army*, by Edward Burr, Occasional Papers, no. 71 (Washington, D.C.: U.S. Government Printing Office, 1939), 42; Hardcastle to Abert, 2 February 1849, Letters

Received by the Topographical Bureau of the War Department, 1824–1865, Microfilm Publication 506, Records of the Office of the Chief of Engineers, Record Group 77, National Archives, Washington, D.C.; Francis R. Stoddard, "Amiel Weeks Whipple," *Chronicles of Oklahoma* 28 (1950): 226–27; Rec'd 27 June 1849, Correspondence of the First U.S. Commissioner, 1849–56, Entry 398, Preliminary Inventory 170, Records Relating to International Boundaries, Record Group 76, National Archives, Washington, D.C.

21. Walter Prescott Webb, ed., *The Handbook of Texas* (Austin: Texas State Historical Association, 1952), 1:722.

22. John Russell Bartlett, *Personal Narrative of Explorations and Incidents in Texas, New Mexico, California, Sonora, and Chihuahua, Connected with the United States and Mexican Boundary Commission, during the Years 1850, '51, '52, and '53* (New York: D. Appleton, 1854; reprint, Chicago: Rio Grande Press, 1965); Robert V. Hine, *Bartlett's West: Drawing the Mexican Boundary* (New Haven: Yale University Press for the Amon Carter Museum, 1968); Dawn Hall, ed., *Drawing the Borderline: Artist-Explorers and the U.S.-Mexico Boundary Survey* (Albuquerque: Albuquerque Museum, 1996).

23. U.S. Congress, 32d Cong., 1st sess., 1852, S. Ex. Doc. 119, 32–33, 241; U.S. Congress, *Report of the Secretary of the Interior, in Compliance with a Resolution of the Senate, of January 22, Communicating a Report and Map of A. B. Gray, Relative to the Mexican Boundary,* 33d Cong., 2d sess., 1855, S. Ex. Doc. 55, 13; To accompany Despatch no. 38, 1852, Letters Relating to Accounts, 1850–60, Entry 437, Preliminary Inventory 170, Records Relating to International Boundaries, Record Group 76, National Archives, Washington, D.C.; Bartlett to Stuart, 17 May 1852, Letters Received from the Third U.S. Commissioner, 1850–1860, Entry 424, Preliminary Inventory 170, Records Relating to International Boundaries, Record Group 76, National Archives, Washington, D.C.

24. Gray to Stuart, 3 August 1851, Journal and Letters of Surveyors, 1849, Entry 429, Preliminary Inventory 170, Records Relating to International Boundaries, Record Group 76, National Archives, Washington, D.C.; U.S. Congress, 33d Cong., 2d sess., 1855, S. Ex. Doc. 55; U.S. Congress, 32d Cong., 1st sess., 1852, S. Ex. Doc. 119, 121.

25. Bartlett, *Personal Narrative,* "List of Members of the United States and Mexican Boundary Commission, as organized in Washington, August, 1850," 2:594–96.

26. Carreño, *México y los Estados Unidos,* 278.

27. Graham to Abert, 16 November 1851, Letters Received from the Head of the U.S. Scientific Corps, 1851–54, Entry 431, Preliminary Inventory 170, Records Relating to International Boundaries, Record Group 76, National Archives, Washington, D.C.

28. Stanley F. Radzyminski, "Charles Radziminski: Patriot, Exile, Pioneer," *Chronicles of Oklahoma* 38 (1960): 354–68; Francis C. Kajencki, "Charles Radziminski and the United States–Mexican Boundary Survey," *New Mexico Historical Review* 63 (1988): 211–40.

29. U.S. Congress, *Report of the Secretary of War, Communicating, in Compliance with a Resolution of the Senate, the Report of Lieutenant Colonel Graham on the Subject of the*

Boundary Line between the United States and Mexico, 32d Cong., 1st sess., 1852, S. Ex. Doc. 121, 87; Herman J. Viola, *Exploring the West* (Washington, D.C.: Smithsonian Institution, 1987), 127–31; Richard W. Stephenson, "The Mapping of the Northwest Boundary of Texas, 1859–1860," *Terrae Incognitae* 6 (1974): 40–42.

30. U.S. Congress, 32d Cong., 1st sess., 1852, S. Ex. Doc. 121, 132–33; W. Turrentine Jackson, *Wagon Roads West: A Study of Federal Road Surveys and Construction in the Transmississippi West, 1846–1869* (New Haven: Yale University Press, 1964; reprint, Lincoln: University of Nebraska Press, 1979), 39–41; Smith to Emory, 22 January 1852, Letters Sent by the Fourth U.S. Commissioner, 1849–58, Entry 399, Preliminary Inventory 170, Records Relating to International Boundaries, Record Group 76, National Archives, Washington, D.C.

31. Cullum, *Biographical Register,* 2:210–11; Ronnie C. Tyler, *The Big Bend: A History of the Last Texas Frontier* (Washington, D.C.: U.S. Department of the Interior, 1975), 77.

32. Clark A. Elliott, *Biographical Dictionary of American Science: The Seventeenth through the Nineteenth Centuries* (Westport, Conn.: Greenwood Press, 1979), 229–30; Bernard L. Fontana, "Drawing the Line between Mexico and the United States: Nineteenth-Century Lithographs of People and Places along the Border," *American West* 20, no. 4 (July–August 1983): 50–56.

33. Emory, *Report,* 1:246–49; Goetzmann, *Army Exploration,* 185; Tyler, *Big Bend,* 82.

34. U.S. Congress, 32d Cong., 1st sess., 1852, S. Ex. Doc. 119, 189–91, 404–5, 410; Robert Taft, *Artists and Illustrators of the Old West, 1850–1900* (Princeton: Princeton University Press, 1953), 277–78.

35. Harkness to Bartlett, 7 June 1850, Applications, Recommendations, Acceptances, and Resignations, 1850, 1860, Entry 405, Preliminary Inventory 170, Records Relating to International Boundaries, Record Group 76, National Archives, Washington, D.C.

36. List, August 1850, Lists of U.S. Personnel, 1850–54, Entry 408, Preliminary Inventory 170, Records Relating to International Boundaries, Record Group 76, National Archives, Washington, D.C.

37. John Bull, "Surveying Book No. 2," 1850, Peter Force Collection, Manuscripts Division, Library of Congress, Washington, D.C., microfilm.

38. "Death of Maj. J. E. Weyss," *Washington Post,* 25 June 1903.

39. Emory to McClelland, 24 October 1854, E 399, RG 76.

40. Emory, *Report,* 1:24, 144; Francis B. Heitman, *Historical Register and Dictionary of the United States Army, from Its Organization, September 29, 1789, to March 2, 1903* (Washington, D.C.: U.S. Government Printing Office, 1903; reprint, Urbana: University of Illinois Press, 1965), 1:974.

41. William H. Emory, *Notes on the Survey of the Boundary Line between Mexico and the United States* (Cincinnati: Morgan and Overend, 1851), 4.

42. Emory, *Report,* 1:5.

43. Emory, *Notes on the Survey,* 6.

44. Emory, *Report*, 1:138.

45. Emory, *Report*, 1:138–42; Derek Howse, "The Lunar-Distance Method of Measuring Longitude," in *The Quest for Longitude: The Proceedings of the Longitude Symposium, Harvard University, Cambridge, Massachusetts, November 4–6, 1993*, ed. William J. H. Andrewes (Cambridge: Collection of Historical Scientific Instruments, Harvard University, 1996), 157–58; National Geodetic Survey, *Geodetic Glossary* (Rockville, Md.: National Oceanic and Atmospheric Administration, 1986), 138, 170.

46. Emory, *Report*, 1:142; Charles H. Cotter, *The Astronomical and Mathematical Foundations of Geography* (New York: American Elsevier, 1966), 12–13, 130–32.

47. U.S. Congress, *Report of the Boundary Commission upon the Survey and Re-Marking of the Boundary between the United States and Mexico West of the Rio Grande, 1891 to 1896*, 55th Cong., 2d sess., 1898, S. Doc. 247, 2:132.

48. William H. Emory, "Boundary between the United States and Mexico," *Bulletin of the American Geographical and Statistical Society*, vol. 1, pt. 3 (1854): 33, 43; Jiménez, "Diario-memoria," 186–88.

49. Jiménez, "Diario-memoria," 187; Emory, *Report*, 1:145; Thomas Jefferson Lee, *A Collection of Tables and Formulae Useful in Surveying, Geodesy, and Practical Astronomy, Including Elements for the Projection of Maps*, 2d ed. (Washington, D.C.: Taylor and Maury, 1849).

50. U.S. Congress, 55th Cong., 2d sess., 1898, S. Doc. 247, 2:113–14.

51. U.S. Bureau of Land Management, *Manual of Instructions for the Survey of the Public Lands of the United States* (Washington, D.C.: U.S. Department of the Interior, 1973), 53–54.

52. Emory, *Report*, 1:143; Emory to Hippel, 2 May 1855, E 399, RG 76.

53. International Boundary and Water Commission, United States and Mexico, *Memoria documentada del juicio de arbitraje del Chamizal celebrado en virtud de la convención de junio 24 de 1910* (Mexico City: Artes Gráficas, Granja Experimental de Zoquipa, 1911), 2:160; Emory to Hippel, 31 March 1855, E 399, RG 76.

54. Whipple to Bull, 26 April 1851, E 424, RG 76.

55. Whipple to Thompson, 26 April 1851, E 424, RG 76.

56. For a list of sample instruments, see Goetzmann, *Army Exploration*, 438–39.

57. Emory, *Report*, 1:5; Hewitt, "Mexican Boundary Survey Team," 172–73, esp. 173 n. 3.

58. Correspondencia recibida por la sección mexicana ante la Comisión de Límites y Aguas con los Estados Unidos de A.—Libro copiador de la misma, en la época del C. Gral. Pedro García Conde, 1849–50, 4–23, Expediente X-2-2, Límites y Aguas Internacionales, Archivo Histórico Genaro Estrada, Secretaría de Relaciones Exteriores, Mexico City; Salazar Ylarregui, *Datos de los trabajos*, 9–10, 15–16.

59. Wright to Emory, 5 May 1856, E 401, RG 76; U.S. Congress, 32d Cong., 1st sess., 1852, S. Ex. Doc. 121, 3–9, 86–87, 90–99.

60. U.S. Congress, 32d Cong., 1st sess., 1852, S. Ex. Doc. 119, 327.

61. Salazar Ylarregui, *Datos de los trabajos,* 16, 39–92.

62. Harry P. Hewitt, "The Mexican Commission and Its Survey of the Rio Grande River Boundary, 1850–1854," *Southwestern Historical Quarterly* 94 (April 1991): 563–64.

63. Jiménez, "Diario-memoria," 3–4.

64. Return of Instruments . . . by Bvt. Major W. H. Emory, 20 December 1852, Lists of and Receipts for Returned Instruments, 1849–60, Entry 436, Preliminary Inventory 170, Records Relating to International Boundaries, Record Group 76, National Archives, Washington, D.C.; Emory, *Report,* 1:171–72, 177–85; Charles E. Smart, *The Makers of Surveying Instruments in America since 1700* (Troy, N.Y.: Regal Art Press, 1962), 170.

65. U.S. Congress, *Report of the Secretary of the Interior, in Answer to a Resolution of the Senate for Information in Relation to the Operations of the Commission Appointed to Run and Mark the Boundary between the United States and Mexico,* 31st Cong., 1st sess., 1850, S. Ex. Doc. 34, pt. 1, 22.

66. Emory, *Report,* 1:138.

67. Jiménez, "Diario-memoria," 127–28; Emory, *Report,* 1:138.

68. Agustín Díaz, "Memoria sobre los trabajos topográficos que de orden del 1er Ing° de la Comisión D. Francisco Jiménez, practicó el 2° Ing° de la misma, D. Agustin Díaz, en la porción del lindero boreal de la República Mexicana, que abraza una parte del curso del Río Colorado y la línea geodésica que va del punto inicial en dicho río (20 millas inglesas abajo de su confluencia con el Gila) a la intersección del meridiano 111° de longitud oeste de Greenwich y el paralelo 31°20′ de latitud norte, año de 1855," 1857, 77, Special Collections, University Library, University of Texas at El Paso.

69. Return of Astronomical and Surveying Instruments &c. &c. Capt. Geo Thom, 30 August 1854, E 401, RG 76.

70. Bartlett, *Personal Narrative,* 2:588–92; Jiménez, "Diario-memoria," 130.

71. Return of Instruments . . . by Bvt. Major W. H. Emory, 20 December 1852, E 436, RG 76; Jiménez, "Diario-memoria," 37–38.

72. Jiménez, "Diario-memoria," 3.

73. William H. Goetzmann, "Science Explores the Big Bend: 1852–1853," *Password* III (1958): 61.

CHAPTER TWO   The Boundary Office: Mapmaking

1. Charles I. Bevans, comp., *Treaties and Other International Agreements of the United States of America, 1776–1949* (Washington, D.C.: Department of State, 1968–76), 9:795, 813.

2. U.S. Congress, *Report of the Secretary of the Interior, in Answer to a Resolution of the Senate for Information in Relation to the Operations of the Commission Appointed to Run and Mark the Boundary between the United States and Mexico,* 31st Cong., 1st sess., 1850, S. Ex. Doc. 34, pt. 1, 5.

3. Alberto María Carreño, *México y los Estados Unidos de America: Apuntaciones para*

la historia del acrecentamiento territorial de los Estados Unidos a costa de México desde la epoca colonial hasta nuestros días (Mexico City: Imprenta Victoria, 1922), 273.

4. Emory to Ewing, 1 March 1850, Letters Received from the Fourth U.S. Commissioner, 1849–60, Entry 425, Preliminary Inventory 170, Records Relating to International Boundaries, Record Group 76, National Archives, Washington, D.C.

5. William H. Emory, *Report on the United States and Mexican Boundary Survey Made under the Direction of the Secretary of the Interior,* 34th Cong., 1st sess., 1857, H. Ex. Doc. 135, 1:XIII; Francisco Jiménez, "Diario-memoria de los trabajos científicos practicados bajo la dirección de Francisco Jiménez, 1er Ingeniero de la Comisión de Límites Mexicana conforme a las instrucciones del Señor Comisionado Don José Salazar Ilarregui, a quien se hace entrega de ellos," 1857, Special Collections, University Library, University of Texas at El Paso; Agustín Díaz, "Memoria sobre los trabajos topográficos que de orden del 1er Ing° de la Comisión D. Francisco Jiménez, practicó el 2° Ing° de la misma, D. Agustin Díaz, en la porción del lindero boreal de la República Mexicana, que abraza una parte del curso del Río Colorado y la línea geodésica que va del punto inicial en dicho río (20 millas inglesas abajo de su confluencia con el Gila) a la intersección del meridiano 111° de longitud oeste de Greenwich y el paralelo 31°20′ de latitud norte, año de 1855," 1857, Special Collections, University Library, University of Texas at El Paso. For the names of the contributors and their roles in the production of the U.S. and Mexican boundary maps, see the Appendix.

6. Ewing to Emory, 29 April 1850, Letters Sent Concerning Boundary Surveys, 1849–1861, Entry 559, Preliminary Inventory, Records of the Office of the Secretary of the Interior, Record Group 48, National Archives, Washington, D.C.

7. Emory to McClelland, 5 March 1856, Letters Sent by the Fourth U.S. Commissioner, 1849–58, Entry 399, Preliminary Inventory 170, Records Relating to International Boundaries, Record Group 76, National Archives, Washington, D.C.

8. Emory to Stuart, 26 May 1851, Letters and Other Communications Received, 1849–1881, Entry 540, Preliminary Inventory, Records of the Office of the Secretary of the Interior, Record Group 48, National Archives, Washington, D.C.; Emory to Stewart [*sic*], 28 March 1851, E 425, RG 76; Clark A. Elliott, *Biographical Dictionary of American Science: The Seventeenth through the Nineteenth Centuries* (Westport, Conn.: Greenwood Press, 1979), 131–32; George C. Groce and David H. Wallace, *The New-York Historical Society's Dictionary of Artists in America, 1564–1860* (New Haven: Yale University Press, 1957), 296.

9. Emory to Hardcastle, 13 September 1851, E 425, RG 76; Seymour I. Schwartz and Ralph E. Ehrenberg, *The Mapping of America* (New York: Harry N. Abrams, 1980), 276.

10. Emory to Hardcastle, 13 September 1851, E 425, RG 76.

11. Emory to McClelland, 5 March 1856, E 399, RG 76.

12. U.S. Coast and Geodetic Survey, *Report of the Superintendent of the Coast Survey, Showing the Progress of the Survey during the Year 1853,* 33d Cong., 1st sess., 1853–54, H. Ex. Doc. 12, 82; U.S. Coast and Geodetic Survey, *Report of the Secretary of the Trea-*

sury, Communicating a Report of the Superintendent of the Coast Survey, Showing the Progress of That Work during the Year Ending November, 1848, 30th Cong., 2d sess., 1848, S. Ex. Doc. 1, 60.

13. Thom to Emory, 5 May 1856, E 399, RG 76; Emory to Secretary of the Interior, 5 March 1857, E 425, RG 76.

14. Emory to Hardcastle, 13 September 1851, E 425, RG 76.

15. Hardcastle to Secretary of the Interior, 23 July 1852, Registers of Letters Received Concerning Boundary Surveys, 1849–1862, Entry 539, Preliminary Inventory, Records of the Office of the Secretary of the Interior, Record Group 48, National Archives, Washington, D.C.; Hardcastle to Stuart, 10 June 1852, Letters Received Relating to Boundary Markers, 1850–52, Entry 427, Preliminary Inventory 170, Records Relating to International Boundaries, Record Group 76, National Archives, Washington, D.C.

16. Stuart to Hardcastle, 25 May 1852, E 559, RG 48; Hardcastle to Stuart, 10 June 1852, E 427, RG 76.

17. Bartlett to Stuart, 16 February 1853, Letters Received from the Third U.S. Commissioner, 1850–1860, Entry 424, Preliminary Inventory 170, Records Relating to International Boundaries, Record Group 76, National Archives, Washington, D.C.; Jiménez, "Diario-memoria," 122.

18. Emory to McClelland, 8 October 1853, E 425, RG 76.

19. Campbell to McClelland, 22 March 1853, Applications, Recommendations, Acceptances, and Resignations, 1850, 1860, Entry 405, Preliminary Inventory 170, Records Relating to International Boundaries, Record Group 76, National Archives, Washington, D.C.; George W. Cullum, *Biographical Register of the Officers and Graduates of the U.S. Military Academy, at West Point, N.Y., from Its Establishment, March 16, 1802 to the Army Re-Organization of 1866–67* (New York: D. Van Nostrand, 1868), 1:575–76; Emory to McClelland, 8 October 1853, E 425, RG 76.

20. Thom to McLellan [*sic*], 18 May 1853, Letters Relating to the Work of the Commission, 1851–55, Entry 426, Preliminary Inventory 170, Records Relating to International Boundaries, Record Group 76, National Archives, Washington, D.C.; Emory to Whiting, 2 June 1856, E 399, RG 76; U.S. Coast and Geodetic Survey, *Annual Report of the Superintendent of the Coast Survey, Showing the Progress of That Work during the Year Ending November, 1851,* 32d Cong., 1st sess., 1851, S. Ex. Doc. 3, 96; U.S. Coast and Geodetic Survey, *Report of the Superintendent of the Coast Survey, Showing the Progress of the Survey during the Year 1852,* 32d Cong., 2d sess., 1852–53, S. Ex. Doc. 58, 61.

21. Emory to Abert, 10 January 1854, Letters Received by the Topographical Bureau of the War Department, 1824–65, Microfilm Publication 506, Records of the Office of the Chief of Engineers, Record Group 77, National Archives, Washington, D.C.; Emory to Abert, 31 January 1854, M 506, RG 77.

22. Thom to McClelland, 27 October 1854, E 426, RG 76.

23. Schedule of Organization, [1854], Copies of Letters Received by the Fourth U.S. Commissioner, 1854–57, Entry 401, Preliminary Inventory 170, Records Relating to In-

ternational Boundaries, Record Group 76, National Archives, Washington, D.C.; Thom to Emory, 14 August 1854, E 401, RG 76.

24. U.S. Coast and Geodetic Survey, *Letter from the Secretary of the Treasury, Communicating the Report of the Superintendent of the Coast Survey, Showing the Progress of That Work during the Year Ending November, 1849,* 31st Cong., 1st sess., 1849, S. Ex. Doc. 5, 59; Emory to McClelland, 5 March 1856, E 399, RG 76; Thom to Emory, 5 May 1856, E 399, RG 76; Emory to Hill, 4 November 1856, E 399, RG 76.

25. Carl Irving Wheat, *Mapping the Transmississippi West, 1540–1861* (San Francisco: Institute of Historical Cartography, 1957–63), 4:207, 209–13, 230, 5:162, 390; Schwartz and Ehrenberg, *Mapping of America,* 287, 291, 307.

26. Thom to Emory, 4 November 1854, E 401, RG 76.

27. Emory to Thom, 26 September 1855, E 399, RG 76; Radziminski to McClelland, 14 September 1855, Letters Relating to Accounts, 1850–60, Entry 437, Preliminary Inventory 170, Records Relating to International Boundaries, Record Group 76, National Archives, Washington, D.C.; McClelland to Thom, 2 May 1856, E 559, RG 48; Emory to Abert, 2 June 1856, M·506, RG 77.

28. Hippel to Emory, 19 April 1856, E 401, RG 76.

29. Emory to McClelland, 20 May 1856, E 539, RG 48; Emory to McClelland, 5 March 1856, E 399, RG 76; Emory, *Report,* vol. 1, following pp. 100 and 120.

30. Emory, *Report,* 1:33; Emory to McClelland, 25 September 1855, E 399, RG 76.

31. Memorandum of an agreement, 16 May 1856, E 399, RG 76; Statements of checks drawn, E 399, RG 76.

32. Jiménez, "Diario-memoria," 230; Emory to Salazar, 6 March 1856, E 399, RG 76; McClelland to Robles Pezuela, 8 July 1856, E 559, RG 48.

33. Sophia A. Saucerman, "The Boundary Maps," in *Treaties and Other International Acts of the United States of America,* ed. Hunter Miller (Washington, D.C.: Department of State, 1942), 6:395; Carreño, *México y los Estados Unidos,* 282.

34. Manuel Orozco y Berra, *Apuntes para la historia de la geografía en México* (Mexico City: Francisco Diaz de Leon, 1881), 496.

35. Orozco y Berra, *Geografía en México,* 497–98. The present location of this document is unknown.

36. Emory to Thompson, 6 June 1857, E 399, RG 76; Carreño, *México y los Estados Unidos,* 284.

37. Jiménez, "Diario-memoria," 231.

38. Groce and Wallace, *Dictionary of Artists in America,* 178; U.S. Coast and Geodetic Survey, *Report of the Superintendent of the Coast Survey, Showing the Progress of the Survey during the Year 1854,* 33d Cong., 2d sess., 1854–55, S. Ex. Doc. 10, 90; Emory to McClelland, 6 December 1856, E 425, RG 76.

39. Emory to McClelland, 2 June 1856, E 425, RG 76; Michler to Siebert, 1 August 1857, E 401, RG 76; Wheat, *Mapping the Transmississippi West,* 4:231–32.

40. Emory, *Report,* 1:37–38.

41. Salazar to Emory (English translation), 12 July 1856, E 401, RG 76.

42. Emory to Thompson, 7 May 1857, E 540, RG 48.

43. Emory to Thompson, 1 October 1857, E 425, RG 76; Memorandum of Proofs Furnished to Mr. Seibert [*sic*], n.d., Letters Relating to Engraving of Prints, 1857–58, Entry 433, Preliminary Inventory 170, Records Relating to International Boundaries, Record Group 76, National Archives, Washington, D.C.

44. 21 and 30 September 1857, Proceedings, 1850–57, Entry 396, Preliminary Inventory 170, Records Relating to International Boundaries, Record Group 76, National Archives, Washington, D.C.

45. Emory to Thompson, 29 September 1857, E 425, RG 76.

46. Santiago Ramírez, *Datos para la historia del Colegio de Minería recogidos y compilados bajo la forma de efemérides* (Mexico City: Imprenta del Gobierno Federal, 1890), 403–4.

47. Emory to Thompson, 19 October 1857, E 399, RG 76.

48. Campbell to Emory, 27 January 1858, E 559, RG 48.

49. Salazar to Emory (English translation), 12 July 1856, E 401, RG 76.

50. John P. Snyder, *Flattening the Earth: Two Thousand Years of Map Projections* (Chicago: University of Chicago Press, 1993), 62, 103–4, 173.

51. [U.S. Boundary Commission], "Boundary between the United States and Mexico" [ms. maps], [1857], Map Records, n.d., Entry 417, Preliminary Inventory 170, Records Relating to International Boundaries, Record Group 76, National Archives, Washington, D.C.; [Comisión de Límites Mexicana], "Línea divisoria entre México y los Estados Unidos" [ms. maps], [1857], Límites, México–Estados Unidos, Mapoteca Manuel Orozco y Berra, Mexico City; [Comisión de Límites Mexicana], "Islands in the Rio Bravo del Norte" [ms. maps], [n.d.], Colección Orozco y Berra—General, Número de control 1120, Mapoteca Manuel Orozco y Berra, Mexico City.

CHAPTER THREE Consultation between the Commissions: Surveys on the Pacific and Gulf Coasts and the Colorado River

1. U.S. Congress, *Report of the Secretary of the Interior Made in Compliance with a Resolution of the Senate Calling for Information in Relation to the Commission Appointed to Run and Mark the Boundary between the United States and Mexico*, 32d Cong., 1st sess., 1852, S. Ex. Doc. 119, 58; José Salazar Ylarregui, *Datos de los trabajos astronómicos y topográficos, dispuestos en forma de diario, practicados durante el año de 1849 y principios de 1850 por la Comisión de Límites Mexicana en la línea que divide esta República de la de los Estados-Unidos* (Mexico City: Imprenta de Juan R. Navarro, 1850), 12–13.

2. William H. Emory, *Report on the United States and Mexican Boundary Survey Made under the Direction of the Secretary of the Interior*, 34th Cong., 1st sess., 1857, H. Ex. Doc. 135, 1:4; Journal of U.S. Surveyor A. B. Gray, p. 7, Journal and Letters of Surveyors, 1849, Entry 429, Preliminary Inventory 170, Records Relating to International Boundaries, Record Group 76, National Archives, Washington, D.C.; Salazar Ylarregui, *Datos*

de los trabajos, 51; Alberto María Carreño, *México y los Estados Unidos de América: Apuntaciones para la historia del acrecentamiento territorial de los Estados Unidos a costa de México desde la época colonial hasta nuestros días* (Mexico City: Imprenta Victoria, 1922), 287.

3. Salazar Ylarregui, *Datos de los trabajos,* 17–18 and map.

4. Journal of U.S. Surveyor A. B. Gray, pp. 7–10, E 429, RG 76; U.S. Congress, *Report of the Secretary of the Interior, in Answer to a Resolution of the Senate for Information in Relation to the Operations of the Commission Appointed to Run and Mark the Boundary between the United States and Mexico,* 31st Cong., 1st sess., 1850, S. Ex. Doc. 34, pt. 1, map.

5. Salazar Ylarregui, *Datos de los trabajos,* 18–19.

6. The length of the *legua marítima* referred to in the treaty would be given a modern equivalent of 5556.6 meters. Roland Chardon, "The Linear League in North America," *Annals of the Association of American Geographers* 70 (1980): 140, 151–52.

7. Harry P. Hewitt, "The Mexican Boundary Survey Team: Pedro García Conde in California," *Western Historical Quarterly* 21 (1990): 185; Salazar Ylarregui, *Datos de los trabajos,* 19; Journal of U.S. Surveyor A. B. Gray, p. 10, E 429, RG 76; Joseph Fr. Michaud, ed., *Biographie universelle ancienne et moderne par J. Fr. Michaud,* nouvelle ed., ed. Louis Gabriel Michaud (Paris, 1854; reprinted Graz, Austria: Akademische Druck- u. Verlagsanstalt, 1966–1968), 14:639–40; List of Instruments and Condition, 20 December 1852, Lists of and Receipts for Returned Instruments, 1849–60, Entry 436, Preliminary Inventory 170, Records Relating to International Boundaries, Record Group 76, National Archives, Washington, D.C.

8. Salazar Ylarregui, *Datos de los trabajos,* 20–22; U.S. Congress, 32d Cong., 1st sess., 1852, S. Ex. Doc. 119, 59.

9. Salazar Ylarregui, *Datos de los trabajos,* 22; William H. Emory, *Notes on the Survey of the Boundary Line between Mexico and the United States* (Cincinnati: Morgan and Overend, 1851), 8–10; William H. Emory, "Boundary between the United States and Mexico," *Bulletin of the American Geographical and Statistical Society* 1, pt. 3 (1854): 41.

10. U.S. Congress, 31st Cong., 1st sess., 1850, S. Ex. Doc. 34, pt. 1, 32–33, esp. 33, and map.

11. U.S. Congress, 31st Cong., 1st sess., 1850, S. Ex. Doc. 34, pt. 1, 37–38 and map; Salazar Ylarregui, *Datos de los trabajos,* 26.

12. Edmund L. F. Hardcastle, Instructions for Flashing at Junction of Gila and Colorado Rivers, 1849, Oct. 5, Folder no. 21; Edmund L. F. Hardcastle, Instructions for Flashing at Los Pinos, [1849], Oct. 5–9, Folder no. 22; Edmund L. F. Hardcastle, Instructions for Flashing at Mt. Wicommon, 1849, Oct. 5–9, Folder no. 23; all in Henderson Collection, MSA SC 501, Maryland State Archives, Annapolis.

13. Emory, *Notes on the Survey,* 9.

14. Emory, *Notes on the Survey,* 9.

15. U.S. Congress, 32d Cong., 1st sess., 1852, S. Ex. Doc. 119, 60.

16. Whipple to Emory, 15 December 1849, Letters Relating to Accounts, 1850–60,

Entry 437, Preliminary Inventory 170, Records Relating to International Boundaries, Record Group 76, National Archives, Washington, D.C.; U.S. Congress, 31st Cong., 1st sess., 1850, S. Ex. Doc. 34, pt. 1, 38.

17. Hunter Miller, ed., *Treaties and Other International Acts of the United States of America* (Washington, D.C.: Department of State, 1937), 5:418 and map; Hewitt, "Mexican Boundary Survey Team," 175, 188.

18. U.S. Congress, *Report of the Secretary of the Interior, with Additional Correspondence Relative to the Operations of the Commission for Running and Marking the Boundary between the United States and Mexico*, 31st Cong., 1st sess., 1850, S. Ex. Doc. 34, pt. 2, 4.

19. Manuel Orozco y Berra, *Apuntes para la historia de la geografía en México* (Mexico City: Francisco Diaz de Leon, 1881), 439; Salazar Ylarregui, *Datos de los trabajos*, 30.

20. U.S. Congress, 32d Cong., 1st sess., 1852, S. Ex. Doc. 119, 65; U.S. Congress, 31st Cong., 1st sess., 1850, S. Ex. Doc. 34, pt. 2, 5–6; Joseph Richard Werne, "Partisan Politics and the Mexican Boundary Survey, 1848–1853," *Southwestern Historical Quarterly* 90 (1987): 334–41; Lewis B. Lesley, "The International Boundary Survey from San Diego to the Gila River, 1849–1850," *Quarterly of the California Historical Society* 9 (1930): 12–14.

21. U.S. Congress, 31st Cong., 1st sess., 1850, S. Ex. Doc. 34, pt. 2, 8.

22. Salazar Ylarregui, *Datos de los trabajos*, 31–32.

23. Emory, *Report*, 1:20.

24. Michler to Emory, 13 December 1854, Copies of Letters Received by the Fourth U.S. Commissioner, 1854–57, Entry 401, Preliminary Inventory 170, Records Relating to International Boundaries, Record Group 76, National Archives, Washington, D.C.; Francisco Jiménez, "Diario-memoria de los trabajos científicos practicados bajo la dirección de Francisco Jiménez, 1er Ingeniero de la Comisión de Límites Mexicana conforme a las instrucciones del Señor Comisionado Don José Salazar Ilarregui, a quien se hace entrega de ellos," 1857, 139–71, Special Collections, University Library, University of Texas at El Paso.

25. Emory to Michler, 29 August 1854, Letters Sent by the Fourth U.S. Commissioner, 1849–58, Entry 399, Preliminary Inventory 170, Records Relating to International Boundaries, Record Group 76, National Archives, Washington, D.C.

26. Michler to Emory, 20 May 1855, E 401, RG 76; Latitude of Astronomical Station no. 2 near Initial Point on Colorado River, 1855, vol. 3, Astronomical Observations, 1850–55, Entry 412, Preliminary Inventory 170, Records Relating to International Boundaries, Record Group 76, National Archives, Washington, D.C.

27. Jiménez, "Diario-memoria," 138, 172–73.

28. Jiménez, "Diario-memoria," 173.

29. Jiménez, "Diario-memoria," 175.

30. Emory to McClelland, 18 August 1855, E 399, RG 76.

31. Jiménez, "Diario-memoria," 181–84, 250–51.

32. Jiménez, "Diario-memoria," 186–87; Emory, *Report*, 1:33–34.

33. Jiménez, "Diario-memoria," 261–62.

34. Emory to Michler, 29 August 1854, E 399, RG 76; Michler to Emory, 12 February 1855, E 401, RG 76.

35. Agustín Díaz, "Memoria sobre los trabajos topográficos que de orden del 1er Ing° de la Comisión D. Francisco Jiménez, practicó el 2° Ing° de la misma, D. Agustin Díaz, en la porción del lindero boreal de la República Mexicana, que abraza una parte del curso del Río Colorado y la línea geodésica que va del punto inicial en dicho río (20 millas inglesas abajo de su confluencia con el Gila) a la intersección del meridiano 111° de longitud oeste de Greenwich y el paralelo 31°20′ de latitud norte, año de 1855," 1857, 1–5, 30–31, Special Collections, University Library, University of Texas at El Paso.

36. Díaz, "Memoria sobre los trabajos topográficos," 31–33.

37. U.S. Congress, *Report of the Secretary of War, Communicating, in Compliance with a Resolution of the Senate, the Report of Lieutenant Colonel Graham on the Subject of the Boundary Line between the United States and Mexico,* 32d Cong., 1st sess., 1852, S. Ex. Doc. 121, 211.

38. U.S. Congress, *Report of the Secretary of the Interior, Communicating, in Further Compliance with a Resolution of the Senate, Certain Papers in Relation to the Mexican Boundary Commission,* 33d Cong., special sess., 1853, S. Ex. Doc. 6, 157.

39. Jiménez, "Diario-memoria," 44–45; International Boundary and Water Commission, United States and Mexico, *Memoria documentada del juicio de arbitraje del Chamizal celebrado en virtud de la convención de junio 24 de 1910* (Mexico City: Artes Gráficas, Granja Experimental de Zoquipa, 1911), 2:157–59.

40. See also Hewitt's analysis of Emory's motives: Harry P. Hewitt, "The Mexican Commission and Its Survey of the Rio Grande River Boundary, 1850–1854," *Southwestern Historical Quarterly* 94 (1991): 574–78; Harry P. Hewitt, "'El deseo de cubrir el honor nacional': Francisco Jiménez and the Survey of the Mexico–United States Boundary, 1849–1857," in *La ciudad y el campo en la historia de México: Memoria de la VII reunión de historiadores mexicanos y norteamericanos, Oaxaca, Oax., 1985* (Mexico City: Universidad Nacional Autónoma de México, 1992), 2:717.

41. Jiménez, "Diario-memoria," 104.

42. Jiménez, "Diario-memoria," 106–7, 238–40.

43. Jiménez, "Diario-memoria," 244–47, esp. 244–45.

44. Frederick Adolphus Wislizenus, *Memoir of a Tour to Northern Mexico, Connected with Col. Doniphan's Expedition, in 1846 and 1847,* 30th Cong., 1st sess., 1848, Misc. Pub. 26 (reprint, Glorieta, N. Mex.: Rio Grande Press, 1969). The quotations that follow are from p. 81.

45. Jiménez, "Diario-memoria," 752; Emory, *Report,* 1:245.

46. U.S. Congress, 32d Cong., 1st sess., 1852, S. Ex. Doc. 121, 211–12.

47. Campbell to McClelland, 22 August 1853, Letters Relating to the Work of the Commission, 1851–55, Entry 426, Preliminary Inventory 170, Records Relating to International Boundaries, Record Group 76, National Archives, Washington, D.C.; A. Hun-

ter Dupree, *Science in the Federal Government: A History of Policies and Activities* (Cambridge: Belknap Press of Harvard University Press, 1957; reprint, Baltimore: Johns Hopkins University Press, 1986), 100-5.

48. Emory, *Report,* 1:58.

49. U.S. Coast and Geodetic Survey, *Report of the Superintendent of the Coast Survey, Showing the Progress of the Survey during the Year 1853,* 33d Cong., 1st sess., 1853-54, H. Ex. Doc. 12, 74-75.

50. [U.S. Boundary Commission], *No. 1, Boundary between the United States and Mexico* [map proofs], 1:60,000 ([Washington, D.C.]: Department of the Interior, [1857]), Map records, n.d., Entry 417, Preliminary Inventory 170, Records Relating to International Boundaries, Record Group 76, National Archives, Washington, D.C.

51. U.S. Coast and Geodetic Survey, *Report of the Superintendent of the Coast Survey, Showing the Progress of the Survey during the Year 1854,* 33d Cong., 2d sess., 1854-55, S. Ex. Doc. 10, 73-74 and map.

52. U.S. Coast and Geodetic Survey, 33d Cong., 2d sess., 1854-55, S. Ex. Doc. 10, 73-75.

53. Aaron L. Shalowitz, *Shore and Sea Boundaries: With Special Reference to the Interpretation and Use of Coast and Geodetic Survey Data* (Washington, D.C.: U.S. Government Printing Office, 1962), 1:151-52.

CHAPTER FOUR   Cooperation in Surveying and Mapping: The Land Boundary

1. U.S. Congress, *Report of the Secretary of the Interior Made in Compliance with a Resolution of the Senate Calling for Information in Relation to the Commission Appointed to Run and Mark the Boundary between the United States and Mexico,* 32d Cong., 1st sess., 1852, S. Ex. Doc. 119, 62-65, esp. 62.

2. Lenerd E. Brown, "Survey of the United States Mexico Boundary—1849-1855: Background Study" ([Washington, D.C.]: United States Department of the Interior, National Park Service, Division of History, Office of Archeology and Historic Preservation, 1969, photocopy), 157-59; Hardcastle to Emory, 2 May 1851, Letters Received from the Fourth U.S. Commissioner, 1849-60, Entry 425, Preliminary Inventory 170, Records Relating to International Boundaries, Record Group 76, National Archives, Washington, D.C.

3. Brown, "Survey of the United States Mexico Boundary," 160-61; Harry P. Hewitt, "'El deseo de cubrir el honor nacional': Francisco Jiménez and the Survey of the Mexico–United States Boundary, 1849-1857," in *La ciudad y el campo en la historia de México: Memoria de la VII reunión de historiadores mexicanos y norteamericanos, Oaxaca, Oax., 1985* (Mexico City: Universidad Nacional Autónoma de México, 1992), 711; Edmund L. F. Hardcastle, 19 March 1851, Minutes of the Meetings between Capt. E. L. F. Hardcastle of the United States and Ricardo Ramírez of Mexico for the Purpose of Locating the Monuments Marking the Boundary between the Two Countries, 1851, Mar. 19–July 30, Folder no. 59, Henderson Collection, MSA SC 501, Maryland State Archives, Annapolis.

4. Hardcastle to Emory, 2 May 1851, E 425, RG 76; Hardcastle, 24 April 1851, Minutes, Folder no. 59.

5. Brown, "Survey of the United States Mexico Boundary," 167–68; Leon Claire Metz, *Border: The U.S.-Mexico Line* (El Paso: Mangan Books, 1989), 28.

6. Hardcastle, 1 June 1851, Minutes, Folder no. 59; International Boundary Commission, United States and Mexico, 1882, *Memoria de la Sección Mexicana de la Comisión Internacional de Límites entre México y los Estados Unidos que restableció los monumentos de El Paso al Pacífico* (New York: John Polhemus and Co., 1901), 98–99; "Remarking the Mexican Boundary," *Science,* n.s., 1 (29 March 1895): 350.

7. Hardcastle to Emory, 2 May 1851, E 425, RG 76.

8. Emory to Hardcastle, 13 September 1851, E 425, RG 76.

9. Harry P. Hewitt, "The Mexican Boundary Survey Team: Pedro García Conde in California," *Western Historical Quarterly* 21 (1990): 194.

10. Hardcastle, 1 June 1851, Minutes, Folder no. 59.

11. U.S. Congress, *Report of the Boundary Commission upon the Survey and Re-Marking of the Boundary between the United States and Mexico West of the Rio Grande, 1891 to 1896,* 55th Cong., 2d sess., 1898, S. Doc. 247, 2:174.

12. Emory to Abert, 20 August 1849, Letters Received by the Topographical Bureau of the War Department, 1824–65, Microfilm Publication 506, Records of the Office of the Chief of Engineers, Record Group 77, National Archives, Washington, D.C.

13. Hardcastle, 7 May 1851, Minutes, Folder no. 59.

14. Wheaton to Emory, 22 October 1854, Copies of Letters Received by the Fourth U.S. Commissioner, 1854–57, Entry 401, Preliminary Inventory 170, Records Relating to International Boundaries, Record Group 76, National Archives, Washington, D.C.

15. Emory to Salazar, 22 January 1855, Letters Sent by the Fourth U.S. Commissioner, 1849–58, Entry 399, Preliminary Inventory 170, Records Relating to International Boundaries, Record Group 76, National Archives, Washington, D.C.

16. William H. Emory, *Report on the United States and Mexican Boundary Survey Made under the Direction of the Secretary of the Interior,* 34th Cong., 1st sess., 1857, H. Ex. Doc. 135, 1:27–28.

17. Charles I. Bevans, comp., *Treaties and Other International Agreements of the United States of America, 1776–1949* (Washington, D.C.: Department of State, 1968–76), 9:813.

18. Emory, *Report,* 1:28.

19. Emory to Clark, 25 January 1855, E 399, RG 76.

20. Hippel to Emory, 4 February 1855, E 401, RG 76.

21. Espia, 24 March 1855 to 31 March 1855, Astronomical Observations, 1850–55, Entry 412, Preliminary Inventory 170, Records Relating to International Boundaries, Record Group 76, National Archives, Washington, D.C.

22. Emory, *Report,* quotation on 1:96, illustrations following; Paula Rebert, "The Gilbert Thompson Collection, Library of Congress," *Meridian* 7 (1992): 30–31.

23. Camp at the Espia, 31°20′, 23 March 1855, E 399, RG 76.

24. Emory to McClelland, 23 March 1855, E 399, RG 76; Emory to McClelland, 19 June 1855, Letters Received from the Fourth U.S. Commissioner, 1849–60, Entry 425, Preliminary Inventory 170, Records Relating to International Boundaries, Record Group 76, National Archives, Washington, D.C.; Emory to McClelland, 9 August 1855, E 399, RG 76.

25. Emory to McClelland, 18 August 1855, E 399, RG 76; Emory, *Report*, 1:30–33, esp. 33.

26. U.S. Congress, *Message of the President of the United States, in Compliance with a Resolution of the Senate of the 20th Ultimo, Calling for Information Relating to the Boundary Line and the Payment of the $3,000,000 under the Treaty with Mexico of June 30, 1853*, 34th Cong., 1st sess., 1856, S. Ex. Doc. 57, 55; Emory, *Report*, 1:32.

27. Manuel Orozco y Berra, *Apuntes para la historia de la geografía en México* (Mexico City: Francisco Diaz de Leon, 1881), 470.

28. Orozco y Berra, *Geografía en México*, 469–81; Emory, *Report*, 1:37–38.

29. Emory, *Report*, 1:37.

30. U.S. Congress, 55th Cong., 2d sess., 1898, S. Doc. 247, 2:175.

31. U.S. Congress, 55th Cong., 2d sess., 1898, S. Doc. 247, 2:118.

32. Emory, *Report*, 1:30.

33. U.S. Congress, 55th Cong., 2d sess., 1898, S. Doc. 247, 1:40; U.S. Section, International Boundary and Water Commission, "List of Western Land Boundary Monuments" (El Paso: United States Section, 1992, photocopy).

34. Emory, *Report*, 1:37–38.

35. U.S. Congress, 55th Cong., 2d sess., 1898, S. Doc. 247, 2:126.

36. Emory to O'Donoghue, 14 June 1855, E 399, RG 76.

37. Emory to Michler, 29 August 1854, E 399, RG 76.

38. Francisco Jiménez, "Diario-memoria de los trabajos científicos practicados bajo la dirección de Francisco Jiménez, 1er Ingeniero de la Comisión de Límites Mexicana conforme a las instrucciones del Señor Comisionado Don José Salazar Ilarregui, a quien se hace entrega de ellos," 1857, 138, Special Collections, University Library, University of Texas at El Paso.

39. Emory, *Report*, 1:34.

40. Jiménez, "Diario-memoria," 188–206; Michler to Emory, 20 May 1855, E 401, RG 76.

41. Emory, *Report*, 1:29.

42. Jiménez, "Diario-memoria," 207–12.

43. Emory, *Report*, 1:30.

44. Jiménez, "Diario-memoria," 272.

45. Emory, *Report*, 1:120.

46. Emory, *Report*, 1:120; Agustín Díaz, "Memoria sobre los trabajos topográficos que de orden del 1er Ing° de la Comisión D. Francisco Jiménez, practicó el 2° Ing° de la misma, D. Agustin Díaz, en la porción del lindero boreal de la República Mexicana, que

abraza una parte del curso del Río Colorado y la línea geodésica que va del punto inicial en dicho río (20 millas inglesas abajo de su confluencia con el Gila) a la intersección del meridiano 111° de longitud oeste de Greenwich y el paralelo 31°20′ de latitud norte, año de 1855," 1857, 7–9, Special Collections, University Library, University of Texas at El Paso; Joseph Richard Werne, "Major Emory and Captain Jiménez: Running the Gadsden Line," *Journal of the Southwest* 29 (1987): 217.

47. Díaz, "Memoria sobre los trabajos topográficos," 9, 17, 78.

48. Jiménez, "Diario-memoria," 212–16.

49. Jiménez, "Diario-memoria," 218; Díaz, "Memoria sobre los trabajos topográficos," 78–79, 92–94; Emory, *Report,* 1:74.

50. Jiménez, "Diario-memoria," 218–19.

51. "Remarking the Mexican Boundary," 349.

52. U.S. Section, International Boundary and Water Commission, "Western Land Boundary Monuments"; Robert R. Humphrey, *Ninety Years and 535 Miles: Vegetation Changes along the Mexican Border* (Albuquerque: University of New Mexico Press, 1987), 272–73; International Boundary Commission, *Monumentos de El Paso al Pacífico,* 302–3; Samuel Whittemore Boggs, "Monument No. 127 (Old Emory Monument No. 27), Intended to Be in North Latitude 31°20′ and West Longitude 111°," in *Treaties and Other International Acts of the United States of America,* ed. Hunter Miller (Washington, D.C.: Department of State, 1942), 6:393.

53. Emory, *Report,* 1:31–32.

54. Luis G. Zorrilla, *Monumentación de la frontera norte en el siglo XIX* (Mexico City: Secretaría de Relaciones Exteriores, 1981), 17–22.

55. Jiménez, "Diario-memoria," 217.

56. Jiménez, "Diario-memoria," 276–77; Díaz, "Memoria sobre los trabajos topográficos," 23. Whether any of the field maps of the azimuth line survey have survived is unknown.

57. Jiménez, "Diario-memoria," 190–91; Díaz, "Memoria sobre los trabajos topográficos," 11–15.

58. U.S. Congress, *Preliminary Reconnaissance of the Boundary Line between the United States and Mexico,* 48th Cong., 1st sess., 1884, S. Misc. Doc. 96, 1:16.

59. Díaz, "Memoria sobre los trabajos topográficos," 14–16.

60. Emory, *Report,* 1:123.

CHAPTER FIVE   Controversy on the Boundary

1. U.S. Congress, *Report of the Secretary of War, Communicating, in Compliance with a Resolution of the Senate, the Report of Lieutenant Colonel Graham on the Subject of the Boundary Line between the United States and Mexico,* 32d Cong., 1st sess., 1852, S. Ex. Doc. 121, 19–20.

2. U.S. Congress, 32d Cong., 1st sess., 1852, S. Ex. Doc. 121, 201.

3. Emory to Bartlett, 14 February 1853, Letters Sent by the Fourth U.S. Commis-

sioner, 1849–58, Entry 399, Preliminary Inventory 170, Records Relating to International Boundaries, Record Group 76, National Archives, Washington, D.C.; Hippel to Emory, 15 May 1852, Letters Received by the Fourth U.S. Commissioner, 1849–57, Entry 400, Preliminary Inventory 170, Records Relating to International Boundaries, Record Group 76, National Archives, Washington, D.C.; Arthur R. Gómez, *A Most Singular Country: A History of Occupation in the Big Bend* ([Salt Lake City]: Charles Redd Center for Western Studies, Brigham Young University, 1990), 17–18.

4. International Boundary and Water Commission, United States and Mexico, *Memoria documentada del juicio de arbitraje del Chamizal celebrado en virtud de la convención de junio 24 de 1910* (Mexico City: Artes Gráficas, Granja Experimental de Zoquipa, 1911), 2:162; Robert V. Hine, *Bartlett's West: Drawing the Mexican Boundary* (New Haven: Yale University Press for the Amon Carter Museum, 1968), 73–74. Vaudricourt's work on the Rio Grande was regarded as a U.S. survey in Harry P. Hewitt, "The Mexican Commission and Its Survey of the Rio Grande River Boundary, 1850–1854," *Southwestern Historical Quarterly* 94 (1991): 567.

5. Agustín Díaz, "Memoria de D. Agustín Díaz," in International Boundary and Water Commission, United States and Mexico, *Memoria documentada del juicio de arbitraje del Chamizal celebrado en virtud de la convención de junio 24 de 1910* (Mexico City: Artes Gráficas, Granja Experimental de Zoquipa, 1911), 2:195–97, esp. 196.

6. Díaz, "Memoria de D. Agustín Díaz," 2:198–247, esp. 206, 230, 246–47.

7. Agreement, 10 April 1852, Letters Received from the Fourth U.S. Commissioner, 1849–60, Entry 425, Preliminary Inventory 170, Records Relating to International Boundaries, Record Group 76, National Archives, Washington, D.C.

8. Rio Grande near mouth of the Cañon, 24 and 25 June 1852, and Opposite Presidio del Norte, 15 and 16 July 1852, Astronomical Observations, 1850–55, Entry 412, Preliminary Inventory 170, Records Relating to International Boundaries, Record Group 76, National Archives, Washington, D.C.; Emory to Stuart, 8 August 1852, E 425, RG 76; Díaz, "Memoria de D. Agustín Díaz," 2:197–98.

9. Francisco Jiménez, "Diario-memoria de los trabajos científicos practicados bajo la dirección de Francisco Jiménez, 1er Ingeniero de la Comisión de Límites Mexicana conforme a las instrucciones del Señor Comisionado Don José Salazar Ilarregui, a quien se hace entrega de ellos," 1857, 93, Special Collections, University Library, University of Texas at El Paso; Emory to McClelland, 8 October 1853, E 425, RG 76.

10. Emory to Bartlett, 14 February 1853, E 399, RG 76.

11. U.S. Congress, *Report of the Secretary of the Interior, Communicating, in Further Compliance with a Resolution of the Senate, Certain Papers in Relation to the Mexican Boundary Commission,* 33d Cong., special sess., 1853, S. Ex. Doc. 6, 161; U.S. Supreme Court, "New Mexico v. Texas," in *United States Reports,* vol. 275, *Cases Adjudged in the Supreme Court at October Term, 1927* (Washington, D.C.: U.S. Government Printing Office, 1928), 279–303; Warren to Secretary of State, 28 August 1925, Letters Received from the Fourth U.S. Commissioner, 1849–60, Entry 425, Preliminary Inventory 170,

Records Relating to International Boundaries, Record Group 76, National Archives, Washington, D.C.

12. There is an error in the numbers given as Gardner's demonstration in the printed record: U.S. Congress, 33d Cong., special sess., 1853, S. Ex. Doc. 6, 156; the correct numbers are given in the manuscript minutes of the meeting: Presidio del Norte, 27 August 1852, E 425, RG 76.

13. U.S. Congress, 33d Cong., special sess., 1853, S. Ex. Doc. 6, 156–57.

14. U.S. Congress, 33d Cong., special sess., 1853, S. Ex. Doc. 6, 155.

15. The placement of decimal points and symbols for degrees, minutes, and seconds is inconsistent in the annotations. At least one scholar has pointed out the annotations but without explanation: see Sophia A. Saucerman, "The Boundary Maps," in *Treaties and Other International Acts of the United States of America,* ed. Hunter Miller (Washington, D.C.: Department of State, 1942), 6:399.

16. Bob Cunningham and Harry P. Hewitt, "A 'Lovely Land Full of Roses and Thorns': Emil Langberg and Mexico, 1835–1866," *Southwestern Historical Quarterly* 98 (1995): 400–5.

17. Emory to Bartlett, 14 February 1853, E 399, RG 76; Ronnie C. Tyler, *The Big Bend: A History of the Last Texas Frontier* (Washington, D.C.: U.S. Department of the Interior, 1975), 80–97; William H. Goetzmann, "Science Explores the Big Bend: 1852–1853," *Password* III (1958): 61–66.

18. Chandler to McClelland, 17 July 1854, Letters Relating to Accounts, 1850–60, Entry 437, Preliminary Inventory 170, Records Relating to International Boundaries, Record Group 76, National Archives, Washington, D.C.

19. William H. Emory, *Report on the United States and Mexican Boundary Survey Made under the Direction of the Secretary of the Interior,* 34th Cong., 1st sess., 1857, H. Ex. Doc. 135, 1:80–85, esp. 83–84; Ronnie C. Tyler, "Exploring the Rio Grande: Lt. Duff C. Green's Report of 1852," *Arizona and the West* 10 (1968): 43–60.

20. Manuel Orozco y Berra, *Apuntes para la historia de la geografía en México* (Mexico City: Francisco Diaz de Leon, 1881), 465–68; [Comisión de Límites Mexicana], [Field Maps] [ms. maps], 7 sheets, scale varies, 1855, Número de control 1124, Colección Orozco y Berra—General, Mapoteca Manuel Orozco y Berra, Mexico City.

21. Emory to Bartlett, 14 February 1853, E 399, RG 76.

22. Emory to McClelland, 8 October 1853, E 425, RG 76; Francis C. Kajencki, "Charles Radziminski and the United States–Mexican Boundary Survey," *New Mexico Historical Review* 63 (1988): 227–29.

23. Kajencki, "Charles Radziminski," 222; Emory, *Report,* 1:191–241.

24. Return of Instruments, 20 December 1852, Lists of and Receipts for Returned Instruments, 1849–60, Entry 436, Preliminary Inventory 170, Records Relating to International Boundaries, Record Group 76, National Archives, Washington, D.C.; Mouth of Rio Bravo, 1853, vol. 6, E 412, RG 76.

25. Emory to McClelland, 8 October 1853, E 425, RG 76.

26. Emory to Abert, 1 August 1853, Letters Received by the Topographical Bureau of the War Department, 1824–1865, Microfilm Publication 506, Records of the Office of the Chief of Engineers, Record Group 77, National Archives, Washington, D.C.; Emory to Abert, 30 June 1853, M 506, RG 77.

27. Orozco y Berra, *Geografía en México*, 442–44; Miguel León-Portilla, ed., *Diccionario Porrúa de historia, biografía y geografía de México*, 5th ed. (Mexico City: Editorial Porrúa, 1986), 2:1217; Hewitt, "Mexican Commission and Its Survey," 572–73; Joseph Richard Werne, "Surveying the Rio Grande, 1850–1853," *Southwestern Historical Quarterly* 94 (1991): 548–49; Harry P. Hewitt, "'El deseo de cubrir el honor nacional': Francisco Jiménez and the Survey of the Mexico–United States Boundary, 1849–1857," in *La ciudad y el campo en la historia de México: Memoria de la VII reunión de historiadores mexicanos y norteamericanos, Oaxaca, Oax., 1985* (Mexico City: Universidad Nacional Autónoma de México, 1992), 2:716.

28. Jiménez, "Diario-memoria," 75, 91, 99, 111–21.

29. Jiménez, "Diario-memoria," 4–5, 95–96, 100, 107, 117–21; Orozco y Berra, *Geografía en México*, 444.

30. Jiménez, "Diario-memoria," 71–75, 100, 109–10.

31. [Agustín Díaz and Luis Díaz], "Río Bravo" [ms. maps], 17 sheets, scale varies, 1853, Número de control 1125, Colección Manuel Orozco y Berra, Entidad Federativa, Parciales 721, Mapoteca Manuel Orozco y Berra, Mexico City; Orozco y Berra, *Geografía en México*, 455–61.

32. Jiménez, "Diario-memoria," 111–35.

33. Orozco y Berra, *Geografía en México*, 445–51.

34. Orozco y Berra, *Geografía en México*, 447.

35. Emory, *Report*, 1:65.

36. Emory to Stuart, 8 January 1852, E 425, RG 76; Emory, *Report*, 1:138.

37. San Elciario [*sic*], 1852, vol. 6, E 412, RG 76; Emory, *Report*, 1:192–93.

38. Jiménez, "Diario-memoria," 5–7; Hewitt, "Mexican Commission and Its Survey," 563–64.

39. Emory to Smith, 15 January 1852, E 399, RG 76.

40. Emory, *Report*, 1:141, 192, 201.

41. Emory to Bartlett, 14 February 1853, E 399, RG 76.

42. Orozco y Berra, *Geografía en México*, 464.

43. Samuel Whittemore Boggs, "The Initial Point on the Rio Grande, Intended to Be in 31°47′ North Latitude," in *Treaties and Other International Acts of the United States of America*, ed. Hunter Miller (Washington, D.C.: Department of State, 1942), 6:392–93.

44. John Russell Bartlett, *Personal Narrative of Explorations and Incidents in Texas, New Mexico, California, Sonora, and Chihuahua, Connected with the United States and Mexican Boundary Commission, during the Years 1850, '51, '52, and '53* (New York: D. Appleton, 1854; reprint, Chicago: Rio Grande Press, 1965), 1:192–95, esp. 193; W. H. Timmons, *El Paso: A Borderlands History* (El Paso: Texas Western Press, 1990), 103–6; An-

gela Moyano Pahissa, *México y Estados Unidos: Orígenes de una relación, 1819–1861* (Mexico City: Secretaría de Educación Pública, 1987), 175–76.

45. [U.S. Boundary Commission], *No. 29, Boundary between the United States and Mexico* [map proofs], 1:60,000 ([Washington, D.C.]: Department of the Interior, [1857]), Map Records, n.d., Entry 417, Preliminary Inventory 170, Records Relating to International Boundaries, Record Group 76, National Archives, Washington, D.C.

46. International Boundary and Water Commission, United States and Mexico, *Chamizal,* 2:162.

47. Anson Mills, *My Story,* 2d ed., ed. C. H. Claudy (Washington, D.C.: Byron S. Adams, 1921), 260–61.

48. Saucerman, "Boundary Maps," 400.

49. U.S. Department of State, International Boundary and Water Commission (United States and Mexico), *Proceedings of the International (Water) Boundary Commission, United States and Mexico, Treaties of 1884 and 1889: Equitable Distribution of the Waters of the Rio Grande. United States Section* (Washington, D.C.: U.S. Government Printing Office, 1903), 1:47.

50. U.S. Department of State, International Boundary and Water Commission (United States and Mexico), *Proceedings,* 1:48.

CHAPTER SIX   Authoritative Maps and the True Line

1. Charles I. Bevans, comp., *Treaties and Other International Agreements of the United States of America, 1776–1949* (Washington, D.C.: Department of State, 1968–76), 9:795.

2. Santa Rita del Cobre, 20 July 1851, Proceedings, 1850–57, Entry 396, Preliminary Inventory 170, Records Relating to International Boundaries, Record Group 76, National Archives, Washington, D.C.

3. Cushing to Emory, 11 November 1856, Copies of Letters Received by the Fourth U.S. Commissioner, 1854–57, Entry 401, Preliminary Inventory 170, Records Relating to International Boundaries, Record Group 76, National Archives, Washington, D.C.

4. 8 November 1856, Letters Sent by the Fourth U.S. Commissioner, 1849–58, Entry 399, Preliminary Inventory 170, Records Relating to International Boundaries, Record Group 76, National Archives, Washington, D.C.

5. Washington, 21 September 1857, E 396, RG 76.

6. U.S. Congress, *Message of the President of the United States, in Compliance with a Resolution of the Senate of the 20th Ultimo, Calling for Information Relating to the Boundary Line and the Payment of the $3,000,000 under the Treaty with Mexico of June 30, 1853,* 34th Cong., 1st sess., 1856, S. Ex. Doc. 57, 62.

7. William H. Emory, *Report on the United States and Mexican Boundary Survey Made under the Direction of the Secretary of the Interior,* 34th Cong., 1st sess., 1857, H. Ex. Doc. 135, 1:38.

8. Carl Irving Wheat, *Mapping the Transmississippi West, 1540–1861* (San Francisco: Institute of Historical Cartography, 1957–63), 3:241.

9. Caleb Cushing, *Opinions of Hon. Caleb Cushing, of Massachusetts, from October 9, 1854, to July 9, 1856,* vol. 7 of *Official Opinions of the Attorneys General of the United States, Advising the President and Heads of Departments, in Relation to Their Official Duties, and Expounding the Constitution, Treaties with Foreign Governments and with Indian Tribes, and the Public Laws of the Country,* ed. C. C. Andrews (Washington, D.C.: Robert Farnham, 1856), 582, 585–86.

10. Cushing to Emory, 11 November 1856, E 401, RG 76.

11. Keith Highet, "Evidence, the Court, and the Nicaragua Case," *American Journal of International Law* 81 (1987): 15–19; Durward V. Sandifer, *Evidence before International Tribunals,* rev. ed. (Charlottesville: University Press of Virginia, 1975), 229–30, 372–73.

12. Gerhard Von Glahn, *Law among Nations: An Introduction to Public International Law,* 6th ed. (New York: Macmillan Publishing Co., 1992), 399–400; L. J. Bouchez, "The Fixing of Boundaries in International Boundary Rivers," *International and Comparative Law Quarterly* 12 (1963): 799–802.

13. Magoffin to Emory, 10 October 1856, E 401, RG 76.

14. Sheldon B. Liss, *A Century of Disagreement: The Chamizal Conflict, 1864–1964* (Washington, D.C.: Latin American Institute, 1965); Charles A. Timm, *The International Boundary Commission: United States and Mexico* (Austin: University of Texas, 1941), 132–74.

15. Timm, *International Boundary Commission,* 149.

16. Bevans, *Treaties,* 9:813.

17. Timm, *International Boundary Commission,* 159.

18. International Boundary and Water Commission, United States and Mexico, *Memoria documentada del juicio de arbitraje del Chamizal celebrado en virtud de la convención de junio 24 de 1910* (Mexico City: Artes Gráficas, Granja Experimental de Zoquipa, 1911), 1:343–49.

19. U.S. Congress, *Preliminary Reconnaissance of the Boundary Line between the United States and Mexico,* 48th Cong., 1st sess., 1884, S. Misc. Doc. 96, 2–3.

20. J[ohn] Ross Browne, *Adventures in the Apache Country: A Tour through Arizona and Sonora, with Notes on the Silver Regions of Nevada* (New York: Harper and Brothers, 1871; reprint, New York: Promontory Press, 1974), 159.

21. Luis G. Zorrilla, *Monumentación de la frontera norte en el siglo XIX* (Mexico City: Secretaría de Relaciones Exteriores, 1981), 15–16.

22. Lawyers Co-operative Publishing Co. and Bancroft-Whitney Co., *State and Local Taxation §§704–1154 to Statute of Frauds §§1–396,* vol. 72 of *American Jurisprudence: A Modern Comprehensive Text Statement of American Law,* 2d ed. (Rochester, N.Y.: Lawyers Co-operative Publishing Co., and San Francisco: Bancroft-Whitney Co., 1974), 428–29; Horacio Herrera, "Estudio sobre el límite internacional terrestre de los Estados Unidos de Norte América con la República Mexicana," *Boletín de la Sociedad Mexicana de Geografía y Estadística* 65, no. 1 (1948): 186–87.

23. Jerry E. Mueller, *Restless River: International Law and the Behavior of the Rio Grande* (El Paso: Texas Western Press, 1975), 33–37.

24. Timm, *International Boundary Commission*, 15, 161–67.

25. U.S. Department of State, *1972*, vol. 23, pt. 1 of *United States Treaties and Other International Agreements* (Washington, D.C.: U.S. Government Printing Office, 1973), 383–93; U.S. Section, International Boundary and Water Commission, *The International Boundary and Water Commission, United States and Mexico* (El Paso: United States Section, 1990, photocopy), 7.

26. U.S. Department of State, *United States Treaties*, vol. 23, pt. 1, 393–98; U.S. Department of State, *1976–77*, vol. 29, pt. 1 of *United States Treaties and Other International Agreements* (Washington, D.C.: U.S. Government Printing Office, 1979), 196–203; Charles E. Harrington, "Maritime Boundaries on National Ocean Service Nautical Charts," *Cartographic Perspectives* 14 (Winter 1993): 9–15.

27. Zorrilla, *Monumentación de la frontera*, 18–21.

28. Wheat, *Mapping the Transmississippi West*, 3:231; John Russell Bartlett, *Personal Narrative of Explorations and Incidents in Texas, New Mexico, California, Sonora, and Chihuahua, Connected with the United States and Mexican Boundary Commission, during the Years 1850, '51, '52, and '53* (New York: D. Appleton, 1854; reprint, Chicago: Rio Grande Press, 1965), 2:542.

29. Paula Rebert, "Mapping the United States–Mexico Boundary: Cooperation and Controversy," *Terrae Incognitae* 28 (1996): 58–71.

30. 8 November 1856, E 399, RG 76.

31. Francisco Jiménez, "Diario-memoria de los trabajos científicos practicados bajo la dirección de Francisco Jiménez, 1er Ingeniero de la Comisión de Límites Mexicana conforme a las instrucciones del Señor Comisionado Don José Salazar Ilarregui, a quien se hace entrega de ellos," 1857, 219–20, Special Collections, University Library, University of Texas at El Paso.

BIBLIOGRAPHY

THE FOLLOWING BIBLIOGRAPHY INCLUDES WORKS CITED IN THIS book, together with a small number of other works providing general ideas and information that I found useful. It is not an exhaustive list of relevant works nor does it include all of the archives and sources I consulted.

The bibliography is arranged in two main sections, containing archival and published materials. Archival materials consist of primary sources, most of which are unpublished, and are organized by archival collection. Maps are listed first under a separate heading, followed by general manuscript sources. The published materials include, in a single list of references, published primary sources, secondary works relating to the United States–Mexico boundary surveys and maps, and general and reference works.

I. Archival Materials

A. MAPS IN ARCHIVAL COLLECTIONS

For a cartobibliography of the original boundary maps made by the U.S. and Mexican commissions, see Paula Rebert, "The United States–Mexico Boundary: Manuscript Maps of 1857," *Bulletin, Special Libraries Association, Geography and Map Division* no. 186 (Summer 1997): 2–35.

1. Mapoteca Manuel Orozco y Berra, Mexico City

Límites, México–Estados Unidos.
   [Comisión de Límites Mexicana]. "Línea divisoria entre México y los Estados Unidos" [ms. maps]. 54 sheets. 1:60,000 (maps "No. 1"–"No. 45") and 1:30,000 (maps "No. 46"–"No. 54"). [1857].
   ———. "Línea divisoria entre México y los Estados Unidos, mapa general" [ms. maps]. 4 sheets. 1:600,000. [1857].
Colección Manuel Orozco y Berra, Entidad Federativa, Parciales 721.
   [Díaz, Agustín, and Luis Díaz]. "Río Bravo" [ms. maps]. 17 sheets. Scale varies. 1853. Número de control 1125.

Colección Orozco y Berra—General.

>[Comisión de Límites Mexicana]. [Field Maps] [ms. maps]. 7 sheets. Scale varies. 1855. Número de control 1124.
>
>———. "Islands in the Rio Bravo del Norte" [ms. maps]. 4 sheets. 1:6,000. N.d. Número de control 1120.
>
>Jiménez, Francisco. "Mapa que representa el camino seguido por la Comisión de Límites, en su vuelta de los pueblos de indies Pimas al Paso del Norte" [ms. map]. 1852. Número de control 1128.
>
>[U.S. Boundary Commission]. *[Index Map] . . . Boundary between the United States and Mexico* [map proofs]. 4 sheets. 1:600,000. [Washington, D.C.]: Department of the Interior, [1857]. Número de control 1104.

2. National Archives, Washington, D.C.

National Archives references are arranged numerically, first by Record Group number, and within each Record Group, by Entry number. Entry numbers refer to items listed in the Preliminary Inventory for the Record Group. For the Preliminary Inventory for Record Group 76, *see* Goggin, *Record Group 76,* listed below under Published Materials.

Record Group 11. Government Documents Having General Legal Effect.

>Disturnell, J. *Mapa de los Estados Unidos de Méjico, segun lo organizado y definido por las varias actas del Congreso de dicha República: Y construido por las mejores autoridades* [map]. Rev. ed. [7th]. 1" = about 70 mi. New York: J. Disturnell, 1847. Treaty Series no. 207.

Record Group 76, Entry 414. Copies of Maps Filed with the Treaty of 1848.

>Pantoja, Juan. "Plano del puerto de S. Diego" [ms. tracing of map]. 1802, copied [n.d.].

Record Group 76, Entry 417. Map Records, n.d.

>[U.S. Boundary Commission]. "Boundary between the United States and Mexico" [ms. maps]. 54 sheets. 1:60,000 (maps "No. 1"–"No. 45") and 1:30,000 (maps "No. 46"–"No. 54"). [1857].
>
>———. "Index Map . . . Boundary between the United States and Mexico" [ms. maps]. 4 sheets. 1:600,000. [1857].
>
>———. *[Index Map] . . . Boundary between the United States and Mexico* [map proofs]. 4 sheets. 1:600,000. [Washington, D.C.]: Department of the Interior, [1857].
>
>———. "Islands in the Rio Bravo del Norte" [ms. maps]. 5 sheets. 1:6,000. [1857].
>
>———. *No. 1, Boundary between the United States and Mexico* [map proofs]. 1:60,000. [Washington, D.C.]: Department of the Interior, [1857].
>
>———. *No. 29, Boundary between the United States and Mexico* [map proofs]. 1:60,000. [Washington, D.C.]: Department of the Interior, [1857].

Record Group 76, Entry 455. Copy of Emory's Map 29 That Was Rejected by the Commissioners of the Treaty of 1853, 1899.

    [International Boundary Commission]. *Photolithographic Copy of Major Emory's Original United States Sheet No. 29 of the Commission of 1853–1855* [map]. 1899.

3. Other Archives

Bancroft Library, University of California, Berkeley

    [U.S. Boundary Commission]. *[Index Map] . . . Boundary between the United States and Mexico* [map proofs]. 4 sheets. 1:600,000. [Washington, D.C.]: Department of the Interior, [1857].

    ———. *No. 1, Boundary between the United States and Mexico* [map proofs]. 1:60,000. [Washington, D.C.]: Department of the Interior, [1857].

Geography and Map Division, Library of Congress, Washington, D.C.

    [U.S. Boundary Commission]. *[Index Map] . . . Boundary between the United States and Mexico* [map proofs]. 4 sheets. 1:600,000. [Washington, D.C.]: Department of the Interior, [1857].

B. MANUSCRIPT SOURCES

1. Archivo Histórico Genaro Estrada, Secretaría de Relaciones Exteriores, Mexico City

Límites y Aguas Internacionales.

    Correspondencia recibida por la sección mexicana ante la Comisión de Límites y Aguas con los Estados Unidos de A.—Libro copiador de la misma, en la época del C. Gral. Pedro García Conde, 1849–50. Expediente X-2-2.

    Espejo, Juan B. "Informe de una expedición para el trazo del meridiano en el extremo occidental del paralelo 32°22′ boreal." 1852. Carpeta no. 43, no. 6. Diario del Gral. Pedro García Conde sobre los límites de las dos Californias—en relación con los trabajos astronómicos y topográficos. Expediente X-2-1.

    Límites entre México y los Estados Unidos de A.—Correspondencia relativa a la proposición de un nuevo tratado (secreto) entre ambos países y en relación con la Comisión Internacional de Límites, 1855. Expediente X-2-5.

2. Library of Congress, Washington, D.C.

Geography and Map Division

    Weyss, John E. [United States–Mexico boundary] [ms. views]. 11 sheets. [1855]. Gilbert Thompson Materials.

Manuscripts Division

    Bartlett, John Russell. "Official Journal." 1849–52. Providence, R.I.: John Carter Brown Library, Brown University. Microfilm.

    Bull, John. "Surveying Book No. 2." 1850. Peter Force Collection. Microfilm.

3. Maryland State Archives, Annapolis

Henderson Collection, MSA SC 501.

Hardcastle, Edmund L. F. Instructions for Flashing at Junction of Gila and Colorado Rivers, 1849, Oct. 5. Folder no. 21.

Hardcastle, Edmund L. F. Instructions for Flashing at Los Pinos, [1849], Oct. 5–9. Folder no. 22.

Hardcastle, Edmund L. F. Instructions for Flashing at Mt. Wicommon, 1849, Oct. 5–9. Folder no. 23.

Hardcastle, Edmund L. F. Minutes of the Meetings between Capt. E. L. F. Hardcastle of the United States and Ricardo Ramírez of Mexico for the Purpose of Locating the Monuments Marking the Boundary between the Two Countries, 1851, Mar. 19–July 30. Folder no. 59.

4. National Archives, Washington, D.C.

National Archives Record Group numbers are followed by Entry numbers, as given in the Preliminary Inventory for the Record Group. For the Preliminary Inventory for Record Group 48, see Hill and Jaussaud, *Record Group 48,* and for Record Group 76, see Goggin, *Record Group 76;* both are listed below under Published Materials.

Record Group 48. Records of the Office of the Secretary of the Interior.

Entry 539. Registers of Letters Received Concerning Boundary Surveys, 1849–62.

Entry 540. Letters and Other Communications Received, 1849–81.

Entry 559. Letters Sent Concerning Boundary Surveys, 1849–61.

Record Group 76. Records Relating to International Boundaries.

Entry 396. Proceedings, 1850–57.

Entry 397. Copy of Proceedings, 1849–50, 1855.

Entry 398. Correspondence of the First U.S. Commissioner, 1849–56.

Entry 399. Letters Sent by the Fourth U.S. Commissioner, 1849–58.

Entry 400. Letters Received by the Fourth U.S. Commissioner, 1849–57.

Entry 401. Copies of Letters Received by the Fourth U.S. Commissioner, 1854–57.

Entry 405. Applications, Recommendations, Acceptances, and Resignations, 1850, 1860.

Entry 408. Lists of U.S. Personnel, 1850–54.

Entry 412. Astronomical Observations, 1850–55.

Entry 424. Letters Received from the Third U.S. Commissioner, 1850–60.

Entry 425. Letters Received from the Fourth U.S. Commissioner, 1849–60.

Entry 426. Letters Relating to the Work of the Commission, 1851–55.

Entry 427. Letters Received Relating to Boundary Markers, 1850–52.

Entry 429. Journal and Letters of Surveyors, 1849.

Entry 431. Letters Received from the Head of the U.S. Scientific Corps, 1851–54.

Entry 432. Letters Relating to the Report of the U.S. Commissioner, 1857–60.

Entry 433. Letters Relating to Engraving of Prints, 1857–58.

Entry 436. Lists of and Receipts for Returned Instruments, 1849–60.

Entry 437. Letters Relating to Accounts, 1850–60.

Entry 486. Records Concerning the Southern Boundary, n.d.

Record Group 77. Records of the Office of the Chief of Engineers.

Microfilm Publication 506. Letters Received by the Topographical Bureau of the War Department, 1824–65.

5. University Library, University of Texas at El Paso

Special Collections.

Díaz, Agustín. "Memoria sobre los trabajos topográficos que de orden del 1er Ing° de la Comisión D. Francisco Jiménez, practicó el 2° Ing° de la misma, D. Agustin Díaz, en la porción del lindero boreal de la República Mexicana, que abraza una parte del curso del Río Colorado y la línea geodésica que va del punto inicial en dicho río (20 millas inglesas abajo de su confluencia con el Gila) a la intersección del meridiano 111° de longitud oeste de Greenwich y el paralelo 31°20' de latitud norte, año de 1855." 1857.

Jiménez, Francisco. "Diario-memoria de los trabajos científicos practicados bajo la dirección de Francisco Jiménez, 1er Ingeniero de la Comisión de Límites Mexicana conforme a las instrucciones del Señor Comisionado Don José Salazar Ilarregui, a quien se hace entrega de ellos." 1857.

II. Published Materials

Bartlett, John Russell. *Personal Narrative of Explorations and Incidents in Texas, New Mexico, California, Sonora, and Chihuahua, Connected with the United States and Mexican Boundary Commission, during the Years 1850, '51, '52, and '53.* 2 vols. New York: D. Appleton, 1854. Reprint. Chicago: Rio Grande Press, 1965.

Bennett, J. A. *The Divided Circle: A History of Instruments for Astronomy, Navigation, and Surveying.* Oxford: Phaidon-Christie's Limited, 1987.

Bevans, Charles I., comp. *Treaties and Other International Agreements of the United States of America, 1776–1949.* 13 vols. Washington, D.C.: Department of State, 1968–76.

Boggs, Samuel Whittemore. "The Initial Point on the Rio Grande, Intended to Be in 31°47' North Latitude." In *Treaties and Other International Acts of the United States of America,* edited by Hunter Miller, 6:392–93. Washington, D.C.: Department of State, 1942.

———. "Monument No. 127 (Old Emory Monument No. 27), Intended to Be in North Latitude 31°20' and West Longitude 111°." In *Treaties and Other International Acts of the United States of America,* edited by Hunter Miller, 6:393. Washington, D.C.: Department of State, 1942.

Bouchez, L. J. "The Fixing of Boundaries in International Boundary Rivers." *International and Comparative Law Quarterly* 12 (1963): 789–817.

Bray, Martha Coleman. *Joseph Nicollet and His Map*. Philadelphia: American Philosophical Society, 1980.

Browne, J[ohn] Ross. *Adventures in the Apache Country: A Tour through Arizona and Sonora, with Notes on the Silver Regions of Nevada*. New York: Harper and Brothers, 1871. Reprint. New York: Promontory Press, 1974.

Brown, Lenerd E. "Survey of the United States Mexico Boundary—1849–1855: Background Study." [Washington, D.C.]: United States Department of the Interior, National Park Service, Division of History, Office of Archeology and Historic Preservation, 1969. Photocopy.

Callet, Jean François. *Tables portatives de logarithmes, contenant les logarithmes des nombres, depuis 1 jusqu'à 108,000; les logarithmes des sinus et tangentes, de seconde en seconde pour les cinq premiers degrés, de dix en dix secondes pour tous les degrés du quart de cercle; et, suivant la nouvelle division centésimale, de dix-millième en dix-millième, précédées d'un discours préliminaire sur l'explication, l'usage et la sommation des logarithmes, et sur leur application à l'astronomie, à la navigation, à la géométrie-pratique, et aux calculs d'intérêts; suivies de nouvelles tables plus approchées, et de plusieurs autres utiles à la recherche de longitudes en mer, etc.* Paris: Firmin Didot, 1795. Reprint. 1855.

Carreño, Alberto María. *México y los Estados Unidos de America: Apuntaciones para la historia del acrecentamiento territorial de los Estados Unidos a costa de México desde la epoca colonial hasta nuestros días*. Mexico City: Imprenta Victoria, 1922.

Chardon, Roland. "The Linear League in North America." *Annals of the Association of American Geographers* 70 (1980): 129–53.

Cotter, Charles H. *The Astronomical and Mathematical Foundations of Geography*. New York: American Elsevier, 1966.

Cuevas, Gabriel. *El glorioso Colegio Militar Mexicano en un siglo (1824–1924)*. Mexico City: S. Turanzas del Valle, 1937.

Cukwurah, A. O. *The Settlement of Boundary Disputes in International Law*. Manchester: Manchester University Press, 1967.

Cullum, George W. *Biographical Register of the Officers and Graduates of the U.S. Military Academy, at West Point, N.Y., from Its Establishment, March 16, 1802, to the Army Re-Organization of 1866–67*. 2 vols. New York: D. Van Nostrand, 1868.

Cunningham, Bob, and Harry P. Hewitt. "A 'Lovely Land Full of Roses and Thorns': Emil Langberg and Mexico, 1835–1866." *Southwestern Historical Quarterly* 98 (1995): 386–425.

Cushing, Caleb. *Opinions of Hon. Caleb Cushing, of Massachusetts, from October 9, 1854, to July 9, 1856*. Vol. 7 of *Official Opinions of the Attorneys General of the United States, Advising the President and Heads of Departments, in Relation to Their Official Duties, and Expounding the Constitution, Treaties with Foreign Governments and with Indian Tribes, and the Public Laws of the Country*. Edited by C. C. Andrews. Washington, D.C.: Robert Farnham, 1856.

Díaz, Agustín. "Memoria de D. Agustín Díaz: A. Copia de las instrucciones relativas del Señor Agrimensor de la Comisión para la ejecución de esta topografía; B. Diario. Memoria de las operaciones practicadas para la topografía del Río Bravo en la parte que comprende de la colonia civil de S. Ignacio á la de los Amoles, en el año de 1852; C. Datos topográficos." In International Boundary and Water Commission, United States and Mexico. *Memoria documentada del juicio de arbitraje del Chamizal celebrado en virtud de la convención de junio 24 de 1910*, 2:195–247. Mexico City: Artes Gráficas, Granja Experimental de Zoquipa, 1911.

Dupree, A. Hunter. *Science in the Federal Government: A History of Policies and Activities.* Cambridge: Belknap Press of Harvard University Press, 1957. Reprint. Baltimore: Johns Hopkins University Press, 1986.

Elliott, Clark A. *Biographical Dictionary of American Science: The Seventeenth through the Nineteenth Centuries.* Westport, Conn.: Greenwood Press, 1979.

Emory, William H. "Boundary between the United States and Mexico." *Bulletin of the American Geographical and Statistical Society* 1, pt. 3 (1854): 32–44.

———. *Notes of a Military Reconnoissance, from Fort Leavenworth, in Missouri, to San Diego, in California, Including Parts of the Arkansas, Del Norte, and Gila Rivers.* 30th Cong., 1st sess., 1848. S. Ex. Doc. 7.

———. *Notes on the Survey of the Boundary Line between Mexico and the United States.* Cincinnati: Morgan and Overend, 1851.

———. *Report on the United States and Mexican Boundary Survey Made under the Direction of the Secretary of the Interior.* 3 vols. 34th Cong., 1st sess., 1857. H. Ex. Doc. 135.

Escoto Ochoa, Humberto. *Integración y desintegración de nuestra frontera norte.* Mexico City: N.p., 1949.

Faulk, Odie B. "The Controversial Boundary Survey and the Gadsden Treaty." *Arizona and the West* 4 (1962): 201–26.

———. *Too Far North . . . Too Far South.* Los Angeles: Westernlore Press, 1967.

———. "William H. Emory and the Mexican Survey." *Pacific Historian* 1, no. 4 (1969): 47–62.

Fontana, Bernard L. "Drawing the Line between Mexico and the United States: Nineteenth-Century Lithographs of People and Places along the Border." *American West* 20, no. 4 (July–August 1983): 50–56.

Francoeur, Louis Benjamin. *Géodésie, ou traité de la figure de la terre et de ses parties; comprenant la topographie, l'arpentage, le nivellement, la géomorphie terrestre et astronomique, la construction des cartes, la navigation.* 5th ed. Paris: Bachelier, 1840.

———. *Uranographie ou traité élémentaire d'astronomie; a l'usage des personnes peu versées dans les mathématiques; accompagné de planisphères.* 5th ed. Paris: Bachelier, 1837.

Fuller, John Douglas Pitts. *The Movement for the Acquisition of All Mexico, 1846–1848.* Johns Hopkins University Studies in Historical and Political Science, ser. 54, no. 1. Baltimore: Johns Hopkins Press, 1936.

Garber, Paul Neff. *The Gadsden Treaty.* Gloucester, Mass.: Peter Smith, 1923. Reprint. 1959.

García Conde, Pedro. *Ensayo estadístico sobre el estado de Chihuahua.* Chihuahua: Imprenta del gobierno a cargo de C. Ramos, 1842.

García y Cubas, Antonio. *Atlas geográfico, estadístico é histórico de la República Mexicana.* Mexico City: Imprenta de José Mariano Fernandez de Lara, 1858.

———. *Memoria para servir á la carta general de la República Mexicana publicada por Antonio García y Cubas.* Mexico City: Imprenta de Andrade y Escalante, 1861.

Goetzmann, William H. *Army Exploration in the American West, 1803–1863.* New Haven, Conn.: Yale University Press, 1959. Reprint. Lincoln: University of Nebraska Press, 1979.

———. "Science Explores the Big Bend: 1852–1853." *Password* III (1958): 60–67.

———. "The United States–Mexican Boundary Survey, 1848–1853." *Southwestern Historical Quarterly* 62 (1958): 164–90.

Goggin, Daniel T., comp. *Preliminary Inventory of the Records Relating to International Boundaries (Record Group 76).* Preliminary Inventories, no. 170. Washington, D.C.: National Archives, 1968.

Gómez, Arthur R. *A Most Singular Country: A History of Occupation in the Big Bend.* [Salt Lake City]: Charles Redd Center for Western Studies, Brigham Young University, 1990.

Gortari, Eli de. *La ciencia en la historia de México.* Mexico City: Fondo de Cultura Económica, 1963. Reprint. Mexico City: Editorial Grijalbo, 1980.

Great Britain. Nautical Almanac Office. *The Nautical Almanac and Astronomical Ephemeris for the Year 1849.* London: The Lords Commissioners of the Admiralty, 1845.

Gregory, Gladys. *The Chamizal Settlement: A View from El Paso.* El Paso: Texas Western College Press, 1963.

Griswold del Castillo, Richard. *The Treaty of Guadalupe Hidalgo: A Legacy of Conflict.* Norman: University of Oklahoma Press, 1990.

Groce, George C., and David H. Wallace. *The New-York Historical Society's Dictionary of Artists in America, 1564–1860.* New Haven, Conn.: Yale University Press, 1957.

Hall, Dawn, ed. *Drawing the Borderline: Artist-Explorers and the U.S.-Mexico Boundary Survey.* Albuquerque: Albuquerque Museum, 1996.

Hammond, George P., ed. *The Treaty of Guadalupe Hidalgo, February Second, 1848.* Berkeley: Friends of the Bancroft Library, 1949.

Harley, J. B., and David Woodward. "Concluding Remarks." In *The History of Cartography.* Vol. 1, *Cartography in Prehistoric, Ancient, and Medieval Europe and the Mediterranean,* edited by J. B. Harley and David Woodward, 502–9. Chicago: University of Chicago Press, 1987.

Harrington, Charles E. "Maritime Boundaries on National Ocean Service Nautical Charts." *Cartographic Perspectives* 14 (Winter 1993): 9–15.

Heitman, Francis B. *Historical Register and Dictionary of the United States Army, from Its Organization, September 29, 1789, to March 2, 1903.* 2 vols. Washington, D.C.: U.S. Government Printing Office, 1903. Reprint. Urbana: University of Illinois Press, 1965.

Herrera, Horacio. "Estudio sobre el límite internacional terrestre de los Estados Unidos de Norte América con la República Mexicana." *Boletín de la Sociedad Mexicana de Geografía y Estadística* 65, no. 1 (1948): 169–87.

Hewitt, Harry P. "'El deseo de cubrir el honor nacional': Francisco Jiménez and the Survey of the Mexico–United States Boundary, 1849–1857." In *La ciudad y el campo en la historia de México: Memoria de la VII reunión de historiadores mexicanos y norteamericanos, Oaxaca, Oax., 1985,* 709–19. Mexico City: Universidad Nacional Autónoma de México, 1992.

———. "The Mexican Boundary Survey Team: Pedro García Conde in California." *Western Historical Quarterly* 21 (1990): 171–96.

———. "The Mexican Commission and Its Survey of the Rio Grande River Boundary, 1850–1854." *Southwestern Historical Quarterly* 94 (1991): 555–80.

Highet, Keith. "Evidence, the Court, and the Nicaragua Case." *American Journal of International Law* 81 (1987): 1–56.

Hill, Edward E., and Renee M. Jaussaud, comps. *Preliminary Inventory: Records of the Office of the Secretary of the Interior (Record Group 48).* Washington, D.C.: National Archives, 1980.

Hine, Robert V. *Bartlett's West: Drawing the Mexican Boundary.* New Haven, Conn.: Yale University Press for the Amon Carter Museum, 1968.

Howse, Derek. "The Lunar-Distance Method of Measuring Longitude." In *The Quest for Longitude: The Proceedings of the Longitude Symposium, Harvard University, Cambridge, Massachusetts, November 4–6, 1993,* edited by William J. H. Andrewes, 149–62. Cambridge: Collection of Historical Scientific Instruments, Harvard University, 1996.

Humphrey, Robert R. *Ninety Years and 535 Miles: Vegetation Changes along the Mexican Border.* Albuquerque: University of New Mexico Press, 1987.

International Boundary and Water Commission, United States and Mexico. *Memoria documentada del juicio de arbitraje del Chamizal celebrado en virtud de la convención de junio 24 de 1910.* 3 vols. Mexico City: Artes Gráficas, Granja Experimental de Zoquipa, 1911.

International Boundary Commission, United States and Mexico, 1882. *Memoria de la Sección Mexicana de la Comisión Internacional de Límites entre México y los Estados Unidos que restableció los monumentos de El Paso al Pacífico.* New York: John Polhemus and Co., 1901.

Izquierdo, José Joaquín. *La primera casa de las ciencias en México: El Real Seminario de Minería (1792–1811).* Mexico City: Ediciones Ciencia, 1958.

Jackson, W. Turrentine. *Wagon Roads West: A Study of Federal Road Surveys and Construction in the Transmississippi West, 1846–1869.* New Haven, Conn.: Yale University Press, 1964. Reprint. Lincoln: University of Nebraska Press, 1979.

Johnson, Richard A. *The Mexican Revolution of Ayutla, 1854–1855: An Analysis of the Evolution and Destruction of Santa Anna's Last Dictatorship.* Rock Island, Ill.: Augustana College Library, 1939.

Jones, Stephen Barr. *Boundary-Making: A Handbook for Statesmen, Treaty Editors, and Boundary Commissioners.* Washington, D.C.: Carnegie Endowment for International Peace, 1945. Reprint. New York: Johnson Reprint, 1971.

Kajencki, Francis C. "Charles Radziminski and the United States–Mexican Boundary Survey." *New Mexico Historical Review* 63 (1988): 211–40.

Lawyers Co-operative Publishing Co., and Bancroft-Whitney Co. *American Jurisprudence: A Modern Comprehensive Text Statement of American Law.* Vol. 72, *State and Local Taxation §§704–1154 to Statute of Frauds §§1–396.* 2d ed. Rochester, N.Y.: Lawyers Co-operative Publishing Co., and San Francisco: Bancroft-Whitney Co., 1974.

Lee, Thomas Jefferson. *A Collection of Tables and Formulae Useful in Surveying, Geodesy, and Practical Astronomy, Including Elements for the Projection of Maps.* 2d ed. Papers Relating to the Duties of the Corps of Topographical Engineers, no. 3. Washington, D.C.: Taylor and Maury, 1849.

León-Portilla, Miguel, ed. *Diccionario Porrúa de historia, biografía y geografía de México.* 5th ed. 3 vols. Mexico City: Editorial Porrúa, 1986.

Lesley, Lewis B. "The International Boundary Survey from San Diego to the Gila River, 1849–1850." *Quarterly of the California Historical Society* 9 (1930): 3–15.

Liss, Sheldon B. *A Century of Disagreement: The Chamizal Conflict, 1864–1964.* Washington, D.C.: Latin American Institute, 1965.

López de Escalera, Juan. *Diccionario biográfico y de historia de México.* Mexico City: Editorial del Magisterio, 1964.

Marchant, Alexander. *Boundaries of the Latin American Republics: An Annotated List of Documents, 1493–1943.* Washington, D.C.: U.S. Government Printing Office, 1944.

Martínez, Oscar J. *Troublesome Border.* Tucson: University of Arizona Press, 1988.

Martin, James C., and Robert S. Martin. *Maps of Texas and the Southwest, 1513–1900.* Albuquerque: University of New Mexico Press for the Amon Carter Museum, 1984.

Martin, Lawrence. "Disturnell's Map." In *Treaties and Other International Acts of the United States of America,* edited by Hunter Miller, 5:340–70. Washington, D.C.: Department of State, 1937.

———. "The Plan of the Port of San Diego." In *Treaties and Other International Acts of the United States of America,* edited by Hunter Miller, 5:371. Washington, D.C.: Department of State, 1937.

Metz, Leon Claire. *Border: The U.S.-Mexico Line.* El Paso: Mangan Books, 1989.

Michaud, Joseph Fr., ed. *Biographie universelle ancienne et moderne par J. Fr. Michaud.* Nouvelle ed. 35 vols. Edited by Louis Gabriel Michaud. Paris, 1854. Reprint. Graz, Austria: Akademische Druck- u. Verlagsanstalt, 1966–68.

Miller, Hunter, ed. "Document 129, Mexico: February 2, 1848." In *Treaties and Other International Acts of the United States of America,* 5:207–428. Washington, D.C.: Department of State, 1937.

Mills, Anson. *My Story.* 2d ed. Edited by C. H. Claudy. Washington, D.C.: Byron S. Adams, 1921.

Moyano Pahissa, Angela. *México y Estados Unidos: Orígenes de una relación, 1819–1861*. Mexico City: Secretaría de Educación Pública, 1987.

Mueller, Jerry E. *Restless River: International Law and the Behavior of the Rio Grande*. El Paso: Texas Western Press, 1975.

Mumme, Stephen. "Innovation and Reform in Transboundary Resource Management: A Critical Look at the International Boundary and Water Commission, United States and Mexico." *Natural Resources Journal* 33 (1993): 93–120.

National Geodetic Survey. *Geodetic Glossary*. Rockville, Md.: National Oceanic and Atmospheric Administration, 1986.

[Office of Pacific Railroad Surveys]. *Map of the Territory of the United States from the Mississippi to the Pacific Ocean* [map]. Compiled by Gouverneur K. Warren. 1: 3,000,000. [Washington, D.C.]: Department of War, 1857.

Oppenheim, Lassa Francis Lawrence. *Peace*. Vol. 1 of *International Law: A Treatise*. 8th ed. Edited by Herah Lauterpacht. New York: David McKay Co., 1955.

Orozco y Berra, Manuel. *Apuntes para la historia de la geografía en México*. Mexico City: Francisco Diaz de Leon, 1881.

———. *Materiales para una cartografia mexicana*. Sociedad de Geografía y Estadística edition. Mexico City: Imprenta del Gobierno, 1871.

Ortega y Espinosa, Vicente. "Díaz Covarrubias, Geodesta." *Memorias de la Academia Nacional de Ciencias Antonio Alzate* 53 (1932–33): 461–66.

Prescott, J. R. V. *The Geography of Frontiers and Boundaries*. Chicago: Aldine, 1965.

Radzyminski, Stanley F. "Charles Radziminski: Patriot, Exile, Pioneer." *Chronicles of Oklahoma* 38 (1960): 354–68.

Ramírez, Santiago. *Datos para la historia del Colegio de Minería recogidos y compilados bajo la forma de efemérides*. Mexico City: Imprenta del Gobierno Federal, 1890.

Rebert, Paula. "The Gilbert Thompson Collection, Library of Congress." *Meridian* 7 (1992): 27–32.

———. "Mapping the United States–Mexico Boundary, 1849–1857." Ph.D. diss., University of Wisconsin, Madison, 1994.

———. "Mapping the United States–Mexico Boundary: Cooperation and Controversy." *Terrae Incognitae* 28 (1996): 58–71.

"Remarking the Mexican Boundary." *Science*, n.s., 1 (29 March 1895): 349–50.

Rippy, J. Fred. *The United States and Mexico*. New York: Alfred A. Knopf, 1926.

Rittenhouse, Jack D. *Disturnell's Treaty Map: The Map That Was Part of the Guadalupe Hidalgo Treaty on Southwestern Boundaries, 1848*. Santa Fe: Stagecoach Press, 1965.

Salazar Ylarregui, José. *Datos de los trabajos astronómicos y topográficos, dispuestos en forma de diario, practicados durante el año de 1849 y principios de 1850 por la Comisión de Límites Mexicana en la línea que divide esta República de la de los Estados-Unidos*. Mexico City: Imprenta de Juan R. Navarro, 1850.

Sánchez Lamego, Miguel A. "Agustín Díaz, ilustre cartógrafo mexicano." *Historia Mexicana* 24 (1975): 556–65.

———. *El Colegio Militar y la defensa de Chapultepec en Septiembre de 1847*. Mexico City: N.p., 1947.

————. *Generales de ingenieros del ejercito mexicano, 1821–1914.* Mexico City: N.p., 1952.

Sandifer, Durward V. *Evidence before International Tribunals.* Rev. ed. Charlottesville: University Press of Virginia, 1975.

Saucerman, Sophia A. "The Boundary Maps." In *Treaties and Other International Acts of the United States of America,* edited by Hunter Miller, 6:394–409. Washington, D.C.: Department of State, 1942.

Schmitt, Karl M. "The Problem of Maritime Boundaries in U.S.-Mexican Relations." *Natural Resources Journal* 22 (1982): 138–53.

Schubert, Frank N. "A Tale of Two Cartographers: Emory, Warren, and Their Maps of the Trans-Mississippi West." In *Exploration and Mapping of the American West,* edited by Donna P. Koepp, 50–59. Chicago: Speculum Orbis Press for the Map and Geography Round Table of the American Library Association, 1986.

————. *Vanguard of Expansion: Army Engineers in the Trans-Mississippi West, 1819–1879.* Washington, D.C.: Department of the Army, Office of the Chief of Engineers, Office of Administrative Services, Historical Division, 1980.

Schwartz, Seymour I., and Ralph E. Ehrenberg. *The Mapping of America.* New York: Harry N. Abrams, 1980.

Sepúlveda, César. *La frontera norte de México: Historia, conflictos, 1762–1975.* Mexico City: Editorial Porrúa, 1976.

Shalowitz, Aaron L. *Shore and Sea Boundaries: With Special Reference to the Interpretation and Use of Coast and Geodetic Survey Data.* 2 vols. Washington, D.C.: U.S. Government Printing Office, 1962–64.

Smart, Charles E. *The Makers of Surveying Instruments in America since 1700.* Troy, N.Y.: Regal Art Press, 1962.

Smith, Ralph A. "Indians in American-Mexican Relations before the War of 1846." *Hispanic American Historical Review* 43 (1963): 34–64.

Snyder, John P. *Flattening the Earth: Two Thousand Years of Map Projections.* Chicago: University of Chicago Press, 1993.

Stephenson, Richard W. "The Mapping of the Northwest Boundary of Texas, 1859–1860." *Terrae Incognitae* 6 (1974): 39–50.

Stoddard, Francis R. "Amiel Weeks Whipple." *Chronicles of Oklahoma* 28 (1950): 226–30.

Szekely, Alberto. "A Commentary with the Mexican View on the Problem of Maritime Boundaries in U.S.-Mexican Relations." *Natural Resources Journal* 22 (1982): 155–59.

Taft, Robert. *Artists and Illustrators of the Old West, 1850–1900.* Princeton: Princeton University Press, 1953.

Tamayo, Jorge L. *Geografía general de México.* 2d ed. 4 vols. Mexico City: Instituto Mexicano de Investigaciones Económicas, 1962.

Thrower, Norman J. W. "William H. Emory and the Mapping of the American Southwest Borderlands." *Terrae Incognitae* 22 (1990): 41–91.

Timm, Charles A. *The International Boundary Commission: United States and Mexico.* Austin: University of Texas, 1941.

Timmons, W. H. *El Paso: A Borderlands History.* El Paso: Texas Western Press, 1990.

Tyler, Ronnie C. *The Big Bend: A History of the Last Texas Frontier.* Washington, D.C.: U.S. Department of the Interior, 1975.

———. "Exploring the Rio Grande: Lt. Duff C. Green's Report of 1852." *Arizona and the West* 10 (1968): 43–60.

[U.S. Boundary Commission]. *Map of the United States and Their Territories between the Mississippi and the Pacific Ocean and Part of Mexico* [map]. 1 : 6,000,000. Washington, D.C.: [Department of the Interior], 1857–58. In William H. Emory, *Report on the United States and Mexican Boundary Survey Made under the Direction of the Secretary of the Interior.* 34th Cong., 1st sess., 1857. H. Ex. Doc. 135.

U.S. Bureau of Land Management. *Manual of Instructions for the Survey of the Public Lands of the United States.* Technical Bulletin no. 6. Washington, D.C.: U.S. Department of the Interior, 1973.

U.S. Coast and Geodetic Survey. *Annual Report of the Superintendent of the Coast Survey, Showing the Progress of That Work during the Year Ending November, 1851.* 32d Cong., 1st sess., 1851. S. Ex. Doc. 3.

———. *Letter from the Acting Secretary of the Treasury, Communicating the Report of the Superintendent of the Coast Survey, Showing the Progress of That Work.* 30th Cong., 1st sess., 1847. S. Ex. Doc. 6.

———. *Letter from the Secretary of the Treasury, Communicating the Report of the Superintendent of the Coast Survey, Showing the Progress of That Work during the Year Ending November, 1849.* 31st Cong., 1st sess., 1849. S. Ex. Doc. 5.

———. *Letter from the Secretary of the Treasury, Transmitting the Report of the Superintendent of the Coast Survey, Showing the Progress of That Work during the Year Ending November, 1850.* 31st Cong., 2d sess., 1850. H. Ex. Doc. 12.

———. *Report of the Secretary of the Treasury, Communicating a Report of the Superintendent of the Coast Survey, Showing the Progress of That Work during the Year Ending November, 1848.* 30th Cong., 2d sess., 1848. S. Ex. Doc. 1.

———. *Report of the Superintendent of the Coast Survey, Showing the Progress of the Survey during the Year 1852.* 32d Cong., 2d sess., 1852–53. S. Ex. Doc. 58.

———. *Report of the Superintendent of the Coast Survey, Showing the Progress of the Survey during the Year 1853.* 33d Cong., 1st sess., 1853–54. H. Ex. Doc. 12.

———. *Report of the Superintendent of the Coast Survey, Showing the Progress of the Survey during the Year 1854.* 33d Cong., 2d sess., 1854–55. S. Ex. Doc. 10.

U.S. Congress. *Message of the President of the United States, in Compliance with a Resolution of the Senate of the 20th Ultimo, Calling for Information Relating to the Boundary Line and the Payment of the $3,000,000 under the Treaty with Mexico of June 30, 1853.* 34th Cong., 1st sess., 1856. S. Ex. Doc. 57.

———. *Preliminary Reconnaissance of the Boundary Line between the United States and Mexico.* 48th Cong., 1st sess., 1884. S. Misc. Doc. 96.

———. *Report of the Boundary Commission upon the Survey and Re-Marking of the Boundary between the United States and Mexico West of the Rio Grande, 1891 to 1896.*

Parts I and II. Part I. Report of the International Commission. Part II. Report of the United States Section. 55th Cong., 2d sess., 1898. S. Doc. 247.

————. *Report of the Secretary of the Interior, Communicating, in Compliance with a Resolution of the Senate, a Report from Mr. Bartlett on the Subject of the Boundary Line between the United States and Mexico.* 32d Cong., 2d sess., 1853. S. Ex. Doc. 41.

————. *Report of the Secretary of the Interior, Communicating, in Further Compliance with a Resolution of the Senate, Certain Papers in Relation to the Mexican Boundary Commission.* 33d Cong., special sess., 1853. S. Ex. Doc. 6.

————. *Report of the Secretary of the Interior, in Answer to a Resolution of the Senate for Information in Relation to the Operations of the Commission Appointed to Run and Mark the Boundary between the United States and Mexico.* 31st Cong., 1st sess., 1850. S. Ex. Doc. 34, pt. 1.

————. *Report of the Secretary of the Interior, in Compliance with a Resolution of the Senate, of January 22, Communicating a Report and Map of A. B. Gray, Relative to the Mexican Boundary.* 33d Cong., 2d sess., 1855. S. Ex. Doc. 55.

————. *Report of the Secretary of the Interior Made in Compliance with a Resolution of the Senate Calling for Information in Relation to the Commission Appointed to Run and Mark the Boundary between the United States and Mexico.* 32d Cong., 1st sess., 1852. S. Ex. Doc. 119.

————. *Report of the Secretary of the Interior, with Additional Correspondence Relative to the Operations of the Commission for Running and Marking the Boundary between the United States and Mexico.* 31st Cong., 1st sess., 1850. S. Ex. Doc. 34, pt. 2.

————. *Report of the Secretary of War, Communicating, in Compliance with a Resolution of the Senate, the Report of Lieutenant Colonel Graham on the Subject of the Boundary Line between the United States and Mexico.* 32d Cong., 1st sess., 1852. S. Ex. Doc. 121.

U.S. Department of State. *Treaties in Force: A List of Treaties and Other International Agreements of the United States in Force on January 1, 1997.* Washington, D.C.: U.S. Government Printing Office, 1997.

————. *United States Treaties and Other International Agreements.* Vol. 23, pt. 1, *1972.* Washington, D.C.: U.S. Government Printing Office, 1973.

————. *United States Treaties and Other International Agreements.* Vol. 29, pt. 1, *1976–77.* Washington, D.C.: U.S. Government Printing Office, 1979.

U.S. Department of State. International Boundary and Water Commission (United States and Mexico). *Proceedings of the International (Water) Boundary Commission, United States and Mexico, Treaties of 1884 and 1889: Equitable Distribution of the Waters of the Rio Grande. United States Section.* 2 vols. Washington, D.C.: U.S. Government Printing Office, 1903.

U.S. Engineer School, United States Army. *Historical Sketch of the Corps of Engineers, U.S. Army,* by Edward Burr. Occasional Papers no. 71. Washington, D.C.: U.S. Government Printing Office, 1939.

U.S. Geological Survey in cooperation with the U.S. Customs Service and the Dirección

General de Geografía, Mexico. *United States–Mexico Border Color Image Maps* [maps]. 203 Sheets. 1:25,000. Reston, Va.: U.S. Geological Survey, 1989.

U.S. Section, International Boundary and Water Commission. *The International Boundary and Water Commission, United States and Mexico.* El Paso: United States Section, 1990. Photocopy.

———. "List of Western Land Boundary Monuments." El Paso: United States Section, 1992. Photocopy.

U.S. Supreme Court. "New Mexico v. Texas." In *United States Reports.* Vol. 275, *Cases Adjudged in the Supreme Court at October Term, 1927,* reporter Ernest Knaebel, 279–303. Washington, D.C.: U.S. Government Printing Office, 1928.

Utley, Robert M. *The International Boundary, United States and Mexico: A History of Frontier Dispute and Cooperation, 1848–1963.* Santa Fe: United States Department of the Interior, National Park Service, Southwest Region, 1964. Photocopy.

Van Zandt, Franklin K. *Boundaries of the United States and the Several States.* U.S. Geological Survey Professional Paper 909. Washington, D.C.: U.S. Government Printing Office, 1976.

Vázquez, Josefina Zoraida, and Lorenzo Meyer. *The United States and Mexico.* Chicago: University of Chicago Press, 1985.

Villasana, J. Alberto, and R. B. Southard. "Cartographic Cooperation along the United States–Mexico Border." *Revista Cartográfica* 32 (1977): 13–24.

Viola, Herman J. *Exploring the West.* Washington, D.C.: Smithsonian Institution, 1987.

Von Glahn, Gerhard. *Law among Nations: An Introduction to Public International Law.* 6th ed. New York: Macmillan Publishing Co., 1992.

Wallace, Edward S. *The Great Reconnaissance: Soldiers, Artists, and Scientists on the Frontier, 1848–1861.* Boston: Little, Brown and Co., 1955.

Warren, Gouverneur K. *Memoir to Accompany the Map of the Territory of the United States from the Mississippi River to the Pacific Ocean, Giving a Brief Account of Each of the Exploring Expeditions since A.D. 1800, with a Detailed Description of the Method Adopted in Compiling the General Map.* Vol. 11 of *Reports of Explorations and Surveys, to Ascertain the Most Practicable and Economical Route for a Railroad from the Mississippi River to the Pacific Ocean, Made under the Direction of the Secretary of War, in 1853–56.* 33d Cong., 2d sess., 1859. S. Ex. Doc. 78.

Washington Post, 4, 25 June 1903.

Webb, Walter Prescott, ed. *The Handbook of Texas.* 2 vols. Austin: Texas State Historical Association, 1952.

Weber, David J. "Conflicts and Accommodations: Hispanic and Anglo-American Borders in Historical Perspective, 1670–1853." *Journal of the Southwest* 39 (1997): 1–32.

———. "Mexico's Far Northern Frontier, 1821–1854: Historiography Askew." *Western Historical Quarterly* 7 (1976): 279–93.

Weissberg, Guenter. "Maps as Evidence in International Boundary Disputes: A Reappraisal." *American Journal of International Law* 57 (1963): 781–803.

Werne, Joseph Richard. "Major Emory and Captain Jiménez: Running the Gadsden Line." *Journal of the Southwest* 29 (1987): 203–21.

———. "Partisan Politics and the Mexican Boundary Survey, 1848–1853." *Southwestern Historical Quarterly* 90 (1987): 329–46.

———. "Pedro García Conde and the Gadsden Treaty." In *La ciudad y el campo en la historia de México: Memoria de la VII reunión de historiadores mexicanos y norteamericanos, Oaxaca, Oax., 1985,* 699–707. Mexico City: Universidad Nacional Autónoma de México, 1992.

———. "Pedro García Conde: El trazado de límites con Estados Unidos desde el punto de vista mexicano (1848–1853)." *Historia Mexicana* 36 (1986): 113–29.

———. "Surveying the Rio Grande, 1850–1853." *Southwestern Historical Quarterly* 94 (1991): 535–54.

Wheat, Carl Irving. *Mapping the American West, 1540–1857.* Worcester, Mass.: American Antiquarian Society, 1954.

———. *Mapping the Transmississippi West, 1540–1861.* Vol. 3, *From the Mexican War to the Boundary Surveys, 1846–1854.* San Francisco: Institute of Historical Cartography, 1959.

Whiting, William Henry Chase. "Journal of William Henry Chase Whiting, 1849." In *Exploring Southwestern Trails, 1846–1854,* edited by Ralph P. Bieber and Averam B. Bender, 241–350. Glendale, Calif.: Arthur H. Clark, 1938.

Wislizenus, Frederick Adolphus. *Memoir of a Tour to Northern Mexico, Connected with Col. Doniphan's Expedition, in 1846 and 1847.* 30th Cong., 1st sess., 1848. Misc. Pub. 26. Reprint. Glorieta, N. Mex.: Rio Grande Press, 1969.

Woodward, David. "The Study of the History of Cartography: A Suggested Framework." *American Cartographer* 1 (1974): 101–15.

Zorrilla, Luis G. *Historia de las relaciones entre México y los Estados Unidos de América, 1800–1958.* 2 vols. Mexico City: Editorial Porrúa, 1965–66.

———. *Monumentación de la frontera norte en el siglo XIX.* Mexico City: Secretaría de Relaciones Exteriores, 1981.

INDEX